Choosing Leaders and Choosing to Lead

To my clients, candidates and colleagues, who taught me.

Choosing Leaders and Choosing to Lead

Science, Politics and Intuition in Executive Selection

DOUGLAS BOARD

GOWER

Published by
Gower Publishing Limited
Wey Court East
Union Road
Farnham
Surrey, GU9 7PT
England

Gower Publishing Company
Suite 420
101 Cherry Street
Burlington,
VT 05401-4405
USA

www.gowerpublishing.com

British Library Cataloguing in Publication Data
Board, Douglas.
  Choosing leaders and choosing to lead : science, politics and intuition in executive selection.
  1. Executives – Recruiting.
  I. Title
  658.4'0711–dc23

Library of Congress Cataloging-in-Publication Data
Board, Douglas, 1957-
  Choosing leaders and choosing to lead : science, politics, and intuition in executive selection / by Douglas Board.
        p. cm.
  Includes bibliographical references and index.
  ISBN 978-1-4094-3648-5 (hard cover) – ISBN 978-1-4094-3649-2 (ebook)
  1. Executive succession. 2. Executive ability. 3. Leadership. I. Title.

  HD38.2.B63 2011
  658.4'07112–dc23

                                                                    2011052063

ISBN 9781409436485 (hbk)
ISBN 9781409436492 (ebk)

Printed and bound in Great Britain by the
MPG Books Group, UK

You Will be Hearing from us Shortly

You feel adequate to the demands of this position?
What qualities do you feel you
Personally have to offer?
                              Ah

Let us consider your application form.
Your qualifications, though impressive, are
Not, we must admit, precisely what
We had in mind. Would you care
To defend their relevance?
                              Indeed

Now your age. Perhaps you feel able
To make your own comment about that,
Too? We are conscious ourselves
Of the need for a candidate with precisely
The right degree of immaturity.
                              So glad we agree

And now a delicate matter: your looks.
You do appreciate this work involves
Contact with the actual public? Might they,
Perhaps, find your appearance
Disturbing?
                              Quite so

And your accent. That is the way
You have always spoken, is it? What
Of your education? Were
You educated? We mean, of course,
Where were you educated?
                              And how

Much of a handicap is that to you,
Would you say?
                              Married, children,

We see. The usual dubious
Desire to perpetrate what had better
Not have happened at all. We do not
Ask what domestic disasters shimmer
Behind that vaguely unsuitable address.
And you were born – ?
                              Yes. Pity.

So glad we agree.

U.A. Fanthorpe
1929–2009

Contents

List of Tables

About the Author

This book draws on the author's experiences as a chooser of leaders, a leader, a researcher and – of course – a candidate. Born in Hong Kong, he received scholarships and degrees from Cambridge and Harvard and for nearly ten years worked on policy advice in the UK Treasury.

Moving to the private sector, he joined a leading UK executive search firm and spent the next 18 years advising on appointments at or near board level across the public, private, non-profit and academic sectors. His specialisms included looking for candidates across sector boundaries and creating leadership teams for new or unusual organisations.

In addition to becoming deputy chairman of this 50-person firm he co-founded a charity, served as treasurer of two others and chaired the board of the Refugee Council, the UK's leading refugee and asylum charity.

He re-thought his experience of selection and leadership as part of studying for a doctorate in management which he received in 2010. He is a senior visiting fellow at Cass Business School in City University, London. He coaches leaders, advises executives and professionals on career change (maslowsattic.com) and writes on management, careers and leadership (douglasboard.com).

He is married to Tricia Sibbons.

Foreword

Baroness Prashar of Runnymede

Towards the end of this book the author, Douglas Board, says,

> *In this book we have stepped back to re-think the process of executive selection so that, returning to the beach of unknowing, we can light a fire of new beginnings. (p. 186)*

As someone involved for many years in making senior appointments, I very much hope that this book will light a fire of new beginnings.

Fresh thinking about selection of senior executives is much needed. It is a truism to say that hiring the right person for the right position is not an easy task and the price of getting such critical hires wrong can be very high.

This book provides an interesting and insightful examination of the theory and practice of selecting people, why methods used for choosing middle managers are not appropriate for selecting senior leaders and why we need to change our game.

A sea change in the way we think about people selection at senior levels is long overdue. This contribution by Douglas Board fills a gap where those appointing individuals at or near board level in every sector have realised that the good practice which is commonly used to select those below senior levels misses the mark.

Given the complexity and importance of getting senior appointments right and inappropriateness of current practice for this level of selection, this book is aimed not just at general management audience and those already involved in choosing senior people but also psychologists and researchers. It argues for a more integral involvement of psychologists and fresh thinking by researchers. It is a refreshing mixture of theory and practical advice, usefully segmented for different sets of audience.

The author does not merely advance his propositions based on his vast practical experience of executive search but combines that with academic analysis. His analysis of what differentiates senior roles from others and why a different marriage of science, politics and intuition is needed is compelling.

This proposed marriage needs more research and innovative thinking but it also needs imaginative consideration of how this can be done openly and with ethical accountability. This will be tricky and challenging but rising to this challenge will pay dividends.

Phenomenal demands on leaders and senior personnel in a fast changing world make it imperative that we devote serious thought to what kind of senior leaders we need and how best to select them openly and with ethical accountability.

This book is a thoughtful invitation to do just that. It is a valuable contribution to kick starting our 'stuck' senior recruitment practices.

I very much hope that it will generate debate, fresh thinking, and the engagement of selection professionals and executives alike in improving the way senior leaders are chosen.

Usha Prashar has served at board level in the public, private, academic and voluntary sectors. As First Civil Service Commissioner (2000–2005) and founding Chair of the Judicial Appointments Commission (2005–2010) she has played a unique leadership role in securing appointment on merit to high public office in Britain. She was made a life peer in 1999.

Preface

Athletes train differently for competitions at high altitude. What about when we are selecting people at high organisational altitude – in other words at or near the board room, whether in the private or the public sectors? Do all of us (selectors, candidates, advisers and researchers) also need to change our game? This book says yes. More specifically, it argues that:

- we often choose people badly for senior roles;

- if we think about this carefully, that outcome will surprise us less;

- today's good selection practice at middle and front-line organisational levels will not be enough to change things; but

- change at the top is necessary and possible.

As applied research, this book seeks to address practitioners and researchers.

The book is firstly addressed to anyone involved in choosing people high up in organisations – chairs and board members, senior executives and human resource (including executive search) professionals – and to psychologists and researchers who seek to bring insight into this activity. Why has the extensive, evidence-backed good selection practice developed over the past 30 years and more – such as competency frameworks – made so little impression on senior selection? How can we do things differently? The book will suggest bringing about a different marriage of science, politics and intuition – one in which the deep experience, courageous openness and ethical accountability of those who choose our leaders will be more important than ever.

The conclusion that new thinking in research is an important element of change took me by surprise. As a practising executive search professional I never imagined such a thing. Psychologists active and influential in senior appointments are rare birds; human resource (HR) professionals who read selection research may knock on the board room door when senior appointments are made, but often they do not get in. Those active in senior appointments who read books informed by research focus, in my experience, on wider literature – organisational behaviour, leadership, changing markets or reforming public services. Nonetheless this book will argue that there is a stuckness in senior selection research which is contributing to the stuckness in senior selection practice. By the same token fresh thinking by researchers will contribute to new and better practice.

In writing this book I have also had in mind middle managers with ambition who are prepared to engage in leading edge thinking. They will already be involved in choosing others to fill front-line and supervisory roles, and will have received training to do this – for example developing person specifications, using competencies and (probably) grimacing at videos of themselves in action. If you are one of these individuals, you will naturally wonder how far you can rise – and how far you want to rise?

For you this book will do several things. It will start where you are. It will explain what makes senior roles senior. If you so choose, it will boost your managerial performance and career potential by helping you make better choices about people and roles. (If you so choose, because no quick-fix gimmick is on offer; quite the opposite.) It will help you be more informed about offering yourself for leadership positions and, if you do offer yourself, handling with confidence the selection processes you may encounter.

Part I of this book establishes our starting point. Having reminded ourselves how badly we tend to make selection decisions when left to our own devices, we reprise the key tools of good practice which science has put at our disposal over the past 30 years. And we observe that while there has been widespread take-up of these tools by selectors at front-line and middle management levels in larger organisations, regardless of sector, that is rarely true near the board room. Senior selection is stuck.

In Part II we explore what differentiates senior roles from others, again regardless of sector, and conclude by arguing that neither existing good practice, however backed by evidence, nor more of the same, is capable of breaking the log-jam. The argument is a fundamental one touching things we take for granted in thinking about selection or concepts like competence or skill. Part III, therefore, entails developing fresh thinking in these and other areas. In particular we will think differently about science, politics, intuition and, indeed, human identity.

Part IV asks, 'So what?' from the perspective of candidates as well as selectors. The core book from Parts I to IV is intended for all readers.

Part V concludes with three sets of more specialised notes – two sets of field notes for the two practitioner audiences identified above and one set of academic notes. The field notes condense what I have learned from my practical experience relevant to two potentially fraught (and lonely) situations: firstly, if one is a candidate for a high-level appointment, and secondly if one is responsible for appointing the CEO of a small to medium-sized organisation with complex stakeholders but limited access to professional advice. The academic notes put the overall argument of the book in context, as well as providing chapter-specific supplementary notes where appropriate.

This book is concerned with selecting people to fill positions at high organisational altitude: at or near the top of organisations large or small, or responsible for substantial numbers of people and budgets. In these positions leadership and management will both be required in varying proportions, and it can be helpful to distinguish them (Zaleznik, 1978). Leaders do not have to be senior managers, nor is everyone with a corner office or an expensive company car a leader. Jim Kotter (1988) suggests that the distinction is between the more controlling and coercive (managerial) and the more motivating and persuasive (leadership) aspects of running an organisation. But given the subject matter of this book, I will treat them as two sides of one coin. Anyone filling a senior management position these days is expected to offer some kind of leadership. Indeed, our unthinking appetite for leadership is problematic – we will consider this in Part III.

This book does not address the election of leaders representing political parties. That said, the cumulative impact over the next 20 years of businesses, public agencies, universities, schools and charities choosing their leaders better could hardly be less than the impact of choosing a prime minister or president. I invite you to be part of that impact.

Douglas Board
March 2012

Acknowledgements

The dedication of this book to the clients, candidates and colleagues who taught me is heartfelt, as are my thanks to Dr Ralph Mortensen ABPP, Peter and Rosemary Drew and Jonathan Morgan. They read the draft chapters with care and great generosity of insight. I am indebted to Dame Janet Paraskeva who worked with me on the book's structure, and to Professors Douglas Griffin and Ralph Stacey, founders of the Complexity and Management Centre at the University of Hertfordshire, who supervised my doctorate. Together with their colleague Professor Patricia Shaw, they unlocked many of the doors through which this book walks. Acknowledgement is also due to my doctoral examiners, Professors Flemming Poulfelt and Keith Randle FCIPD, of Copenhagen Business School and the University of Hertfordshire respectively. However none of those named are responsible for the errors, omissions and idiosyncrasies in the path taken.

You Will be Hearing from us Shortly by U.A. Fanthorpe, from *New and Collected Poems*. London: Enitharmon, 2010. (ISBN: 978-1-907587-00-9) is reproduced by permission of Dr R.V. Bailey.

Notes on Usage

All emphases within quotations are original unless stated otherwise. Where examples from the author's experience are not on the public record, details which identify organisations or people have been withheld or changed. The work of signifying both genders is shared in different chapters between 'he' and 'she'.

PART I

From Bad to Good to Stuck

1

From Bad ...

Difficult Choices

Stories of difficulty in choosing leaders are all around us. Here are three, spanning organisations small to large, which surfaced in less than six weeks.

In February 2011, Time Warner chief executive fired Jack Griffin, chief executive of the group's Time Inc. magazine publishing business, after less than six months on the job. Previously Griffin had worked at a competitor. He succeeded someone who had been with Time for more than 30 years. Within 24 hours *Harvard Business Review* editor Julia Kirby had crystallised six lessons for would-be corporate change agents – including not hiring cronies into the positions around you (2011).

Later that month, biographer of Warren Buffett, Alice Schroeder wrote in *The Financial Times* about the increasing murk surrounding the succession to the renowned investment guru (2011). Within a month the murk had deepened – Buffett's company, Berkshire Hathaway, announced the acquisition for $10 billion of Lubrizol followed by the resignation under a cloud of David L. Sokol, one of Buffett's key lieutenants. Since Buffett has had his 80th birthday and controls over $160 billion of invested assets, who should succeed him (and why) is a leadership choice question to rival the succession to the Pope.

These choices are no easier at the smaller, non-profit end of the scale. How difficult can it be, bankrolled by some of the world's wealthiest and best-known individuals, to set up and build a school in a developing country? More specifically, in a country with a per capita income of less than $3 a day, how much is it possible to spend on architects, design, salaries, cars and golf course memberships without even acquiring the site for the school, now never to be built? Answer: $3.8 million. So reported Adam Nagourney in March in *The New York Times* (2011) on Madonna's project to build a girls' school in Malawi.

According to an independent assessment quoted by Nagourney, the choice of person to head the planned school was one of the contributing factors. 'Her charisma masks a lack of substantive knowledge of the practical application of education development and her weak management skills are a major contributor to the current financial and programmatic chaos.' The former head was barred by a confidentiality agreement from replying.

Every day board committees, senior executives and others have to choose individuals to fill positions at or near the top of organisations. As the Madonna example illustrates, even if the organisation to be headed up is small, things can go wrong. And every day these decisions have to be made by individuals and groups who cannot afford – in contrast to the examples just given – costly professional advice.

This book aims to be readable by people in the situation of having to choose leaders with limited or no access to professional advice. But it also aims to change the advice which selection professionals and researchers into the practice give. For this reason academic readers might wish to start with the introductory section of the academic notes in Chapter 14 before returning here.

The book sets its sights on fundamentally improving how we choose people for senior roles, not tricks or quick-fixes which must at best be zero-sum gimmicks as between selectors and selectees. Therefore a thread throughout the book is to take seriously the players on both sides of the selection net. After all, tomorrow's top managers are today's middle managers, already appointing people and offering themselves for selection.

Since its readers will already have experience (and in many cases training) in selection, the review of current good practice in Chapter 2 will concentrate on principal features: other sources will be referred to for more detail. The book's thesis will be that it is time to choose our leaders differently: when we get to senior roles, that existing good practice lets us down. But that good practice came about through science dragging this human activity out of the Dark Ages. Not only to understand what makes our good practice effective (without which we will not understand when it might become ineffective), but also because a return to the Dark Ages is the last thing we need, that is where our journey should start: how we choose people when we do not know any better.

From the Playground to the Drawing Room

In the next section we will look at some of the scientific evidence, but first let us use our common sense. Throughout this book I will try to work with both science and common sense, including pointing out where there is reason to believe that one of the two is letting us down. I hope this will help make the book readable and practical; but in Part III there will turn out to be deeper reasons for approaching our subject in this way.

A microcosm of human selection can be found in the school playground. Many of us have memories of lining up and being picked by two captains alternately in order to form two teams. Who gets picked early and why? Most of selection is here. Someone who kicks or throws like a dream. Someone on a winning streak in their last few games. Someone influential or cool, or at least not nerdy or laughed at; someone whose group you want to be in. Someone who is already friends with one of the captains. Someone good-looking. Someone tall. Someone keen. Someone who flatters and sucks up. Someone intimidating or handy in a fight. Above all someone similar to the existing group, who fits in. Despite being tall I was always one of the dregs at the end of the process, barely worth the two captains flipping a coin over, so my memories are still vivid (sociologists call this 'the lucidity of the excluded'). If you look beneath the disciplined language of a Harvard professor, it is easy to see many of the same playground factors at work in Rakesh Khurana's study of how CEOs are recruited at the top of America's largest corporates (2002).

As we grow up, we get taught how to use the correct knives and forks, but unless we are trained in interviewing, the way we select in the playground moves effortlessly into the drawing room or board room. This is beautifully captured in the poem *You Will Be Hearing From Us Shortly* by U. A. Fanthorpe reproduced at the beginning of this book. What she captures – the sense of interviews as a process of social gradation, with class as one significant factor – is no fantasy. As late as the 1970s this was established British good practice.

Consider this example from research at that time by David Silverman and Jill Jones (1973). They studied the graduate recruitment process of a large public sector organisation. The process was thoughtful and structured. First interviews were carried out at universities by a single representative of the employer, out of which 150 candidates (about one-fifth of those interviewed) were invited to a group process at the employer's offices. Groups of eight candidates spent the morning in two group discussions (one on a concrete administrative problem and one on a general topic) and were observed by a panel of three selectors (senior administrators). In the afternoon each candidate had an individual 20 minute interview by the panel. Typically two or three of the eight candidates would be selected.

The organisation had decided that beyond the scheme's degree requirements, they did not wish to select on intelligence. Instead 'acceptability' was key, as reflected in the mark-sheets which selectors used in making and recording their decisions. 'Chadwick' and 'James' are respectively one of the first-round candidates and his interviewer. This was the mark-sheet James completed on Chadwick. The interview was one of a number which were taped and later discussed with the interviewer and with other senior administrators.

Table 1.1   Chadwick's mark-sheet

Appearance	Tall, slim, spotty faced, black hair, dirty grey suit.
Acceptability	Non-existent. Rather uncouth.
Confidence	Awful. Not at all sure of himself.
Effort	High.
Motivation	None that really counts.
Any other comments	Reject.

Source: Silverman and Jones, 1973: 70

Chadwick had a cockney accent. Part of the interview noted that few people from Chadwick's school had gone to university, to which he had applied behind his parents' backs. In a closing exchange in which Chadwick objected to the interview itself:

> J: *Now, any other points?*
> C: *Er ... basically no. Interviews to me – this type of interview – I object to most strongly actually. (Silverman and Jones, 1973: 74–75)*

Chadwick went on to assert – from the perspective of Chapter 2 we might say presciently – that by the end of the interview James still did not know whether a person was suitable for a position in administration, but when challenged he was unable to suggest another way of selecting people. Nevertheless Chadwick had a perspective:

> J: *Put it another way, what would you be looking for?*

C: A logical mind.
J: That's the mental equipment. But what kind of bloke would you look for?' (Silverman and Jones, 1973: 76)

James reflected subsequently that he had been amused by Chadwick's criticism of the interview while lacking an alternative approach, although neither of the things to which Chadwick arguing more effectively might have pointed (intelligence or knowledge of selection) were on the organisation's wanted list.

Three senior administrators who reviewed the tape for the purposes of the research concurred with James's overall judgement. Their discussion includes these exchanges:

A1: ... And bear in mind, of course, that the chap, admittedly he comes from, he is slightly less well-mannered than the other people James has interviewed because of his background ...

A2: I wouldn't say well-mannered necessarily. We've interviewed one or two Etonians whose manners have been absolutely dreadful. But, uh, you know (laughs) ... (Silverman and Jones, 1973: 71–72)

A3: What an excellent interviewer James is!

A2: Yes I liked the way he squashed the attempt of the candidate to interview him at the end of the interview [when Chadwick criticises the interview]. He just killed it stone-dead really without being rude, which is terribly difficult to do in fact ... (Silverman and Jones, 1973: 94)

All this indicates that James is not a rogue interviewer but interpreting the thoughtful good practice of 1973. 'Acceptability' in all its nebulousness does indeed seem to be the key to this selection process. In coming from the playground into the drawing room we do not seem to have travelled far. By contrast the indignation which anyone trained in selection today may feel towards these exchanges shows how far we have moved in the past 40 years.

We make that journey in Chapter 2. What prepared us to move were scientific flashes of light in the dark, snapshots which showed us what we well-meaning selectors were in fact doing.

Scientific Snapshots in the Dark

Worrying evidence about untrained selection, and in particular interviewing, abounds.

Important in Chapter 2 will be the idea of competencies as a basis for selection and HR management more broadly. This concept was developed by Richard Boyatzis (1982), motivated in part by a scientific study of the Broadway Manufacturing Company in America. The study took people who had joined the company as supervisory managers 20 years previously and looked for objective factors which distinguished those who had been promoted most within the company from their less successful peers. Only one objective difference could be found: the more successful supervisors were taller.

Height continues to matter. Judge and Cable looked at four studies (three American, one British) totalling 8,590 individuals. Basing their calculations on the value of US dollars in 2002, they found that:

> ... an individual who is 72 in. [1.83 m] tall could be expected to earn $5,525 more per year than someone who is 65 in. [1.65 m] tall, even after controlling for gender, weight, and age. (Judge and Cable, 2004: 435)

Speaking of weight – more recently Judge and Cable (2011) have explored the gendered impact of weight on earnings. They conclude that across a 25-year career, American women who are 25 lbs (11.4 kg) below average weight earn $389,300 more than American women of average weight, while for American men the difference is $210,925 and reversed (the heavier men earn more).

Or – a small sample from a cornucopia of possible material – women candidates facing male interviewers should wear dark jackets (and preferably blue rather than red), while female interviewers are relatively uninfluenced by colour (Damhorst and Reed, 1986) (Scherbaum and Shepherd, 1987). Studies among managers in utility companies suggest that physical attractiveness is correlated with interview ratings as well as with assessed job performance (Motowidlo and Burnett, 1995) (Burnett and Motowidlo, 1998) (DeGroot and Motowidlo, 1999).

For many years there has been evidence that untrained interviewers are drawn to intuitive conclusions in the opening minutes of an interview and use the rest of the time to assemble confirmatory evidence. That initial judgement time was estimated at four minutes by Springbett (1958) and nine minutes by Tucker and Rowe (1977).[1]

Some judgements formed even before the interview starts prove difficult to displace. Huguenard, Sager and Ferguson (1970) simulated 377 employment interviews where one person interviews another. Before meeting the candidates the interviewers were given (artificial) results from a 'personality test' which suggested that the candidates they were about to meet were 'cold' or 'warm'. Whether the interviews lasted 10, 20 or 30 minutes, the interviewers persisted in describing the candidates in terms consistent with the initial label.

In fact the selection interview is a doubly dangerous breeding ground for early impressions. However we react to someone's height, weight, jacket colour or physical attractiveness, these things are unlikely to change during the interview. That is not so with the complex interpersonal factors with which interviews are concerned. Most interviewers' early impressions are leaky. They rapidly communicate themselves to the candidate in different ways – eye contact, posture, tone of voice, frequency of interruption not to mention choice of words. Consciously or unconsciously the candidate is affected. The interviewer plays a major part in creating the interview 'performance' which she assesses. An early critique on these lines was made by Dipboye (1982). Fanthorpe's poem in the opening pages of the book expresses this eloquently: we see the candidate vividly through the interviewer's eyes without reading a single word of the candidate's own.

Indeed, Arvey and Campion (1982) were able to say in what became one of the most frequently cited articles of the 1980s in the journal *Personnel Psychology*:

> *Perhaps the glaring 'black hole' in all previous reviews and in the current literature concerns the issue of why use of the interview persists in view of evidence of its relatively low validity, reliability, and its susceptibility to bias and distortion. (1982: 314)*

That landscape has not changed. As Wood and Payne (1998) observed:

---

1   Gladwell (2005) has noted that we are capable of astonishingly complex judgements within a few minutes, seconds or fractions of a second. These are ideas to which we will return in re-thinking skill and intuition in Chapter 7, but for the moment we may note that Gladwell devotes a chapter and his central conclusion to emphasising how badly wrong our rapid judgements about people and their abilities can be.

*Many studies have shown the predictive validity of unstructured
interviews to be around zero. (1998: 96)*

One would be as well off choosing people by tossing a coin.

To all the selection-specific research we can add the extensive body of
knowledge which, thanks to science, we have gained about more general
problems with human decision-making. For example there have been many
studies of the processes of clinical judgement which trained professionals – for
example psychologists – use to assimilate complex, incomplete and possibly
discrepant information about particular individuals and make a decision.
Writing in the context of psychologists who assess and counsel individuals,
Spengler and three colleagues (1995) highlight several recurrent problems in
the formation of clinical judgements including:

- availability – paying too much attention to the parts of the evidence
  which come easily to mind;

- anchoring – over-weighting information which is presented early;

- overshadowing – one major diagnosis leads other complicating
  factors to be ignored;

- confirmation – seeking and finding evidence to support initial
  hypotheses rather than noticing contra-indications;

- attribution – too easily interpreting events or actions as signs of
  personal traits at the expense of external or situational factors.

These potential errors easily translate into selection interviews, particularly the
'halo' effect in which the flaws of candidates who appear good disappear from
view. Only careful re-reading of interview notes which are sufficiently detailed
to bring back to mind the dull as well as the vivid parts of a candidate's answers
will combat availability: taking such notes as well as participating in an engaged
way in the questioning is beyond the ability of most occasional interviewers.
Anchoring, overshadowing and confirmation are obvious suspects behind the
overpowering effect of early interview impressions. An attribution error so
often made that it masquerades as common sense is deciding that someone is
indecisive who hesitates and fumbles an interview question, despite years of
contrary evidence from their actions in the field.

In any of these respects, the judgements even of trained employment interviewers are hardly likely to be better than that of clinical professionals – quite apart from the lack of objectivity involved if the decision will be whether to make the candidate a colleague of the interviewer's.

Selection at Senior Levels

By now it would be reasonable to accept that, at least in the absence of contemporary good practices, selection can be a fraught activity. The Dark Ages were dark.

However they were also some time ago. Good practices along the lines of those summarised in Chapter 2 have been around in some form for 20 or 30 years. Moreover the reasonable person might expect more than average care, effort and expense in the way selection people are chosen for leading roles. After all, a recent financial modelling exercise estimated that boards of US corporations behaved as if replacing the CEO cost shareholders at least $200 million (Taylor, 2010). So it seems improbable that school playground behaviour would have much to do with this. The stories with which this chapter opened – Jack Griffin's departure from Time Inc., the Warren Buffett succession at Berkshire Hathaway, Madonna's girls' school in Malawi – at best hinted indirectly and anecdotally at problems. Why should we think the Dark Ages are anywhere nearby when we choose leaders today?

To be clear about this book's claim, it is not that every top appointment is filled badly. Chapter 3 will give examples of good, indeed exceptional, board room selection. However the spread of such laudable examples is patchy. Behind the corporate confidentiality which cloaks most top appointments, standards often fall below those taken for granted in far less lofty places. I am suggesting that this is both surprising and significant.

I will use three sources of evidence which cover different sectors and different countries: the study by Rakesh Khurana (2002) of how CEO positions are filled at the pinnacle of corporate America referred to earlier in this chapter; the first reports in Britain of how individuals were chosen for judicial office; and my own 18 years in executive search.

Corporate America

If the confidentiality of senior appointments is fiercely guarded, that of CEOs of major US corporations – a world of private jets, closed doors and wariness about stories which might move the stock price unintentionally is particularly so. No doubt the cachet of Harvard Business School was helpful to Khurana in breaking in. He interviewed 40 directors with experience between them of some one-fifth of the *Fortune* 1000 companies. The interviews explored in depth 40 separate CEO succession events which took place between 1990 and 2001. Khurana supplemented this with interviews with 30 executive search consultants. His analysis is thoughtful and his conclusions trenchant, conveyed quite clearly by his study's title: *Searching for a Corporate Savior: The Irrational Quest for Charismatic CEOs.*

The terrain reeks of confidentiality and money. After all we are in the territory of the Warren Buffett story at this chapter's opening. To set the scene Khurana reconstructs the appointment on 27 March 2000 of Jamie Dimon (at the time of writing chairman and CEO of J. P. Morgan Chase & Co) to be CEO of Chicago-based Bank One. In the final stages of the process, the choreography required to assure confidentiality was extreme – for example scheduling interviews and shortlisted candidates' flights so as to eliminate any possibility of candidates seeing one another at the airport.

As for money, within a week Bank One's market capitalisation had soared by nearly one-third. Dimon himself was assured $3.5 million in cash in his first year plus future, variable bonuses and a guaranteed minimum of $7 million annually in bank shares. Suffice to say that using industry standard benchmarks, search professionals at this level would charge the hiring companies (their clients) more than $1 million in fees, little or none of which would be contingent on future company results.

For sums like this, one might expect the search firms to work extremely hard at finding and attracting obvious and less obvious candidates, and to assess them meticulously. Given what was at stake for their clients (the appointing boards and their nominations committees), one would expect them also to be rigorous and challenging to a fault in their assessment of candidates. Khurana so expected.

He was surprised. He observed that predominantly it was the client boards who suggested the candidates: having paid for very expensive dogs, they barked themselves. The role of the search firms was to approach the candidates and to invest prodigious effort in managing multiple, delicate, separate courtships, protecting both candidates and the hiring firm from embarrassment at any stage. Since discovering that a wooed candidate was unsuitable or incompetent would be such an embarrassment, search firms tended not to do much of this, the rational pretext being that candidates of this eminence were already very well known within their industries.

More surprising was that this lack of challenge to the candidates extended to the hiring companies. Board directors described interview processes in which their main concern was not to ask a question which might inadvertently put a top candidate off. Khurana ended up summarising the archetype of the processes which he found as crowning Napoleon – a coronation whose finishing touch is that the candidate takes the crown out of his anointers' hands and places it on his own head. Recall that this is to appoint someone whose removal, if a mistake has been made, would apparently cost shareholders at least $200 million – according to the same board members' actions interrogated by Taylor's research above. The following is also a reasonable surmise: if after the new CEO's arrival the HR director recommended the appointment of someone important but lesser – say a director of research and development – with the same lack of scrutiny, she would be out on her ear.

Is Khurana's picture exaggerated? Fellow Harvard professor Joseph Bower (2007) drew on his own extensive board as well as academic experience to take a less negative view of search firms and board succession processes, but nevertheless described as 'quite typical' a selection process for corporate CEOs which he characterises as 'blindfolded parking' (Bower 2007: 84). He meant by this that an internal candidate is inadequately prepared for the role in advance. At the time of appointment these deficiencies become apparent but the candidate is appointed anyway. For Bower this amounts to:

> You back into the space until you hit the car behind you, then you go forward until you hit the car in front of you, and you repeat the process until you're close enough to the curb. It is almost always costly to both the company and the candidate. (Bower, 2007: 84)

Filling senior roles in this way may cost shareholders hundreds of millions of dollars of value and many other employees their jobs.

I think Khurana's picture should be qualified as to scope, but taken as fair at the dizzy corporate heights which he was studying. My experience at senior but less dizzy levels is that good search firms do more finding of creative candidates, and that both clients and search firms do more testing of candidates' strengths and weaknesses, than Khurana found. But within the terrain he was surveying, there is good reason to believe that his picture is not exaggerated.

For example, the study was retrospective. Therefore interviewees (anonymity notwithstanding) probably gave accounts which to some degree flattered themselves. If so, we can draw unflattering conclusions all the more confidently. Reality may be worse than Khurana's picture, but not better. On that assumption, there is more of the school playground in how we get our top commercial chief executives than most of us care to think.

Judicial Britain

Khurana's account still allows that a key function of search consultants is to stir up individuals to become interested in roles which do not immediately catch their attention. Normally, however, the search consultant will be delighted to find a candidate who is already enthusiastic. One search I led where that was not the case was to find a group of Britons with diverse backgrounds and professional skills, including experience of making senior appointments, who could become interested in the appointment of judges but who were initially lukewarm on the subject. The result was the appointment in 2001 of the Commission for Judicial Appointments with Professor Sir Colin Campbell, then Vice-Chancellor of Nottingham University, as chair.

The curious requirement for potential but not developed interest was because the function of the Commission was akin to that of a jury. People highly interested in the subject would already have formed views. The Commissioners were to make history: the first group with independent standing empowered to audit and report on how judges were chosen in England and Wales. Judicial appointments had been a closeted function of the Lord Chancellor for many centuries. The Commissioners would also inspect the arrangements, also in the Lord Chancellor's hands, for awarding exceptional advocates and leaders of the legal profession the title 'Queen's Counsel' (QC), also known as taking silk.

Judicial appointments in England span several tiers including magistrates, district judges and chairs of tribunals, but the system's apex is appointments to the High Court, the Court of Appeal and what is now the Supreme Court. High Court judges often sit alone without a jury. Their decisions may include whether an individual's deportation should be stopped or their life support turned off, determining that one party should pay another damages worth hundreds of millions of pounds or quashing a government action as unlawful. Traditionally they are an elite group drawn from male court room advocates (barristers) educated at the country's most prestigious universities.

Without doubt the historical process of appointment produced High Court judges who, with few exceptions, commanded national and international respect for their knowledge, sharp reasoning and impartiality. But were the appointments made at lower tiers as consistently effective? And at all levels were equally effective candidates who were women, or from ethnic minorities, or doing less prestigious types of legal work (such as solicitors who mainly dealt with clients rather than court room jousting), being overlooked?

The historical process presumed that, firstly, the best training ground and competitive assessment process to be a High Court judge was to earn your living over many years as a premier division court advocate, and secondly, the people who could best assess these individuals were their peers (as opposed, for example, to their clients). From this perspective how could the results of any interview compare with individuals' professional track record (cases won and lost) over many years, evaluated by those who had worked alongside and against them?

The core elements of this social-professional rating structure are common to many elite groups. For example it is similar to the way in which academics who are candidates for high university roles rate each other; indeed the cachet attached to research by comparison with teaching is reminiscent of the distinction in the English system between court room advocates and other lawyers. There are also echoes in the way bishops are appointed in the Church of England, through the confidential assembling of views rather than interview or any other direct assessment procedure.

The pattern has the clear potential to become self-serving, complacent or indeed corrupt but equally it does not need to be so. If I need specialist surgery and know how specialist surgeons are rated by each other, I would not obviously be better off choosing my surgeon by studying each one's credentials myself. How would I decide whether to attribute higher patient death rates to lower skill, or a more difficult case load reflecting higher skill?

In the case of the processes audited by the Commissioners for Judicial Appointments, we should acknowledge that they involved some of the country's most intelligent individuals (although almost exclusively white men) – and moreover individuals dedicated by career choice to delivering public, impartial and accountable fairness. The importance of the selections made was heightened by the difficulty of removing judges from office.

In personnel selection terms, the Commission found themselves peering into the Dark Ages. In one year alone (2003) they found all of the following (by no means an exhaustive list). A judge had been unfairly rejected for promotion by a panel whose:

> ... *comments did not relate to the criteria [of the competition], cited no evidence to support their views, appeared highly subjective and moreover were couched in offensive and inappropriate language. (2003: 10)*

Moreover:

> *We have seen evidence of senior consultees [high-ranking lawyers and judges] expressing their views about female candidates in inappropriate terms, referring to their dress sense or marital status. (2003: 41)*

They found the 2003 High Court judge appointments to be so lacking in transparency and accountability that they hoped no further appointments would be made on that model.

In their review of the process for awarding QC status (silk) in the same year, they found those involved frequently unable to articulate what they were doing – 'silk quality' was stated to be impossible to describe but you know one when you see one – and they observed a lot of off-the-record discussion of irrelevant material, descriptions of candidates as buffoons or (in the case of a woman) comments on her dress sense. One official part of the process was a discussion of the papers summarising the 394 candidates with the Attorney General, which was cut short to 20 minutes because of an urgent Cabinet meeting. The final discussion between the Lord Chancellor, the Lord Chief Justice and other senior judges, which was observed by the Commissioners, in several cases petered out with no evident conclusion or consensus. (Since they were being observed it is clear that the distinguished individuals involved believed they were acting conscientiously and appropriately.) The Commissioners reached the strong conclusion that not only could they not describe the system as meritocratic, but they could not see how adjustments short of wholesale reform could make it meritocratic.

By 2005 there had been a complete overhaul of the process for 'silk'. Selection remained in the Lord Chancellor's hands, but guided by an independent panel. However legislation removed judicial appointments from the Lord Chancellor's gift and placed them in the hands of a new, independent Judicial Appointments Commission.

My Experience

Throughout this book I draw on my experience particularly as a search consultant (although also as a leader, a candidate, a careers adviser and a researcher). It is therefore relevant to give an insight into my search work. This true account does that. It also shows me failing to master a professional challenge and introduces a summary of personal encounters with the 'Dark Ages' in senior selection – unprofessional behaviour which would not be tolerated lower down in organisations.

XPA has a worldwide turnover of more than $100 million and operates in more than 50 countries. It is also a professional body with a large membership, qualification-awarding powers and substantial commercial operations. At the time in question XPA had grown dramatically in size and reputation under its workaholic chief executive for more than the previous ten years, Patrick, who was now approaching retirement. Like many professional bodies, governance (including the appointment of the next chief executive) was in the hands of a large and unwieldy elected board, further weakened by the annual rotation of officers. In other words each person who became chair did so for one year only.

Along with three or four competitors, my search firm was invited to submit a proposal for the recruitment of Patrick's successor. This needed to include a timetable and all key steps for making the selection decision, including the evaluation of any internal candidates. In addition, the commercial success of XPA meant that the board attached a lot of importance to searching out growth-oriented, international, commercial and other candidates of stature who might ordinarily consider the chief executiveship of a professional body too dull.

Already, on the facts already summarised and without having met Patrick, we sensed as a potentially important risk factor the possibility of a too-powerful incumbent. The risk was that the incumbent would dominate the process of attracting and selecting his successor. I had been in the business long enough to identify quite a range of problems, some of them grave, which could arise.

We made our presentation to the relevant committee. It was no surprise to see Patrick sitting alongside them – silent but clearly influential. That scenario was familiar and could be turned to advantage. Politely but bluntly, after covering other more predictable issues, we expressed strongly that while an incumbent had a critical role to play in certain early stages of the process, in our view it was inappropriate for them to be involved in shortlisting, final interviewing or the committee's final decision. Normally the presence of an incumbent during such a presentation was an advantage. If we failed to persuade the committee members, or if the incumbent was more powerful than the committee and wanted to be involved in the final stages, then one of our competitors would be given the assignment. In one sense all this could not be simpler or more rational: having gained sufficient experience to learn certain lessons, by placing these (including the possible issue of a powerful incumbent) on the table before our services were contracted, then – problem solved.

Not so. My firm was appointed on the terms we had proposed. The search was international and creative, and took several months. A high-quality international field was identified. Throughout these stages we involved Patrick in all the ways which we had agreed and he behaved impeccably. But as the final stages approached, this rapidly changed. Previous agreements and rational discussions failed to stop Patrick pressuring the committee at short notice to let him sit in on the final candidates' interviews and the committee's deliberations. XPA's chairman simply caved in. As a result shortlisted candidates were constrained by Patrick's presence in presenting in a frank way their analyses of XPA's shortcomings. They were also somewhat concerned by this departure from etiquette (as well as previous plan). Although things were now tense, Patrick's job was offered to an individual who accepted it and resigned publicly from a high-profile position elsewhere. He accepted the congratulations of friends on winning his first chief executive role and began a round of leaving parties. A few weeks later he 'unresigned' and took his old job back; although he had only started doing induction visits to XPA and had not yet had his first employed day in the organisation, he felt Patrick had made his position intolerable.

Patrick stayed on and another search firm started afresh. Within a year that too turned out problematically. Ultimately Patrick was succeeded by an internal candidate. Considerable damage had been done to XPA by behaviour which would not have been tolerated from a junior or middle manager, but which behind closed board room doors rode rough-shod over the interests of the organisation and many reputations.

A reasonable estimate is that during my 18 years in executive search I interviewed over 7,500 candidates and advised on over 1,000 appointments. Of these 70 per cent were at board or senior management team level. While most of the appointments were UK-based it was frequently the case (as it was with XPA) that the candidates came from, and had to be searched for in, many countries. The work ranged widely across the private, public, academic and non-profit sectors.

XPA was an extreme case. Another extreme was sitting in the office of the British Cabinet Secretary listening to a knight of the realm argue that Vanessa, whom they had just interviewed and rated highly, was not the best choice because if her appointment was announced, it would be thought that she had been appointed because she was black. I was the most junior person in the room but I'm sure it would have been easy to find a policeman outside had I gone looking for one. I bit my lip and later found a way of getting the decision reversed.

Eschewing extremes, my experience has been that in all the main stages of top-level recruitments, from the identification of requirements through selection to negotiation with candidates, most months I encountered things which in many organisations would not have been acceptable in less senior recruitments.

Explaining inexplicable delays, apologising for lack of basic information, clients changing meetings at short notice and grappling with opacity about, or U-turns in, what the organisation is 'really' looking for are bread and butter for search consultants and their candidates. They speak to a shoddiness, discourtesy and lack of attention to what it feels like to be the candidate; but shoddiness can be elevated into an art form. How about in the private sector taking a candidate whose remuneration expectations are made clear from the outset, interviewing her ten times and then offering her the role at half the expected money. The equivalent in the public sector, where the salary is usually known from the outset, might be reading your name along with the rest of the shortlist in a newspaper, and then still being kept in the dark for weeks.

Why is this worth saying? Firstly, to offer context (certainly not an excuse), should you be a candidate in a senior appointment process and experience rudeness or bizarre twists. And secondly, as a stimulus to curiosity: why is the world like this? In Chapter 3 we will ask if it is just an accident that senior selection lags behind good practice which is well-established elsewhere. Next we turn – perhaps with some relief – to that good practice.

2

... To Good

Rigorous Practice

An example of rigorous practice in choosing leaders was reported by Craig Russell (1990) in the *Journal of Management*. A *Fortune* 50 company was selecting staff for promotion to its general management tier, where those chosen would run businesses each of which, had they been independent companies, would have ranked in the middle half of the *Fortune* 1000. The average age of the 66 candidates was 47.5 years, all insiders (and all men) with 22 years' previous service with the company. Some had run business units, some had spent their careers within a functional role, such as marketing, while others had moved between different kinds of role.

The first task was taken to be, to identify as objectively as possible what capabilities successful performance in a general management role within this company required. Those concerned led an intensive process of discussion with 12 general managers perceived to be amongst the highest performing in the company, focussing on concrete incidents which had happened. The results were distilled into nine attributes or abilities whose importance was verified by a questionnaire to a wider group of 75 general managers. Examples of the attributes which emerged were short-term business execution, customer relations and strategic planning. Each of the nine was carefully defined and supported by concrete examples of the attribute in action.

The second task was to assess, again as objectively as possible, the candidates' strengths and weaknesses against each of the defined attributes. The candidates underwent tape-recorded interviews which lasted between four and 8.5 hours (average 4.5). The interviews concentrated on the main challenges, achievements and learning of the candidates in their current role and earlier in their career. Transcripts of each interview were prepared and assessments made independently by five raters against the nine defined attributes.

This information was combined with assessments by direct superiors and a range of other colleagues. Interviews with superiors lasted between two and three hours; other respondents (subordinates, peers and previous superiors) were interrogated by questionnaire. The five raters – one a human resource specialist within the firm, four independent academics or consultants – assessed all the material on all the candidates individually, and then met to produce a consensus report on each candidate. These reports were debriefed to the candidates and their direct superiors.

At the time of writing up his work, Russell noted that 12 candidates had been appointed to the target roles but insufficient time had elapsed to make a judgement about the success of the selection process. However it would be hard to imagine a more rigorous attempt to select candidates objectively against the best available understanding of the organisation's needs. Self-evidently, the process was time-consuming and expensive; equally its hoped-for benefits would not have been limited to better performances in the 12 business units with new leaders (better than if the process had been more cursory). Among the 54 executives not selected, each already in a demanding role, there should have been dividends in the form of greater self-awareness, better focused personal development and a strengthened sense of the company's fairness. To a yet wider managerial group, the selection process would have made a significant statement about the company's confidence in its in-house talent and the diversity of possible career routes within the company which could reach the top.

At a different corporate scale, Kaplan, Klebanov and Sorensen (2008) reported on a commercial database of assessments of 316 CEO candidates for positions in private equity or venture capital-financed businesses. The assessments were prepared by a specialist consulting firm, ghSMART, which produced 20 to 40-page reports on each candidate covering 30 specific characteristics. These reports were based on four-hour interviews conducted by individuals with doctorates or MBAs from leading business schools who had worked in strategy consultancies such as McKinsey or Bain. The interviewers asked for specific examples of actions and behaviour at every job and life stage of the candidates, from childhood onwards.

Both of these approaches examine past actions at a level of detail which, while not immune to selective memory, demonstrably get beyond candidates making wishful generalisations about their achievements. The interviews demanded facts in a quantity beyond most candidates' ability simply to fabricate. This detailed, granular, behavioural approach is not the only one which could be adopted. For example an approach which interrogates candidates' careers in terms of the level of complexity and the time horizon for decisions taken will be introduced in Chapter 4. This approach has recently been used in filling some of the most senior appointments in the British public service. Another recognised approach is the in-depth assessment of candidates by a psychologist, reviewed by Silzer and Jeanneret (2011). While the evidence which validates the use of each of these approaches is often patchy or mixed, there clearly are outbreaks of rigorous selection practice at senior levels, even if the conclusion of Chapter 1 remains that their coverage is limited. However the kinds of detailed, behaviour-based assessment described by Russell and by Kaplan exemplify particularly well an approach to selection which is today nearly synonymous with 'good practice': namely the use of competencies.

Given the risks described by Khurana in Chapter 1, most large private sector organisations will go to great lengths to avoid reliance on an external search as the way to fill a CEO vacancy.[1] Here the emphasis will be on having planned five or ten years ahead, and having sufficient breadth and depth of talent inside the company in the one (or two) ranks below the CEO. However, even with successful succession planning, at some point a selection decision among the internal candidates is required. I agree with Bower (2007) that the idea of a 'baton passing' succession, in which at an early stage one internal candidate emerges head and shoulders above her peers and is anointed heir-apparent, simply shifts the time at which the competition and the selection decision take place. Only monarchies have (in theory) at all times an already-known successor.

In the next section we will come down to earth. I will sketch an understanding of good selection practice today in ordinary, everyday terms. Then we will examine the idea of competencies, including why the idea has proved so powerful as to dominate human resource management. We will note some of the strengths and weaknesses of thinking in this way, and in particular highlight the scientific foundations on which not only competencies but virtually all selection research and good practice rest.

---

1   In contrast, universities even of the highest rank will commonly conduct a major external search to find their CEO's successor.

Good Selection Practice Today

If the two examples in the preceding section represent the Lexus and the BMW of good, contemporary selection practice, I now want to sketch something closer to the Fiat Punto.

This section will not try to provide the detail you might need to design a high-quality recruitment process for, say, managers of out-patient clinics. This material is widely available elsewhere, for example in the guides to best practice by Wood and Payne (1998) or Howard (2007), and in training courses organised by HR departments. Nor is this the place where I try to distil all the practical help I can offer to someone responsible for recruiting, say, a chief executive of a stand-alone small or medium-sized organisation. What I have to offer in that vein is in Chapter 13. Here I simply want to give the flavour of today's generally accepted good practice.

The first step is to fix one's eyes not simply on the post to be filled but the wider organisation, its strengths and weaknesses, its priorities and challenges for the next three years (or the consequences of the fact that these are unclear, if that is the case). The expected degree and direction of change in the organisation's environment (or its chaotic quality) will be important. A senior post is part of a group of people with wide and to some extent unpredictable responsibilities.

The second step will be to look at (and in most cases involve in discussion) other members of that senior group, and consider to what extent the person to be appointed needs to fit with, complement or challenge the dynamic which is there already.

None of these things are likely to appear in the one document which can normally be relied upon to surface at this stage: a job description of the post, possibly some years out of date. In a larger organisation a set of competencies to be included in all posts in the corporate leadership cadre may be available and may prove useful.

The third focus will be the group, activity or business unit of which the new person will take charge – here the current business plan and the performance history of the group needs to be digested. There may be debates about what qualifications or professional experience are essential, desirable or perhaps neither.

The line manager, or someone from HR or a recruitment consultant, takes the lead in converting all of the above into a draft *person specification* – a statement of what knowledge, skills, abilities and other attributes it is considered that the candidate either must, or preferably should, have. While the person specification is not the only important document in a recruitment – for example it matters that there is an adequate formal statement of the job's responsibilities, including to whom the person will be accountable – the person specification is the hinge of the whole selection process. It should drive whether, where and how the position is advertised, and where search is carried out if relevant. Made known to potential candidates, the person specification enables them to decide whether to put themselves forward for the role. And, if they do, it tells them which of their past achievements and other potentially relevant information to offer the selectors. It should shape what kind of interview questions are asked and what other selection procedures are used. It should also be the measuring rod against which candidates are compared.

Good person specifications take time and experience to produce. Normally at least a couple of iterations will be needed to construct something that is clear, focused on the six to ten (maximum) most important attributes, avoiding duplication and contradiction as well as fatuous platitudes. It is also vital that, taken with the responsibility and remuneration offered, the person specification is at least half-way compatible with the relevant labour market. Taking into account the prestige and the riskiness of the role, what chance is there of finding someone with everything which the specification says is essential and at least some of what it says is desirable for the salary and other benefits offered?

Most person specifications fail badly against several of these criteria. This is unsurprising because they are produced as a rush job and with little sense of how much hangs on the quality of the thought which goes into this critical stage. Apart from being overlong, unclear or poorly prioritised, person specifications can fail through being unnecessarily restrictive as well as too lax. By demanding qualifications which are not needed, the process may miss out on the best candidates as well as be discriminatory.

At the end of Chapter 13 is a person specification for the recruitment by a small national organisation of a chief executive, set out in a form which could be used as an interview checklist and assessment sheet. Although small the organisation needed to set the pace in its field and wield national influence. It had relationships with a wide range of specialist and larger organisations in two disciplines (to maintain anonymity these appear as 'P' and 'Q'), as well as government and many members of the public. In preparing the form I was encouraging the selectors to assess what all the evidence on each candidate told them about two aspects of the candidate's drives and values, three aspects of their track record of achievements and five skills. Five of these ten attributes were highlighted as priorities. Skills where more is always better (for example being persuasive) were distinguished from ones where the essence of the skill lies in striking a balance (for example risk-taking).

As well as interviews, the costs and benefits of a number of other selection elements will have been considered as part of the process – for example what information to ask from candidates as part of the process before interview, whether to use telephone screening or psychometric tests or work simulation exercises, the nature and kind of reference checks, and so on. Cost, likely value, the time required and likely acceptability to good candidates will have to be weighed up. In the final mix, different selection elements will be targeted against particular parts of the person specification, so that for example precious interview time is not wasted covering things better explored another way.

The number of interviewers in any interview will reflect thought about the kind of exchanges desired with the candidates. Adequate note-taking will be seen as critical. Most people on their own have great difficulty conducting an interview, listening to what is said and note-taking at the same time, but there are diminishing returns as the number of interviewers increases beyond two or three. The interviewers' questions will follow a structure which is consistent between the candidates, with appropriate use of open and closed questions and a lot of asking for specific examples from the person's experience. Use of hypothetical fantasies 'what would you do if … ' will be very sparing.

Some strict expressions of good practice suggest that the detailed interview questions should be identical between candidates. I think it is preferable to cover consistent areas in a way which gives different candidates equal opportunity to show their best – which means putting questions in a way which recognises what they have already written or said, and follows up unclear or unexpected answers. The interviewers need to do all this keeping their positive energy and conversational engagement with each candidate as consistent as they can manage.

The interviewers will not think that having reached a firm conclusion about the candidate before the interview has ended is testimony to their interviewing prowess, rather the opposite. They will maximise the opportunity of the interview to let the candidate put forward relevant evidence, including evidence which disconfirms early suppositions. The time after the candidate has gone – which should not be rushed – is the time when judgements should be reached. The final judgement will pull together evidence from all the different parts of the process to reach a reasoned assessment of the candidate against the person specification (and not extraneous or spontaneously created criteria).

Finally training will have been necessary to embed these points into selectors' practice. That training will have highlighted how good selection practice is vital if an organisation is to achieve a diverse leadership cadre and to avoid direct as well as indirect discrimination on inappropriate grounds, such as gender, ethnicity, sexuality and age, as well as appropriate adaptations for candidates with disabilities.

Timeliness and detail of feedback to unsuccessful as well as successful candidates will be a hallmark of a quality selection process. Not only is this ethical behaviour but also every selection is a two-way process: the selector needs the preferred candidate to choose to take up the role. Since the unsuccessful candidates will also be senior how they experience the process will affect the hiring organisation's reputation. From the beginning what kind of information to give candidates about the organisation (and what opportunities to give them for probing in depth) will have been carefully considered, and not left to a perfunctory few minutes at an interview's end.

Chapter 14 provides suggestions if you would like to inquire in more detail into what is today's good practice. Instead my purpose has been to produce a recognisable sketch, albeit with personal variations and emphases, about what good practice is for people working in selection today. If I have done that task justice, then recalling from Chapter 1 Chadwick's mark-sheet ('[Acceptability] non-existent. Rather uncouth') and *that* selection process, good practice has moved a long way since 1973.

A competency-based approach will go further in requiring that all or most of the person specification should not be as general as 'knowledge, skills, abilities and other attributes' (KSAOs) but be more narrowly drawn, with an emphasis on observable actions and outcomes and with distinctions between levels of skill clearly pinned down in objective terms. The emphasis in a competency-based application form or interview is on asking the individual to give in some detail concrete instances in which they demonstrated this skill in action, stating the context, what they did, what part others played, what happened and with what consequences. Wood and Payne give the following example of a competency in detail (Table 2.1).

Table 2.1   A competency in detail

Planning and Organizing

Definition: the ability to visualize a sequence of actions needed to achieve a goal and to estimate the resources required. A preference for acting in a structured, thorough manner.

Indicators: Level 1 – junior manager
- manages own time and personal activities
- breaks complex activities into manageable tasks
- identifies possible obstacles to planned achievement.

Level 2 – middle manager
- produces contingency plans for possible future occurrences
- estimates in advance the resources and time scales needed to meet objectives
- co-ordinates team activities to make the best use of individual skills and specialisms.

Level 3 – senior manager
- identifies longer term operational implications of business plans
- effectively plans utilisation of all resources.

Source: Wood and Payne, 1998: 28

Competencies are the flagship of the flotilla of good practices which this section has described.

Competencies

Richard Boyatzis based his book *The Competent Manager: A Model for Effective Performance* (1982) on studies involving over 2,000 managers working in eight *Fortune* 500 companies in different sectors together with four federal agencies. Stung by the appalling results of cumulative ad hoc selection over time, including the discovery of height as the only objectively discernible characteristic differentiating more promoted from less promoted managers at the Broadway Manufacturing Company (see Chapter 1), Boyatzis and his colleagues devised a rigorous process for doing better. Both the approach he took and the results he obtained have proved influential.

Boyatzis started his quest by attempting to think clearly about what effective managerial performance might consist of. He saw this as produced by the conjunction of a job's demands, the organisational environment and the individual's competencies. He summarised the overlap like this:

> The job demands component reveals primarily what a person in the job is expected to do. The organizational environment component reveals some aspects of what a person in a management job is expected to do, but primarily reveals how a person is expected to respond to the job demands. The individual's competencies component reveals what a person is capable of doing: it reveals why he or she may act in certain ways. (Boyatzis, 1982: 16)

For example, the job of a finance director includes supervising the production of an annual set of audited accounts which comply with applicable accounting standards. Is it 'effective performance' to do this quickly or slowly, transparently or opaquely, with excruciating attention to detail or with just enough attention to get by? That will be decided by the organisational environment. Whether a particular finance director is capable of delivering what the job and the organisation jointly demand will be down to that person's competencies.

What Boyaztis meant by 'competencies' was more than just skill, meaning to emphasise by this word that one can observe certain actions producing certain results. Thus, what in soccer might be the competencies of a striker? They will include skill in kicking an awkardly moving ball with accuracy and power. Targeting the goal reliably at different speeds, angles and distances – all these are measurable and are in the realm of skill. That is also true of all the aspects of planning and organising given in Wood and Payne's table above. The points they list are observable behaviours, with explicitly or implicitly observable results: 'effectively plans utilisation of all resources' involves a plan being produced about whose likely effectiveness we can have a view. For Boyatzis this level or dimension of skill is one dimension of a competency.

But Boytazis argues that:

> ... to define a competency, we must determine what the actions were and their place in a system and sequence of behaviour and what the results or effects were and what the intent or meaning of the actions and results were. (Boyatzis, 1982: 22)

What induces people to act in this way? What motivates or drives them? How do they see themselves and how do others see them in the light of their actions? These other dimensions of a competency Boyatzis calls motives, traits, self-image and social role. Thus a full picture of a striker's competence needs to say something about when and why he exercises his skill of accurate kicking – does he always shoot for goal however low the odds or does he give chances to better placed colleagues? Is he motivated by personal glory or the team's success? Does he keep the skill of shooting accurately, or even raise his game, when things are going badly or is he easily thrown off his stride? Does he see himself as a leader, and is he seen by his colleagues like that, or as a prima donna?

How would Wood and Payne's planning and organising competency look if it was fleshed out in this multi-dimensional way? Boyatzis does not have a competency in identical terms, but one which relates closely to planning and organising is proactivity. For Boyaztis proactivity is one of four competencies which comprise a 'goal and action management cluster', the other three being concerned with impact, diagnostic use of concepts and efficiency orientation. Proactive people take actions (including diagnostic and information-gathering actions) early, without waiting for problems to become fully formed, and they readily accept personal responsibility.

By making a multi-dimensional analysis of proactivity, Boyatzis was able to draw from the managers he studied a more nuanced picture than he could if, like Wood and Payne, he had limited himself to the dimension of observable skill (Boyatzis, 1982: 77–78). He found that in the dimension of observable actions (skill), proactivity was associated with superior managerial performance. This was also true in the dimension of social role: being perceived by others in terms such as 'initiating change' or 'acting as a catalyst' was associated in the same way. But in the dimension of personality trait (assessed by a psychological test), superior and poor performers appeared to have similar high levels of this trait. Boyatzis speculated that poor performers might have a personality which encourages them to instigate too much of the wrong kind of activity, for example solving problems which they should be allowing their subordinates to solve. The detail of this speculation need not concern us: what is apparent is the richness that is possible in a multi-dimensional competency as opposed to one which is flat, restricted to the plane of skill.

Now we are in a position to see the fullness of Boyatzis's contribution. Working with data on more than 2,000 people in 12 organisations, Boyatzis first engaged with a subsample of these to generate possible competencies from managers' own perceptions and experiences. Managers were then asked to rate these possibilities, saying whether they thought each differentiated between superior and average performance in the job, or was needed to reach a threshold level of competence. Statistical analysis of the results led to a list of 21 possible competencies. Then, further data corresponding to observable behaviour was collected by asking managers to undertake interviews lasting about two hours in which they were asked to describe in detail three incidents in which they felt effective in the job and three in which they felt ineffective. The interviews were transcribed and then coded by independent assessors, whose consistency with each other in coding was checked, to show how often specific observable actions were described as occurring. To explore the managers' personality traits two psychological instruments were administered, one indicating the strength of different kinds of motive and the other capturing how individuals saw themselves in terms of learning style.

All of this information was analysed statistically for connections with superior, average or poor performance. The information available to Boyatzis on performance was a mixture of objective outcome measures, supervisory nominations (spontaneously named by one or more supervisors as an example of a superior performer) and supervisory ratings (line managers' assessments of subordinates' performance). Boyatzis adopted these as the best available guide to performance and rejected:

> ... *imposing some arbitrary, theoretical or value-based assumption as to what constitutes effectiveness as a manager, each organization involved in these studies determined what effectiveness was, or who was demonstrating it, in the context of its goals and objectives. (Boyatzis, 1982: 44)*

Of the 21 possible ideas for competencies he concluded that 12 were significantly associated with superior compared with average managerial performance. They included the goal and action management cluster cited above – concern with impact, diagnostic use of concepts, efficiency orientation and proactivity. He also identified clusters in leadership, human resource management and focus on others. These competencies were: conceptualisation, self-confidence and the use of oral presentations; managing group process and the use of socialised power; perceptual objectivity, self-control and stamina/adaptability.

He identified seven additional 'threshold competencies', associated with average compared with poor performance: logical thought, accurate self-assessment, positive regard, developing others, spontaneity, use of unilateral power and specialised knowledge (Boyatzis, 1982: 229–230).

As with proactivity, for each of these he produced not merely a label but an articulation of the competency in multiple dimensions (motivation, trait, skill, self-image and social role) and an examination of the supporting statistical evidence.

This was a landmark piece of work. Of course the competency approach and specific aspects of Boyatzis' study, like anything else, have their limits. For example, the price of scientific rigour is being backward-looking, taking one's cue from what appears to have worked in the past. Given that creating a fully worked up and researched competency framework for a company costs a lot of money and senior management time, this risks being like the Maginot Line which the French constructed after the First World War, a formidable edifice which proved worthless in the face of unexpected innovation. For more critiques see Chapter 14; but the good which competencies have done is huge.

Competencies' Transformational Impact

In the past 30 years competencies – multi-dimensional or flattened into observable behaviours – have achieved a commanding position in HR management. Reflecting on a career practising and writing as an organisational psychologist, George Hollenbeck (2009) noted:

> Behavioral competency models – a benchmarking study by the American Productivity and Quality Council in 2004 found that every one of their best practice organizations had developed a behavioral competency model, designed to guide their selection and development efforts. It is difficult to find any organization today that doesn't have its competency model. (Hollenbeck, 2009: 132)

Writing about leader selection, Howard notes that organisational practice has shifted 'dramatically' towards competencies and concludes that best practice is to define in advance the characteristics of effective leadership in terms of competencies (Howard, 2007: 19, 39). However the relevance of competencies to selection has been only one part of the story.

Forty years ago the idea that large corporations should be diversified collections of unconnected businesses – conglomerates – was much more popular than it is now. The increasing size and sophistication of capital markets has exploded this view: savers (or fund managers on their behalves) prefer to decide for themselves the relative exposure they wish as between aircraft manufacture, say, and citrus farming, or Asian markets relative to South American ones. They can diversify their investment portfolios more flexibly than by investing in Conglomerate Inc. which makes airframes in Indonesia as well as growing oranges in Brazil (and has an expensive headquarters in New York).

Capital markets are also more aggressive than they were 40 years ago. They more frequently challenge (or depress the share price of) managements whom they suspect of building empires without creating shareholder value. Corporations have increasingly needed a clear rationale for the businesses they are in, backed up by active engagement in aspects of the management of those businesses. To use the term coined by Campbell, Goold and Alexander (1995), large corporations need to explain what their 'parenting advantage' is: why does it benefit shareholders to have *this* business overseen by *that* group headquarters?

At the same time the globalisation of many businesses has been dramatic, not only in the skin-deep terms of personnel and offices ('flags on the map') but more profoundly in terms of intricate, technology-enabled international processes such as supply chains. So achieving coherent, consistent performance across national boundaries has shot up in importance. The same was true when businesses bought each other on the strength of promised synergies.

In this context competency-based HR management systems were a very potent idea. They promised a triple win for senior management, HR professionals and employees. If jobs in disparate businesses and countries could be analysed in a consistent, objective way into generic competencies, then senior management could assemble a coherent overall picture of their human capital and its skills, and redeploy that capital according to need. Moreover, emphasising particular competencies to be achieved in the future – for example in leadership or customer service – and having HR machinery in place so that staff worldwide would be measured, rewarded and promoted in the light of their delivering these competencies in action gave corporate leaders scope to create powerful stories of group-wide transformation, with themselves in the driving seat.

To be able to offer something this eye-catching to senior management was highly attractive to HR professionals, always struggling to make the impact of their work on shareholder value more apparent. If competencies could underpin pay and reward systems and investment in training and development as well as performance appraisal, resourcing (putting people into jobs) and succession planning, and do all of this with measurability, objectivity and consistency across different businesses and countries, then even within the HR function the prize of getting all these activities 'in synch' was captivating. Of course, once a corporation makes competencies part of its organisational DNA, it would be crazy not to recruit and select on the basis of competencies as well.

To employees and individual executives, a competency-based HR system offers not just fairness but increased mobility. Skills become a recognised ticket to move or be promoted elsewhere within the organisation. Part of this gain is illusory, because increased transferability for everyone means correspondingly increased competition for any particular vacancy. Nevertheless to be recognised by your organisation as possessing skills applicable outside your present context is a real boost.

This is Wood and Payne's summary of the benefits of competencies, first to HR at large and then to selection in particular:

> Competencies, then, offer a way of binding together and integrating the elements of a progressive human resources strategy. If competencies are defined, as they should be, with reference to the needs of the business, then a competency-based appraisal system can help to reinforce particular approaches to work (for example, continuous improvement or customer focus). Delivered in this way, competencies can be a powerful tool when trying to change the culture of an organization. The overall effect is to oblige everyone in the organization to focus on their performance in specific, common areas, to develop their skills accordingly and ultimately to improve the performance of the organization. (Wood and Payne, 1998: 22)

> Experience with a range of organizations shows [competencies] improve our accuracy in assessing people's suitability or potential for different jobs.

They facilitate a closer match between a person's skills and interests and the demands of the job.

They help prevent interviewers and assessors from making 'snap' judgements about people or from judging them on characteristics that are irrelevant to the job in question.

They can be used to underpin and structure the full range of assessment and development techniques – application forms, interviews, tests, assessment centres and appraisal ratings.

By disaggregating an individual's profile into specific skills and characteristics, development plans can more accurately be targeted to areas of true development need. (Wood and Payne, 1998: 22–23)

The foregoing suggestions as to why competencies have changed the HR landscape are, I think, plausible and relevant, but they are only suggestions. What is undeniable is that the impact of competencies has been wide and deep.

Good Selection Practice Revisited

We can now revisit the examples with which this chapter opened and describe the landscape of good, contemporary selection practice of which they are a part. We have seen that competencies were originally multi-dimensional but in practice they are often flattened – reduced to the plane of observable actions and results. They can be the product of extensive research into a specific organisation at a specific time, or they can be taken from a researched list (such as Boyatzis's) which has some claim to be more widely applicable. If they are researched, they are necessarily backward-looking. Alternatively competencies can be proposed conjecturally, as best guesses at what the organisation may need in the future. To the extent that the evidential basis for any particular set of competencies becomes weaker, and to the extent that the assessment process becomes less focused on the candidate's accounts of specific past actions, at some point the connection with competencies becomes too weak for that term to be useful; one might better speak of a person specification expressed more loosely in terms of KSAOs.

Viewed like this, the senior management assessment process in a *Fortune* 50 company described by Craig Russell can be seen as a fully-fledged competency assessment based on research into the specific organisation's needs. The data collected was sufficiently rich to address competencies in a multi-dimensional way, embracing how individuals saw themselves and how others saw them as well as detailed assessment of actions and results. At least one of the raters had human resources expertise (and no other expertise is mentioned as relevant), suggesting an attempt to take a multi-dimensional, nuanced view.

The 316 CEO assessments studied by Kaplan and his colleagues were also strongly research based, with the research focused on what leads to superior performance in companies in private equity or venture capital contexts. However it seems likely that the skills element was dominant, since the raters were qualified in the high-scoring MBA mould (so by supposition well able to assess business situations, strategies and results) but no mention is made of psychological or human resource expertise.

An example of a flat competency or skill is the example of 'planning and organizing' from Wood and Payne. By design all the indicators listed are observable actions with outcomes. Such a competency could arise from studying the specific management needs of the organisation in question or it could have been selected from a list of common or generalisable competencies (for example Wood and Payne, 1998: 27).

We might describe the person specification at the end of Chapter 13 as a KSAO specification influenced by competencies. It is multi-dimensional, including values and drives, track record and skills. For a senior role 'track record' commonly provides both evidence of knowledge, skills and abilities and can be a requirement of its own (an 'other attribute') speaking to credibility: someone with no relevant track record, however skilled they may be, may not be accepted by stakeholders in the role. The specification is forward-looking and has no research underpinning: its quality or lack of it rests on the combined product of the skills and experience of the consultant who produced it and the perspicacity and candour of the directors and staff of the organisation to whom he spoke. An important influence of competencies lay in the encouragement given to the interviewing panel to place at the centre of their questioning asking candidates for specific, relevant and if necessary detailed examples of actions taken by them.

The Centrality of Science

If Chapter 1 described selection's Dark Ages, Chapter 2 describes something very different. Much has changed since Arvey and Campion (1982) concluded:

> There is a dearth of guidelines and suggestions concerning the improvement of interview effectiveness based on research findings. Instead, many guidelines, suggestions, 'how to interview' workshops and techniques are founded on intuition, beliefs, and what seems more comfortable rather than on research results. (Arvey and Campion, 1982: 317)

Science has been central to this change, not only in yielding specific research results (such as Boyatzis's competencies) but in the framing of the whole selection challenge as a twofold task of objectification and measurement. Firstly, what the organisation needs from the person who will fill the role is to be specified in the form of criteria which are fixed as objectively as possible. Secondly, candidates should be measured as accurately and fairly as possible against those criteria. Provided all the essential criteria are met, the candidate who best fits the criteria should be offered the job. And, as Arvey and Campion make explicit, where science advances, intuition should retreat.

Neal Schmitt was a former President of the Society for Industrial and Organizational Psychology in the US. He wrote a book-length assessment of the state of personnel selection research in 1998. In their opening pages he and his co-author give this clear statement of the scientific approach and its rightness:

> Personnel selection research has been conducted for most of the twentieth century ... This research has followed the [following] general paradigm ... The job for which individuals will be chosen is examined to determine what tasks and responsibilities will be required. This specification of the domain of job tasks is followed by the generation of hypotheses concerning the knowledge, skills, abilities and other characteristics (KSAOs) required of individuals who must perform these tasks. Specification of the tasks and KSAOs leads to the development of measures of both job performance variables and predictor variables and evaluation of the hypotheses about ability-performance relationships proposed during the job analysis phase of the project. Assuming some confirmation of these hypotheses, various steps are taken to implement

*the selection procedures and to assess their practical costs and benefits
in an organizational context.*

This basic paradigm appropriately underlies good personnel selection or
staffing research (Schmitt and Chan, 1998: 1–2).

The advance of science in personnel selection, as well as the advances in
personnel selection made possible by science, are two sides of the same coin.
They did not take place in a bloodless realm of ideas but through the struggles
of selectors and managers in organisations who wanted to do things better, the
professional and research contributions of psychologists, and the competition
of institutions, firms and consultants to offer training or other 'good practice'
interventions (such as ghSMART's) in the marketplace. So let me tell this story
of the advance of science in a more personal way.

The advance of science was reflected in growing respect for certain
institutions and by training and socialising managers like myself. The British
Civil Service Selection Board was one such institution whose origins went back
to the Second World War or earlier. It selected entrants for the high-potential
stream of the British Government service. One of the research studies noted
by Arvey and Campion is a study by Anstey (1977) of this body, which I first
encountered around that year as an undergraduate candidate. Ten years later
my formative experience as a recruiter was spending one year working for the
organisation full-time. Both encounters were career-shaping, leading me firstly
to join government service and secondly lighting the fuse of an intense interest
in people and their selection, which contributed to my going into executive
search.

At that time the Civil Service Selection Board operated like this. Candidates,
having already been through a written test, spent two days at a centre in
London in groups of five or six, assessed by a panel of three comprising two
civil servants (one senior) and a psychologist. The name given to the role of one
of the civil servant interviewers 'the Observer' pointed to the scientific ethos
of the institution. The exercises performed over two days in London included
further written work, group work and three individual interviews each of about
40 minutes. Some of these exercises were based on a file of papers prepared as
a job simulation. The assessors met on the third day to review the evidence and
to make their judgements against what was defined as an objective standard
(in other words none, some or all of the candidates in any one group might be

recommended for final interview). Final interviews by a panel of senior civil servants and distinguished outsiders took place some weeks later.

My year in that environment was formative. I was an observer interviewing three days out of five. I also had to write the job simulation case file and create the related group and written exercises for the following year. I worked intensively alongside psychologists. All the time I was picking up the idea that this was how to do selection *properly*.

Arvey and Campion quoted Anstey's study because it compared the assessments made of candidates by my predecessors three decades before with where the appointed candidates' careers had taken them 30 years later – by any standards an impressive length of time. It found that the assessments made had significant predictive validity. They were a triumph of science.

3

... To Stuck

The Argument of this Chapter

Chapter 1 was about the Dark Ages, the selection practices of the playground. Judged by today's standards of good practice, Chapter 1 looked at unreformed ways of choosing people – and even the good practice of 40 years ago – and found it wanting. It also gave instances of people being chosen badly for senior roles.

Chapter 2 was about scientific progress. It examined what constitutes today's standards, particularly objective job descriptions and person specifications. The latter might be framed in terms of people's KSAOs or more technically in terms of competencies. The latter could be multi-dimensional or simplified and relatively flat. Propelling these changes was scientific research, generating evidence, creating new tools and validating these in practice.

Competencies have spread rapidly in a relatively short time. Chapter 2 suggested that they enabled a way of thinking about HR which was not only scientific and comprehensive, but offered gains to senior managers, HR professionals and employees in the circumstances of a globalising and technology-enabled world increasingly concerned with shareholder value.

Finally, Chapter 2 pointed to some examples of rigorous practice in choosing people for senior roles.

The argument in this chapter has three parts. Firstly, that selection at senior levels has been very little affected by the transformation just described. The examples of rigorous practice at this level are atypical. While competencies (and other attempts to think more objectively about HR) have burst the banks of scientific research and changed management practice at front-line and middle management levels like a flood, the peaks have hardly been touched. We look at this both within the public and the private sectors.

Secondly, that research into senior selection is caught in a position from which it cannot easily escape, and from which it can offer little convincing help or challenge to the practice. It is in the light of these factors that I describe senior selection as stuck.

Thirdly, we look at who should be worried about this stuckness, and who is, and why. I will suggest that major groups such as investment fund managers and the ordinary public who are not concerned should be, while the efforts of the most vocal advocates for change in fact contribute significantly to stuckness. I have in mind those concerned about diversity in boards and leadership cadres: diversity of professional experience and thinking, as well as social categories such as gender, ethnicity or class. I count myself among them.

Senior Selection Has Changed Little

Across large swathes of the private, public, academic or voluntary sectors, in organisations both large and small, a consequence of Chapter 2 has been significant changes over the last 30–40 years in the way people are selected into front-line or middle management roles. What is being looked for in candidates will be more clearly and openly specified; the process will be more open to candidates who can meet the specification coming from broader backgrounds; interviews will not be the only or primary selection tool; and the interviews themselves will be more structured.

Retailers and customer service organisations might use personality profiling or drill-down, behavioural questioning ('Tell me about a situation when you had to deal with an angry customer'); strategy consultancies and technical organisations may present candidates with examples of advanced problems; military and emergency service organisations may use psychological assessment to look for traits such as calmness under pressure; and so on. While the details will vary from case to case, it would now be quite surprising to encounter a selection process at front-line or middle management level for a quality organisation which comprised simply one or two relatively unstructured interviews.

Nor have these changes been limited to the more quantitative or analytic occupations. To be accepted as a candidate for training for the priesthood in the Church of England involves attending a selection conference where groups of candidates will spend time over three days with groups of assessors and be observed in a wide range of activities (Archbishops' Council: Ministry Division, 2010).

Or, consider selection as a musician for a top-tier orchestra. Gladwell (2005) describes vividly the introduction of blind auditions and the positive impact which this change, in many cases fiercely contested, had on the selection of women.

Selection processes at the top of organisations have remained remarkably impervious to this trend. Here, while the specific details vary between sectors and countries, the typical final story remains the same – an emphasis on selectors' knowledge of (or assumptions about) candidates gained outside of an explicit process designed on the basis of an objective specification and a small number of interviews structured loosely (if at all) and falling far short of the probing rigour exemplified in Chapter 2.

As we will see in the last section of this chapter, not only does comprehensive research into senior selection not exist, but that fact itself is both symptomatic of and a contributor to the stuckness which is this chapter's subject. But there is evidence which combines to make a strongly suggestive picture.

In the Public Sector

In the UK the Civil Service Commissioners are charged with overseeing Civil Service appointments and driving forward the principle of appointment on merit. (The Civil Service Selection Board described at the end of the preceding chapter operated under their auspices.) The Commissioners charged Clive Fletcher (2005), a psychologist and a leading British scholar of selection, with producing a review on:

> ... the most reliable, validated techniques for recruiting and selecting senior staff in the private, public and voluntary sectors. (Fletcher, 2005: 5)

He concluded that:

... 85% of external [non-Civil Service] organisations still use just interviews and references for top posts. (Fletcher, 2005: 8)

Fletcher was commenting on what happens outside the government sector. Within that sector, progress has been made in the UK to introduce additional selection tools at senior levels, including psychological assessments and sometimes job simulation (such as briefing an actor playing the part of a politician). The Civil Service Commissioners' annual reports show continuing progress. Judicial appointments – described in Chapter 1 – now make use of competencies.

However the heart of the selection process for the highest-level UK public appointments – such as the permanent secretary in charge of a government department or the chair of the board of a major public authority, such as the BBC or the Financial Services Authority – typically remains a 40 or 50 minute semi-structured interview conducted by a selection panel with four or five members. Of these three will be senior officials involved with or responsible for the job which is to be filled, and one or two will be independent members. It would be unusual for more than one of the panel to have specialist experience in selection interviewing.

My experience has been that this model also provides the core of senior selection in the academic and voluntary sectors, on occasion supplemented by shortlisted candidates moving in rapid sequence (every 20 minutes or so) between groups of staff from different departments or having dinner with their selectors and fellow candidates. My comments on these selection devices are in Chapter 13. The point here is that even if some of the models have stretched bodies or sun roofs, the selection engine is the same.

Time and again when I had to explain the public sector interviewing model to private sector candidates they found it surprising that senior roles could be filled satisfactorily after such a formal and potentially cursory process. For them the most striking characteristic was the very limited opportunity for the selectors and candidates to have an extended conversation about the role, or to get to know each other as people.

They would find even more peculiar the process by which the Church of England appoints the bishops in charge of dioceses. While most churches in the Anglican Communion make these appointments by a process of structured open election, in the Church of England a panel is appointed to put forward two names to the Prime Minister, after a process in which no-one is interviewed and (in theory) no-one knows whether they are being considered as a candidate.[1] Contrast this with the process mentioned earlier to be selected for training as an ordinary priest. Of course the Church is in many ways an anachronistic organisation. Its relevance here is how the pattern of difference between selection at the top and selection at the bottom still applies.

In the Private Sector

While top-level processes in the private sector differ from those above (certainly there is more time spent in conversation), they too are problematic.

The situation in the private sector where an external search is engaged to find the next CEO was the subject of the study by Khurana (2002) introduced in Chapter 1. Khurana's account of search firms who do not 'find' candidates, who are instead suggested by board members on the basis of prior personal impressions, and of search firms and board search committees which together engage not in challenging scrutiny but in obsequiousness and the avoidance of embarrassment, was graphic.

The more common practice in private sector organisations which are large enough will normally be to develop internal candidates as possible successors to the CEO, with the relevant committee of the board observing them and the performance of their business units over a period of years. Where possible external search will be avoided at the point of ultimate succession but used a few (or even ten) years earlier to strengthen or diversify the internal succession pool. Collins (2001) counselled against finding CEOs outside. Howard (2007) noted that insiders run two-thirds of *Fortune* 1,000 companies and cited a 2003 study in which the median shareholder return was 3 per cent in companies run by insiders compared with -5 per cent for outsiders.

The process of building and selecting from an internal succession pool is explored in detail by Khurana's Harvard colleague Joseph Bower (2007), briefly mentioned in Chapter 2.

From Bower's work two important points emerge. Firstly, this extended internally-oriented process – at its best thoughtful and data-rich, and the

---

1   No-one apart from women priests who, at the time of writing, know that they have been disregarded en bloc.

source of the disbelief in selection by 50-minute interview – often stumbles. Secondly, it *still* relies on the twin pillars of an emphasis on untested knowledge of candidates gained outside of an explicit, specification-driven process and a small number of loosely structured interviews. We can see this not only in processes which go spectacularly awry, such as the succession to Richard Greenbury as CEO of Marks and Spencer in 1999, for which the board began to prepare in 1994 (Bower, 2007: 45–50, 143–145) – but in the less fiery example (Brown Shoe) which Bower holds up as an example of the process reaching a successful outcome. In this case he managed the process himself as a member of the board (Bower, 2007: 40–45).

In this example, looking ahead to the retirement of the Brown Shoe CEO in 1999, the full board regularly discussed the leading executives of the successor generation. By 1998 they had identified a clear frontrunner.

> One executive seemed particularly talented. He had joined the company as part of the team that managed the overseas sourcing business that was acquired in the mid-1980s. On more than one occasion, I met with him between board meetings and soon developed an appreciation for his talents. (Bower, 2007: 41)

In 1998 the board moved to make this individual president (a standard US title approximating to deputy CEO and chief operating officer) while:

> ... at dinners the night before board meetings and on-site visits, the board continued its practices of meeting two or three times a year with other executives. (Bower, 2007: 42)

Later that year a series of surprises surfaced in the international division which raised serious questions about the front-runner, leading to his resignation. Bower was then asked by the board to chair an external search process while the best of the remaining internal candidates (Ron Fromm) became acting president. The search process eventually led to the decision to offer the role of president and CEO-designate to:

> ... one very attractive candidate who was serving as a group executive in a company that made unrelated consumer products.[2] (Bower, 2007: 43)

---

2   That is, from outside the shoe industry, a somewhat illogical outcome since the board had chosen to work with a search consultant because of his (or her) 'special knowledge of the

In other words by this point the board had twice passed over Fromm in favour of someone else. However the negotiations on remuneration with the attractive external candidate took months. Finally they collapsed over the candidate's insistence that he should still receive the package offered even in the rare event that he was asked to leave because of inadequate performance. In the meantime Fromm:

> ... was doing a good job managing those parts of the business with which he had not been familiar. Confronted with the choice of returning to the external search or helping Fromm succeed, we embraced Fromm and the opportunity he presented. (Bower, 2007: 43)

In other words Fromm was chosen at the third time of asking, *faute de mieux*. In the event Brown Shoe's stock then appreciated more than five times over a number of years. In hindsight Bower judges that Fromm not only re-energised the company but transformed it, in Jim Collins' famous terminology, from good to great (Collins, 2001).

We should not quarrel with Bower's choice of this example as a flagship for internal selection. Instead we should congratulate him for his candour. If from the comfort of front row spectator seats we are tempted to mock the twofold misreading by the board of the talent that was under their noses, we should pause. The Brown Shoe story could be explained by board competence or snobbery (Bower contrasts Fromm, a heart and soul upper Midwesterner, with his predecessor who dressed like a Wall Street patrician). But quite often Brown-like outcomes are produced by sincere, competent and experienced individuals employing contemporary good practice. When that happens, clues are put in front of our own noses that our way of thinking about choosing leaders is not yet adequate.

In Summary

To summarise, while the processes of selection at the most senior levels are not identical in all contexts, my experience and available research suggest the following common pattern. The processes have changed much less over the last 40 years than the processes at front-line and middle management levels of

---

shoe industry' (Bower, 2007: 42). But by Khurana's assessment of search processes and my own, neither this nor the immediately following twist in the process are unusual in top-level searches.

the same organisations. Interviews of some kind are normally central. Nothing in any sector remotely approaches the rigour of the general management selection process described in Chapter 2 by Russell. Instead the index of the role's seniority becomes, instead of the rigour of the selection process, the assumption that only someone within an approximately known universe of proximately senior jobs could be a credible candidate; and that the selectors (or some of them) should have or be able to get insight into that candidate from what they have done in that proximate role.

This proximate universe need not be as firmly defined as the college of cardinals who, in the Roman Catholic Church, elect the pope from their number. The field might be nearly as rigid – for example conceivable candidates for president of the European Central Bank will be heads of the central banks of the smaller euro countries and only a slightly wider field in the larger ones. In the case of Brown Shoe, the field seems initially to have been senior management team members in the shoe industry (possibly the American shoe industry), but widened to their equivalents in consumer products companies.

In any event, however fuzzy or permeable this possible universe, in relation to filling the most senior roles our thinking and action seem to shift in this direction. Correspondingly, relative to junior and middle management levels, our selection practices remain remarkably untouched by the scientific revolution. At the tops of our organisations we stick close to the Dark Ages.

Help is Not Being Sought – Nor is it at Hand

The stuckness which this chapter portrays is more than historic immobility. There is every reason to expect the stuckness to continue. The practitioners of senior selection, taken as a whole, are not seeking help. Nor are they being challenged by appropriate research – the research which would also need to be done to offer practitioners meaningful help were they to request it. And, not only is the research cupboard bare: the research practice itself is stuck. Without a fundamental change of approach, the cupboard is bound to remain bare – so far as selection for senior roles is concerned.

In other words the stuckness in how we choose our leaders – the way selection practice at senior levels has barely been touched by the advances of the past 40 years – is not like the stuckness of a traffic jam, where, for reasons which those of us stuck in our cars do not see, suddenly the traffic flows again.

It is more like being stuck in a big ditch while the only tractor available within miles has a broken axle. Let us put the pieces of this picture together.

Notwithstanding the approach of ghSMART in Chapter 2, it is clear where practitioners would turn for help if they wanted it – to psychologists. In terms of academic research, psychology is far ahead of any other science in having studied personnel selection extensively. In terms of offering practical help backed by research in assessing individuals, whether by tests or talk, psychologists are the only professionally qualified game in town. Psychology is also a broad field embracing different perspectives, such as clinical psychology, cognitive psychology, social psychology and organisational psychology as well as the identification of personality or work-related traits in individuals.

At the end of Chapter 2 I described the formative year I spent working with and alongside psychologists at the Civil Service Selection Board. Knowing full well the limitations of interviews, the executive search firm which I joined only recruited researchers (many of whom joined straight from university) as well as consultants after an individual assessment by a psychologist lasting two or three hours. In fact we regularly flew a particular psychologist over from Sweden for the purpose, because of his knowledge of executive search as well as his knowledge of the firm. Although for various business reasons things were different at the start and at the end of my 18 years with the firm, for the greater part of that time we did not ourselves employ any psychologists. So when I explain that throughout this time my colleagues and I sought to persuade clients making senior appointments to use additional psychological help, we can defend the proposition that we meant this sincerely and not simply to boost our income. Only infrequently was the advice taken up. Most practitioners in senior selection do not want rigorous professional help.

That this is so is well expressed by George Hollenbeck (2009) reflecting candidly in *Industrial and Organizational Psychology* on a lifetime's work trying to help organisations. Talking specifically about the selection of individuals for senior roles, he notes that industrial–organisational psychologists are 'largely absent from the table' (Hollenbeck, 2009: 134) when decisions are made. And this is not the self-pity of a professional bemoaning that clients have failed to be hoodwinked into paying his kind large fees: he argues that the reason is the relevant psychological research cupboard is bare:

> *That we get no respect and don't have a seat at the table are the symptoms, not the cause of our problems. Nobody is buying because*

we don't have much to sell. This is not a marketing problem; our
traditional psychometric selection model has led us down the wrong
paths. (Hollenbeck, 2009: 140)

The advances which were made and proved powerful in Chapter 2 were based
on a way of thinking about personnel selection and practising science which
lent itself to studies of large groups, typically of entry-level or supervisory staff
(extensive studies like Boyatzis's at middle management level were rarer), or
experiments in which university undergraduates were given token incentives to
be interviewed or undergo particular tests. Large sample sizes ('*N*' in statistical
parlance) were essential to producing compelling research and, for obvious
reasons, these are very difficult to obtain in senior-level work.

> *... Our field has stuck with our classical personnel selection model,*
> *seeking to correlate predictors with criteria, hoping for large samples.*
> *We do this even though it continues to disappoint us in terms of*
> *research, results, or respect. Our model is so thoroughly ingrained*
> *in all of us that we keep hoping that the right set of predictors and*
> *criteria and a large enough N will (finally) produce the results we seek.*
> *(Hollenbeck, 2009: 138)*

Instead Hollenbeck argues for a multi-disciplinary approach reaching beyond
psychology. McCall and Hollenbeck (2007) also argue that thinking about
leadership in terms of competencies is a mistake; in their view the activity of
leading a group to overcome difficult challenges is not decomposable in this
way. But most of all Hollenbeck argues that senior selection has dropped off
psychology's radar and needs to be put back, otherwise the cupboard will
remain bare.

Chapter 2 quoted the book-length assessment of personnel selection research
by Schmitt and Chan (1998). Inadvertently they corroborate Hollenbeck's point.
They refer to the practice of assessing senior executives individually and state
that this 'is rarely, if ever, described in research reports' (Schmitt and Chan,
1998: 33) – but none of the 11 key research issues for the future with which they
conclude call for any repair of this gap.

Howard (2007) notes that individual assessment of executives by a
psychologist is frequently used for higher management. However:

There is little research to support [it] ... but small samples and other factors make such research difficult. (Howard, 2007: 34)

In other words there is a major research gap but it is difficult to see scientific research getting access to very senior appointments in the numbers necessary to practise science. The relevant people are hard to reach, hard to persuade and highly sensitive about confidentiality. Which chair of a board faced with the fraught situation of recruiting a CEO would complicate life not only by admitting third parties into the board room, but ask candidates to consent to their presence in (or recording of) interviews? Khurana's study was a rare achievement but it relied on *ex post* accounts and rationalisations (nor is he a psychologist).

Who Should Be Worried about This?

To complete the picture of the car stuck in a big ditch with no help but a broken tractor we should therefore add two elements – most of the occupants of the car are not worried and neither are most of the owners of the tractor. Nothing in this picture shows any sign of changing in a hurry. Worse, several elements would have to change for the car to get out of the ditch.

We might explain the unconcern of most of the occupants of the car in this way. The principals involved in selecting for senior roles are themselves senior: the processes which selected them cannot be all bad, can they? Those advising them, such as search professionals, earn a living by servicing the marketplace as it exists. Some may not wish to undermine their clients' (or their own) faith in their own expert judgement by seeking independent opinions. Others may encourage their clients to seek additional help, but if this is not wanted, that is the client's prerogative.[3]

The unconcern of researchers is different. Here the problem may not be straightforward unconcern – in any case qualified by the presence of voices such as Hollenbeck's – so much as the lack of any obvious way forward. Scientific research and the classical personnel selection model make various

---

3   Even where a psychologist's assessment is sought, senior clients' attitudes may not quite be one of seeking help. At the conclusion of one senior appointment process in the public sector, the chair of the panel asked me to congratulate the psychologist who had prepared reports on the shortlisted candidates. I was to tell the psychologist that her reports had been impressively accurate, terminology which implies that the panel knew best.

demands and it is not easy to see how they can be satisfied in researching at the most senior levels.

Those who rely on the quality of organisations' leaderships should be concerned – for example fund managers in the private sector, the shareholders in whose name value is being created. And there is concern about the adequacy of succession plans, expressed privately or sometimes publicly – for example the Warren Buffett example in Chapter 1. However my observation is that if a private sector company appoints a CEO from outside, the investor reaction to the candidate chosen will depend on whether the person chosen comes from a perceived stable of talent like GE, or has led a business during a period when its share price has risen relatively uninterruptedly. Groysberg, McLean and Nohria (2006) have looked at the problems in the former while the latter is frankly bizarre: most fund managers would be sacked for buying shares in a company simply because of its recent uninterrupted rise, yet they will push up the market value of a company which buys the CEO associated with the same rise. Senior executive appointments need to be understood at a deeper level.

Candidates might be worried. Selection decisions at these levels make crucial differences to the perceived success of individuals' careers. However they often do not know on what the critical moments of the decision which affected them turned (if the reason is too embarrassing for polite company the client or the search professional will probably substitute something more reasonable). Even if they are worried, so long as they are open to seeking further promotions (whether within the same organisation or outside) it pays not to rock the boat, and once that period is past their views may be treated as sour grapes.

Frequently in-house HR professionals are worried about the way senior selection decisions are made in their own organisation. However in most organisations HR is a relatively low-status function. In any case, recommending procedures which were developed and validated mainly on junior jobs – such as asking differing candidates the same questions in interviews, or perhaps scoring the answers numerically – will usually settle any doubts in the mind of those in charge. At the most critical points in the process, the board room door will be closed and the HR professional – like the psychologist – will probably be on the outside of it. Of course there are contrary examples of HR directors who command exceptional respect; I have had the pleasure of meeting several. But in my experience they are the exception rather than the rule.[4]

The groups most worried about stuckness in senior appointments have been concerned with the lack of diversity in leadership cadres, for example in terms of gender, ethnicity, disability, sexuality and so forth. The need for diversity in class is often forgotten but at least in Britain it should not be. I include myself in this concerned category and would extend diversity to include diversity of professional or other relevant experience. Lack of diversity was an important driving force behind the changes to judicial appointments discussed in Chapter 1. At the time of writing, a focus for debate in Britain has been the slow rate of increase in gender diversity on private sector boards – currently 87.5 per cent male for FTSE 100 companies – and whether the country should follow Norway's example of a compulsory minimum quota. The report commissioned by the Government from business leader Mervyn Davies (Lord Davies of Abersoch, 2011) said not yet but challenged leading companies, as a matter of urgency, to do better.

This book will not replicate the extensive literature on diversity, but make a different argument whose implications for diversity are drawn out in Chapter 11. At this stage I simply note two consequences of pro-diversity changes (one intended, one not so) which entrench the present stuckness. I am not suggesting that the changes should not have been made, but having been made, they compound our predicament.

The first consequence, and an intended one, is legal. Riding on the back of the scientific progress and the development of competencies in Chapter 2 has been legislation and court judgements on discrimination which make it harder to think about fundamentally different ways of making selection decisions. Nervousness about change exists at two levels – whether thinking differently can be good (or may it let discrimination in by the back door) and whether it can be safe (can we be seen to have thought in a new way in case our selection decision is challenged in court).

The second consequence, unintended, particularly when arguments are advanced for quotas, is that a wedge is driven between diversity and merit.

---

4   I am not making the ridiculous suggestion that search professionals command more respect than HR directors. At certain points the search professional may be behind the closed board room door when the HR director is not, but that does not make her a trusted advisor. Usually search professionals are there to do a task and then thrown out. But, as with HR directors, some individuals do better than this.

Many proponents of diversity make their argument in terms of merit or a business case, suggesting for example that more diverse boards are less prone to 'group think' and will do a better job of understanding a company's diverse customer base or workforce. But progress has been slow, so arguments have been made for quotas, which encourages some of the majority group in power (affluent, educated, older white men) to dig in their intellectual heels. In their view they have been *appointed* on merit, they have been *appointing* on merit, and diversity reflects a contaminating political agenda.

This book is about thinking differently. Certainly if we do not, we are stuck.

Re-stating a simple point, how we choose our leaders has been remarkably unaffected by the leaps we have taken in choosing people for other roles in our society from the playground and the Dark Ages (Chapter 1) into scientific light (Chapter 2). This chapter suggests that waiting around for the elites in our societies to catch on will not do the trick. Something is stopping the force of scientific progress from doing for senior roles in all sectors what it has done very powerfully at the front-line and middle levels of organisations. Our inquiry in Part II will be to ask why this is.

In the meantime all of us as citizens, unless we think the way we choose our leaders is the best it could be, should be concerned. At a theoretical level, part of the social cohesion of a modern society springs from all of us being able to believe in a certain, albeit imperfect, level of openness and meritocracy in the filling of positions of power (Walzer, 1983). But more simply how we choose our leaders affects whether our businesses thrive, whether we have jobs, whether we discover new things, how our schools and hospitals are run, and whether we protect vulnerable people and the environment. It also affects whether it is worth ourselves, and our children, having ambitions to shape the world and not only to be shaped by it.

Howard puts it like this: 'Selection matters. Leader selection matters much more' (Howard, 2007: 40).

PART II

What's Different about Senior Roles?

4

Complexity, Humility and Responsibility

Introduction

Part I proposed that, across sectors and organisations as unlike each other as churches and shoe manufacturers, the way we choose people for senior roles has changed little during the past 40 years. By contrast, at other levels in the same organisations there has often been a lot of change, reflecting scientific advances which enabled us to move beyond the antics of the playground when we choose people for roles. I also called this unreformed stage the Dark Ages. If we take into account the importance (even the exaggerated importance) of very senior roles in our society; the desire in our society, even if it only represents passing fashion, to do things the latest way ('my organisation's leadership roles are more important than yours'); and the money spent (for example on search firms) on filling vacancies at the top which could not be afforded elsewhere in the organisation; then this pattern is curious and ought to be of concern.

Compounding the situation, there is little research about selection at senior levels. It is difficult to imagine that this will change. To complete the picture, most practitioners in senior selection and most selection researchers seem either happy with the situation or resigned to it. This is the situation which Part I characterised as stuckness and described as similar to a car being stuck in a deep ditch, the only tractor in the vicinity having a broken axle and none of the parties involved trying particularly to change the situation.

To address this situation we need to ask, what is different about filling senior roles? To start with, what differentiates the roles themselves? To explore these questions is my purpose in the next three chapters which comprise Part II. This chapter will be practice-led, while nevertheless posing challenging questions and making connections with theory. The approach in Chapter 5 will be the reverse: theory-led, while making connections with experience. In Chapter 6 we will test what has emerged from our exploration against a larger body of theory and take stock of the whole argument thus far. If the stuckness in the way we choose leaders starts to look unsurprising, that will be because we start to see it as part of a deeper crisis which we had not expected.

Are Senior Jobs Different or Just Better Paid?

The more we are persuaded that senior jobs are genuinely different from front-line and middle-level jobs, the more we may be persuaded that selection research (the bulk of it based on more junior roles or experiments with university students) has simply proved not up to the job. We might say, the equipment was neither designed to work nor tested at high organisational altitudes. From this point of view we should study what is different about senior roles – what constitutes organisational altitude. That is the journey we are about to make. But in order that we make it with our eyes open, consider the suggestion that there may be less to senior jobs than meets the eye. Let us sketch what this suggestion might look like.

The suggestion might be that modern work structures are like a disguised lottery or exploitative talent quest in which winning – getting a top job – is tough (in the sense of unlikely), but not a matter of deep skill. What might this society look like?

On the planet Delusio there is a pyramid of increasingly well-paid jobs. Delusians believe that the better-paid jobs are harder, requiring high levels of skill as well as the training which comes from working up the pyramid from one level of difficulty to the next. As the economy grows and vacancies arise, they are filled by senior individuals choosing from those who have shown promise at the level below. But the opportunities are few and this makes it tough for ordinary Delusians to have a go at a top job. However, if they could, they would find it no more difficult than the job they are doing already. That is what distinguishes the planet from its neighbour, Earth, where there is a similar structure but the top jobs are in fact more difficult.

At this point one could posit a grand conspiracy in which senior Delusians realise that their status and wealth depend upon a grand lie, and swear themselves to secrecy on pain of death. That might make an excellent film but an unsustainable society. Instead several elements combine to ensure that

Delusians, as they climb the pyramid, find the higher jobs do demand special skills and are more difficult.

Firstly, as in a talent show, the intense competition for each vacancy predisposes promoted Delusians to believe they are special. Secondly, the competitions are run by professionals (headhunters for example) who claim arcane powers of discernment which they exercise in identifying the winners. Since these professionals are paid a proportion of the earnings of the winning class, they have every incentive to believe in what they are doing and to make a song and dance about it. Thirdly, the selection process always includes a ritual in which the keenest candidates affirm in word and deed that they truly believe that the vacancy to which they wish to be promoted is a difficult and challenging job, for which it would be a great honour to be selected. This ritual might be called an interview. Fourthly, once appointed, those keen to progress further apply themselves to a great supply of books and courses. Many of them say contradictory things but that is not important because what the contradictions prove, which the books and courses also say, is that this higher-level activity (often called 'leadership') is tricky and difficult stuff.

Moreover the higher up jobs are *only* easy to do if those doing them can convince themselves that they are nearly infallibly gifted at doing them. For example, one of the very top Delusian jobs involves deciding from time to time whether to send an armed force to pacify one of the circling moons. This is not a difficult job to do in the sense that (provided one sticks to relatively small and underdeveloped moons) the armed force never wins or loses, and life continues much as before. No senior Delusian ever visibly screws up in the sense that every junior Delusian who has to pick up one child from school while taking another to the doctor and working a late shift will definitely screw up. However this is only true if the senior Delusian can convince themselves that they were absolutely right to cause quite a few deaths on this particular moon; this happens quite quickly because otherwise the responsibilities of the job become crushing.

In the perfect Delusian society, senior Delusians would *only* be appointed in the way described. But nothing is perfect. From time to time some senior Delusians build their own pyramids and become so powerful within them that their children can queue-jump into positions of power. Of course if this happened too often and too successfully, the scales might fall from everybody's eyes; but this has not happened yet.

How should you decide whether you are living on Earth or on Delusio? We will return to this question at the end of this chapter, after hearing three accounts of ways in which senior roles differ from front-line and middle management roles. For short call them IQ, EQ and UQ.

Intelligence and Complexity

On Delusio leaders would not fail, but here they do. Studying why carefully selected high-achieving individuals fail (often called derailment) should tell us something about the particular challenges of senior roles. Furnham (2010) has written about this, particularly in relation to personality types and disorders. But he is at pains to emphasise that an overwhelming body of psychological research backs the idea of general intelligence or cognitive ability (or IQ), not only in terms of its reliability but its unmatched ability to predict performance in a wide range of contexts, including senior roles. This includes comparing such measures with tests of more specialised intellectual capabilities. Intelligence defined in this way tends to be stable in each individual from late childhood onwards.

> The data on general intelligence as a predictor of work-related behaviors are, however, very clear. There are very few researchers who have inspected recent meta-analyses who could not be impressed by the fact that without doubt the best single predictor of success at work (particularly in senior complex jobs) is intelligence. This is not to deny that there are not other important factors nor that it is patently obvious that not all intelligent people do particularly well in the workplace. Intelligence is relatively easy to measure reliably and accurately. Intelligence test scores are influenced by other factors (like personality) but not to any great extent. Intelligence is cognitive capacity and refers to both efficient problem solving and accumulated knowledge. (Furnham, 2010: 232)

More specifically to succeed in senior positions Furnham considers that individuals need to be in the top 10–20 per cent of the population. Notice the link made between intelligence and 'senior complex jobs'.

This perspective is strongly echoed by Howard (2007):

Positions of leadership, particularly high up in an organization, are
unquestionably complex and are strongly predictive (sic) from cognitive
tests. (Howard, 2007: 22)

Underlying this is the differentiation of senior from junior roles probably most widely used by practitioners and a range of researchers, namely that senior roles are more strategic. Howard presents a pyramid with five tiers below the CEO, in descending order: strategic leaders; operational leaders; middle managers; supervisors; employees (Howard, 2007: 13).

A different analysis but with common ground is the levels of complexity model developed by Professor Gillian Stamp and colleagues at BIOSS (see Chapter 14 for information and acknowledgements). Developed and tested over more than 40 years and in many different countries, unlike the bulk of personnel selection research these tools reflect a close analysis of what top-level executives do. In the BIOSS framework, at each successive level decisions of a broader nature are made in increasingly complex and ambiguous environments. The features of the BIOSS levels most relevant to the present discussion are:

Level 1. Direct and immediate service to the external or internal customer. Judgements are needed about the quality of materials, the way to handle equipment or the specific characteristics of particular customers.

Level 2. Managerially, puts the right people in the right place to respond to short-term fluctuations in demand; or professionally deals with individual cases which require specialist expertise.

Level 3. Integrates subsystems and resources so that a whole operational system functions effectively and efficiently and improves continuously. Typical time horizon a couple of years. Uncertainty is seen as containable as long as it is temporary.

Level 4. Takes a step back from the operational perspective to see 'the big picture', identifying typically over a three to five year horizon what in the organisation needs to change and what should remain intact. This level is defined as operational strategy.

Level 5. This involves extracting for the organisation and communicating a clear strategic intent and identity: providing effective 'givens' for an organisation in a turbulent environment which has no 'givens', in which problems do not yield to rational solutions and complex interactions mean that unanticipated consequences will unfold over many years.

Distinguishing senior jobs according to the complexity or strategic nature of the problems which they need to confront is therefore not only a widely held difference but one supported by research. It is also noteworthy that the distinction is not tied to any particular sector or size of organisation. Wikipedia is a complex non-profit organisation whose income and staff numbers[1] are tiny compared to those of many regional supermarket managers, but the leadership of one is a strategic or Level 5 challenge while the other is likely to be middle management or Level 3.

However I believe Furnham is wrong to emphasise intelligence to the degree he does as the key to succeeding in the face of complexity. To recommend that top managers have intelligence in the top 10–20 per cent of the general population is one thing; in British terms that might equate (for those who had the opportunity to go to university) to a good, but not spectacular, first degree. To suggest that organisations are helped by having very clever people at the top is quite another. To my mind Furnham implies this in passages such as the following:

> Leaders have to 'size up the situation'. This may involve analyzing analyzing data or trends. They also have to make plans, often of considerable complexity. In business they must be good at 'tumbling numbers', understanding spreadsheets, understanding and mastering new technology. More importantly, they have to make wise, timely, informed and often risky decisions. They need to accurately examine and appraise complex, ill-defined and new problems. ... In short, they need to be bright, bright enough to cope with all aspects of the job.
>
> The more complex the task, the more things change; the more novel the problems presented, the brighter leaders have to be. (Furnham, 2010: 199–200)

This approach underestimates the extent to which it is the collective intelligence of a team which a senior leader must be able to muster and harness. Only in certain kinds of specialist consultancy, investment business or perhaps university (and not always even there) will we find the cleverest person at the top of the

---

1   http://en.wikipedia.org/wiki/Wikimedia_foundation. Accessed 18 February 2012. 65 employees in May 2011 is still the latest information shown today.

pyramid. The challenge of motivating, guiding and challenging people cleverer than oneself is a tricky one, requiring a threshold level of intelligence but much else besides. Having to be cleverer than your subordinates is a managerial dead end, likely to leave the person unable to move beyond Level 3.

That conclusion is reinforced by the limitations of resorting to ever more complicated thinking in the face of complexity. That thinking may try to master something which, of the essence of complexity, cannot be mastered or made safely predictable, or coped with predominantly intellectually. For that reason, Stamp notes that the capabilities indicated by the BIOSS levels equate neither to intellect as measured by IQ nor to the intelligence we use to solve well-structured practical problems.

An example of a relevant study by Kaplan, Klebanov and Sorensen (2008) was mentioned in Chapter 2, which looked at 316 CEO candidates for positions in private equity or venture capital-financed businesses. The candidates had been measured on 30 specific characteristics (of which five were classified as intellectual – brainpower, analytical skills, strategic vision, creative and attention to detail). A statistical analysis was done to identify which small number of key factors best explained the differences in performance. The authors described the dominant factor which explained 53 per cent of the variation as general talent or ability. This included intellectual abilities but only in broad step with, or slightly behind, a wide range of other attributes such as hiring and developing people, efficiency, flexibility, speed, commitment, persistence, proactivity, high standards and accountability. The factor which best explained the next 20 per cent of performance variation was slightly negatively related to intellect. Intellect was prominent (and positive) in the next two factors but these only explained 11 and 8 per cent of performance respectively.

To summarise, senior jobs pose more complex, less tractable challenges over longer time horizons than front-line or middle management roles. In facing these challenges intelligence is helpful up to a point, but not sufficient. Not for nothing is Elkind and McLean's riveting account of Enron entitled *The Smartest Guys in the Room* (2004). We now turn from IQ to EQ.

Relationships, Emotions and Humility

Daniel Goleman (1996) introduced the term 'emotional intelligence'. How do senior jobs differ from more junior ones in terms of the emotional and relationship challenges which they place on their holders?

Every so often in selection you come across an individual who is exceptionally talented in a number of respects but has not managed more than a small team, say eight people, within the context of a larger organisation (for example a consultancy). In interview they quite often argue that having done this successfully, they can take on much larger responsibilities, because they have the necessary skills and the primary management task of anyone, however high in a hierarchy, is to manage their direct reports (usually fewer than a dozen).

My experience is that this argument is badly mistaken on two counts, which we may call the loneliness of command and size.

The first point is the difference between being captain of a small boat (crew eight) on the open sea and being, say, chief engineer or purser (in charge of a team of eight) on an ocean liner. As captain you are not only more likely, as just discussed, to face Level 5 challenges;[2] you lack peers with whom you can share your quandaries, and your decisions not only need to be taken but also lived out. While a coach or a sympathetic chair of your board can help, both activities can be extremely lonely. As CEO of an independent organisation of eight you can expect to have exhausting days and sleepless nights trying to lead in situations from which you were previously protected – for example as income dips below the level needed to pay salaries at the end of the month. This work is not just intellectually but emotionally draining, with few relational resources to support you.

The second point connects with size. Perhaps you have eight direct reports, but each runs a business of 100 people. It is possible to manage eight people, knowing roughly what it is they are doing and ought to be doing. (The leadership saying which goes with this is 'I'd never ask someone to do something which I'm not prepared to do myself.') But not 800 people. The problems which your direct reports will bring you will be of quite a different order than if your total team is eight, not just intellectually but emotionally. For example a customer service problem emerges which was supposed to have been fixed two years ago, but it turns out it was not; now your company is at risk of becoming a national news story and being sued by thousands of customers. Another challenge: if you are to get any advance warning of such problems you will need to earn your direct reports' respect – why do you have your job instead of one of them? And how will you be visible to and help motivate the 800 people under your overall charge, without taking your subordinates' leadership space?

---

2   Whereas a chief engineer or purser might be operating at Level 2 or 3.

By the time you are responsible for 8,000 people the problems are multiplying. The information which reaches you is increasingly filtered, consciously and subconsciously. You are likely to be fed more of what you like and less of what you dislike. The situation is like that of a pressure vessel. More responsibility tends to amplify any cracks or weaknesses in your personality while reducing your relational support, such as your opportunities to spend time with people with whom you can drop the brave front. As you climb the pyramid you have fewer peers, and some or all of them may be competitors. Above you there is always someone saying, is this the best you can do – I want more. Or the demands may come from a voice inside your own head. Outside work, family and friends are increasingly impressed with the jobs you get but see less of you. Of course it need not be like this but what I have described is more the rule than the exception. In sum the challenge is not to be a well-balanced, emotionally intelligent person at the start, but to remain one. Organisational altitude disrupts EQ.

Let us look at just one dimension of this. Furnham devotes a chapter to narcissistic leadership which according to one source is probably the major cause of why CEOs fail (Furnham, 2010: 125). He sees self-confidence which is something we are keen to have in our leaders, because it may rub off on us: narcissists have a surplus of it. (Furnham, 2010: 113). He cites Rosenthal and Pittinsky (2006) who argue that we should think broadly of narcissistic leadership as produced by all of us, followers as well as leaders, in particular situations, rather than fixing it purely in one personality, and following Brown (1997) offers six traits which can characterise narcissism at individual, group and organisational levels:

> Denial: *the denial of facts about oneself, the realities of the constraints around one's work, and about the details of past occurrences in order for their ego ideal not to be challenged.*

> Rationalization: *the development of plausible justifications for explaining behaviour that does not support the belief in the ego ideal. This can come in the form of rationalizing failures, and justifying self-serving policies and decisions as if they were done in the interest of the group.*

> Self-aggrandizement: *engaging in behavior that serves to convince both oneself and others of one's fantasy of power, control and greatness. This includes over-stating one's virtues, merits and achievements.*

Attributional egoism: *attributing positive organizational outcomes to one's own efforts, and unfavourable outcomes to external factors or other people, regardless of one's own role. Such false attributions seek to defend the ego ideal of the narcissist.*

Sense of entitlement: *a feeling that one is entitled to organizational privileges such as success, power and admirations, whilst at the same time lacking in empathy for others and exploiting people in the pursuit of self-interest.*

Anxiety: *the experience of ongoing difficulty in maintaining self-esteem accompanied by hypersensitivity to criticism, and persistent feelings of insecurity. (Furnham, 2010: 115–116)*

My own experience suggests that narcissism is a significant leadership challenge in our society, and not just for individuals of a predefined personality type. In reflecting on the global financial crisis and my own experience in search, it seemed to me that we are frequently complicit in creating leadership roles which require – or only become easy to perform if one acquires – hubristic over-self-confidence (Board, 2010b). But you may wonder whether all of us are not prone to diagnose that which falls within our expertise; psychologists are well placed to diagnose narcissism. To my mind an important corroboration comes from the identification of the same issue from a completely different source.

Jim Collins (2001) and his colleagues carried out a five-year programme of research in which they studied 28 companies, 11 of which had made a transition from average performance (in terms of stock market appreciation) to sustained outperformance over at least 15 years. Each of the so-called 'good to great' companies was compared with a company as nearly similar as possible in its sector which did not outperform. At the outset Collins, sceptical of the fashionability of leadership as an explanation, gave the research team 'explicit instructions to *downplay* the role of top executives' (Collins, 2001: 21). But in the end they made their top finding that each of the 'good to great' companies had had, during the relevant period, Level 5 leadership which they defined as follows:

Level 5 Executive. *Builds enduring greatness through a paradoxical blend of personal humility and professional will.*

Level 4 Effective leader. *Catalyzes commitment to and vigorous pursuit of a clear and compelling vision, stimulating higher performance standards.*

Level 3 Competent manager. *Organizes people and resources toward the effective and efficient pursuit of pre-determined objectives.*

Level 2 Contributing team member. *Contributes individual capabilities to the achievement of group objectives and works effectively with others in a group setting.*

Level 1 Highly capable individual. *Makes productive contributions through talent, knowledge, skills, and good work habits. (Collins, 2001: 20)*

What caught the attention of Collins and his readers was the articulation of Level 5 and, within it, the unexpected appearance of humility. What Collins explains by humility is not timidity (in facing obstacles and overcoming them he described something more like tenacity), but in terms of the place of the self-humility describes the opposite of the narcissistic traits cited by Furnham from Brown. I take this as a strong non-psychological corroboration of the psychological focus on narcissism. Moreover there is a suggestive congruence between Collins's five leadership levels and the quite separate BIOSS levels which focus on levels of work. To be sure they represent gradations of different kinds of things, but things which are connected; and without seeking a one-to-one correspondence I think they point us clearly towards some of the emotional, relational and non-intellectual challenges of leading in the face of complexity – and therefore of differences between senior and more junior roles.

Our final exploration of difference is about UQ – or the ulcer quotient.

Track Record and Responsibility

I would like to note two different relationships between individuals and their track records which grow in significance at high organisational altitude and pursue one of them.

As leaders grow in seniority, so does the importance of what they symbolise as opposed to what they do. The symbolic work of leaders has as much to do with being as acting. The process does not have to be conceived of as quasi-magical. For example, it concerns the allocation of time. In a world sceptical of (although at the same time addicted to) various communication techniques – for example the 'town hall' meetings of a CEO or presidential candidate which are made available in real time, or very shortly afterwards, to supporters on video – time is a hard currency, or gold standard. If you are responsible for 8,000 people and you spend ten minutes in a meaningful conversation, one on one, with one of your front-line staff, you signal something which cynicism finds hard to debase: however many noughts in your pay packet, you only have 24 hours in a day.

At times it will mean you have the opportunity, or obligation, to speak for a large group (and will be judged harshly if you fail). Equally certainly you will be the donkey to which all kinds of other tails – events, contingencies, how things turn out with which you had little to do – will be pinned. All this will form part of your track record: what you are associated with. President Barack Obama needed to be ready to speak to the American people and carry responsibility whether the helicopter assault on Osama bin Laden succeeded or failed. Sometimes for the good of the community the leader will be sacrificed (Girard, 1979). If you don't want to pick up the leadership bill, don't eat in the restaurant.

The effectiveness of senior leaders is judged by others on more than their skills, and they themselves must take the same approach. In 2007 the distinguished British public servant, Paul Gray, resigned while he was in charge of Her Majesty's Revenue and Customs with over 100,000 staff. One staff member sent two password-protected discs, with personal records including bank account details for 25 million people, to the auditors by the internal mail. They never arrived. Whether you think you would have done that or not, if you cannot conceive of circumstances in which you would have done the same, then you do not understand the symbolic work of leaders. Of course, you may still become one – for example Italy's Prime Minister Silvio Berlusconi.

These remarks speak about responsibility and an acceptance that, as a senior leader, your track record will comprise events and results over some of which you had no influence. Fundamentally this is a shift of degree rather than kind from more junior roles: sales representatives carry the can for good luck and bad luck in their territories. But it is a shift. Not many sales representatives would expect to resign because someone they had never met accidentally lost something. But I would now like to draw between experience and potential leadership a second, different, and speculative strand. I do not know of research which bears on the point.

The 'ulcer quotient' refers to an old headhunters' saying, 'a three ulcer person in a five ulcer job'. To different headhunters the saying will mean different things. To me it says something about experience which is different from reputation, intellect, skill or emotional capability. It is to do with the likelihood that if you are around a fair amount of time, unpredictable stuff happens. It is to do with the capacity to cope conferred by challenging past events *separate from* reputation, intellect, skill or emotional capability. It is (so far as I know) unsupported by research; other practitioners may reject the saying or interpret it differently.

Over time, life throws 'stuff' at you. Some of it is related to your job, some is tangentially connected and some is unconnected. Overcoming severe challenges may enhance your reputation, build your conscious or unconscious grasp of situations and response strategies or strengthen your emotional capability. But walking through an unexpected fire can confer a different survival quality. Perhaps some years ago you coped with one of your children having a cancer scare, while behind the scenes at work your boss undermined you while you led a ferocious budget round. This is not reputation, because no-one at work may know all the facts. This is not intellect and skills, because they do not get you through a cancer scare. This is not emotional capability, at least in the sense of having chosen your parents well or learned to overcome reasonable setbacks. This is (my experience leads me to posit) something from your track record which enables you to put new, outrageously unexpected, challenges in perspective because you know you have survived something else outrageous. However much it irritates the exceptionally brilliant and the lucky, some things only come with time.

This is not only an academically unsupported concept but one which fits the Delusio model – the keepers barricade the gates of privilege by inventing vague and unsupported entry requirements.

I knew Henry for some years. A rising executive in a major British clearing bank, he had been variously both a candidate and a client in some executive search assignments. He was very keen to become a CEO and in my view he had the appropriate skills. With no involvement of mine he had an opportunity to become CEO of a financial services company, not on the scale of a clearing bank but a quoted, entrepreneurial company with a stable senior executive team and track record of a decade or more of profitability. He took it.

Within a year he had lost nearly all of his several million pounds of net worth, his job and his homes, and his marriage was at risk. It turned out that the long-standing executive team and the equally long-standing track record of profitability were more closely connected than anyone, including the auditors, had realised. After some months Henry had the shock of realising that he had to suspend all of his team and call in the police. It would take some time and most of his money to clear his name.

We might call that a five ulcer job. Survive that, and it puts a lot of other things into perspective. My own experience has not been on that scale, but the closest has been being a trustee of the Diana, Princess of Wales Memorial Fund, and having to tell my wife one evening that the combination of US litigation and unlimited personal liability meant that this unpaid role could bankrupt us. It took two years or more to live through that mess and come out the other side.

The ulcer quotient may be meaningless but, if it has meaning, its merit lies in the untidy way it points beyond skills and transgresses narrow boundaries of 'work' or 'the job'. To differing degrees holders of senior roles face such transgressions. The ulcer quotient is a folkloric way of saying that at high organisational altitudes storms can be violent, and there may be risks which will not emerge from a competency analysis from appointing to an exposed role a *wunderkind* whose skills are impeccable, whose track record is glowing (but brief) and whose life experience has been relatively protected. Appreciating those risks can be valuable to the *wunderkind* herself, if she accepts that the advice is not simply the dismal product of an older generation congratulating itself for having survived.

Earth or Delusio?

The simplest way to escape the Delusian snare is to point to an objective skill required for success. Basketball players are not living on Delusio because there are measurable skills – shooting hoops quickly from difficult distances and angles – which underpin success, whatever the pundits say. On this ground we could defend senior leadership as a real talent if we embraced Furnham's focus on the need for IQ; but I have accepted this only to a partial degree.

Another way to know that we are not on Delusio is that senior leaders fail, because on Delusio everyone succeeds. Furnham cites Kellerman (2004) as saying that corporate leaders are being held increasingly to account – leaders of 100 of the 2,500 world's largest companies were replaced in 2002, four times the number in 1995. Kellerman concluded:

> *Convictions, dismissals, recall movements and forced resignations such as these seem to signal a growing intolerance of bad leadership, as well as a trend in which bad leaders and followers are increasingly held to account. But let's not kid ourselves. Change is slow. (Kellerman, 2004: 231)*

Yet the objective evidence is mixed. Furnham cites with approval an estimate by Hogan and colleagues of $1–3 million as the cost of a failed executive (Furnham, 2010: 3). Hogan produces diagnostic tools for leadership selection and is therefore unlikely to underestimate this figure. Conversely a recent financial study (Taylor, 2010) concludes that boards of directors behave as if firing the CEO cost shareholders several hundred million dollars – in other words, as on Delusio, it happens rarely. My own experience leans towards the latter conclusion.

Of course Delusio is an artificially cynical creation. But in truth it hits too close to home for my comfort: particularly the link between narcissism and the pressures on top Delusian leaders to inflate their views of their own prowess. Another cynical creation is the infamous Peter Principle: in any hierarchy, individuals tend to rise to their level of incompetence (Peter, 1985). Of course, on Delusio there are no levels of incompetence to which to rise. But just as the Peter Principle can give us insightful glimpses into reality even while it fails to make the grade as a universal law, so in Part III we may decide that we have done a better job of explaining reality if we can show why Delusio and the Earth resemble each other so closely.

Power and Politics

Introduction

Chapter 4 suggested ways in which senior roles differ from front-line and middle management roles. We explored the complexity of the challenges senior leaders face, the emotional and relational content of those challenges and the symbolic work we ask leaders to perform, for example when we expect them to accept responsibility for fickle and unforeseen events. These differences that make up seniority may be matters of kind, may be matters of degree. But let us agree that the differences are marked and go on to notice something curious.

Imagine a collection of pizza recipe books from around the world, from a diversity of authors from the amateur to the professional, none of which mention making dough. Or a collection of aerial photographs of Paris, all missing the Eiffel Tower. Once we notice it, that is the situation we face in senior selection. One can write and read at length about senior selection – for example see any of the guides to good practice referred to in Chapter 2 – and there will be no discussion of power and politics. We have just done the same thing in Chapter 4. Yet power and politics constitute one of the most characteristic features of senior appointments.

In this chapter we shall ask three questions. Why is this dimension so characteristic? Why is it so absent from good practice books, training courses and research? And consequently, how is it in fact being learned? Because if something is intrinsic to an activity but missing from this literature, something else must be happening. If there are pizzas, somehow people are learning to make dough.

This chapter will look at how power is written about (or not) in management literature. In Chapter 6 we will test what emerges against a wider body of thinking on power in sociology, political science and philosophy.

But our starting point will be some practical examples of the power and politics surrounding the choosing of leaders.

Practical Examples

Occasionally power and politics reveal themselves like flashes of lightning. For a moment the organisational landscape we have been working in is illuminated with unnatural clarity. The story in Chapter 1 of painful, unsuccessful attempts to find a successor chief executive for a $100 million-turnover professional body is, to my mind, the story of Patrick's inability to give up power. To an extent which may have surprised Patrick as much as anyone else, he and power turned out to have a merciless grip on each other. What stood revealed in the landscape through successive painful but illuminating events was a rising body count: more individuals retired hurt, more damage to a respected organisation's reputation.

Another example sticks out in my mind, of a major government department with diverse, complex operations. Adrian, a new permanent secretary (CEO) was appointed promising change. He was a civil servant but without experience of the department's work. His predecessor had spent several years building senior managerial capability and teamwork. Adrian reversed this. Within six months he had moved all the heads of business units who reported to him. The most knowledgeable direct reports were moved outside the department or rotated into roles about which they knew nothing. Key roles were filled by talented but equally ignorant outsiders. Within six months Adrian had done the equivalent of taking over a ballet company, sending the artistic director abroad, switching the musical director to run administration and hiring a management consultant as choreographer. No-one could doubt that Adrian wanted change, but what kind of change? The destruction of a senior team and its knowledge and teamwork was total – and probably not accidental.

All the following were predictable and political consequences of Adrian's actions. Firstly, within six months all Adrian's direct reports knew less about their roles than he (himself ignorant) did: alarming for organisational performance but promising for Adrian's power over them. Secondly, his new lieutenants, chosen by him, owed him personal loyalty; the old-timers had seen the fate of their colleagues and been warned. Thirdly, Adrian had written on the wall what kind of change he wanted – quick changes which made him look dynamic. His strategy was rash if he was concerned with sustainable change in organisational capability; it made sense if he was concerned with 'action this day'. The risks for him were less than the risks for the department. Adrian might prove lucky but even if he did not, the CEO's office was the perfect place to investigate any emerging problems and pick which of his subordinates should shoulder the blame. (Crucial to such a tactic was that his subordinates should know less about their jobs than Adrian did.)

None of this was said, of course. Adrian was full of praise for the department's achievements under his predecessor. The pattern did not emerge straight away. But six months in I saw things differently. Abruptly the familiar organisational landscape showed itself in a new way and I thought (rightly or wrongly) 'So that's what the b---- is up to.'

Regardless of my interpretation, within a few months the world of the organisation's managers had been turned upside down by the choosing of a leader. There were not only new people but a new sense of up and down, important and unimportant, right and wrong.

For a vivid example at the top of a quoted private sector corporation we can turn to the example cited in Chapter 3, that is the problematic succession to Richard Greenbury as CEO of Marks and Spencer, described by Bower (2007). In formal terms the process began in 1994, with Keith Oates, vice chairman and CFO, as a leading contender among a number of internal possibilities. In 1995 Marks and Spencer broke UK retail records with profits of £1 billion; by 1999 the financial and commercial weather had become much stormier.

> As the poor results piled up, the London financial markets were further stunned by a leaked letter from Keith Oates to M&S's nonexecutive board members. The letter called for Greenbury's replacement as chief executive by Oates, with Greenbury to remain on as chairman.

> In the ensuing months of crisis, Oates resigned, Salsbury was appointed chief executive, and, after it became clear to Greenbury that he could not work with Salsbury, Greenbury resigned. After a search, Luc Vandevelde, a Belgian food retailer, was appointed nonexecutive chairman in February 2000. After seven more months, Salsbury departed, and Vandevelde assumed the chief executive's role as well. While Vandevelde was able to stabilize the turbulent situation, his tenure was not destined to be long. His own choice to succeed him as chief executive was asked to leave, at which point Vandevelde resigned

as chairman, and a new team was installed by the spring of 2004.
(Bower, 2007: 48)

Dramatic stories have their advantages and their disadvantages. They capture the collision of events with political struggles in which not merely the jobs but, thanks to reputational impact, the professional survival of key players may be at stake. But for most Wagnerian opera is not a weekly treat. Emphasising those associations may lead us to miss how power and politics are equally present (and unstoppable) in quieter, better behaved situations.

Theresa[1] was a general manager in a multi-division private sector group whose acclaimed CEO was due to retire. There had been effective succession planning and the senior management team included two or three plausible successors, one externally recruited a few years previously. The CEO stood down as anticipated on a bravura final set of financial results, and the external recruit took over. All the potential successors had been at pains to emphasise commitment to the organisation ahead of their own personal futures. This was no lip service: they might not have qualified for Collins's description of humble but they took seriously the good of the organisation. Each studiously eschewed Adrian-style tactics. This was music to Theresa's ears since she disliked politics. The 'day job' of serving customers and shareholders was difficult enough without added problems. And Theresa's peers felt the same way.

Nonetheless, as the likely time of succession approached, politics reared its head anyway.

In relation to the departing CEO, business decisions came up (each with objective rationales) which had the incidental effect of shifting likely profits or losses between years. For example, certain operations were regularly reviewed to ensure compliance with set standards; but there was a case for conducting every so often a more rigorous review. Its results might (but no-one could be sure) require lower profits in the current year. But there were other pressing priorities and no impropriety would be involved in putting the decision off to next year. A competent executive could see these implications in advance; in part that is what being competent at a senior level in a large organisation means. The departing CEO never asked for his final year results to be flattered and he never took blatant decisions which had that effect. Probably such a thought never had occurred to him in his dreams. It did not need to.

---

1   Theresa is a composite of individuals whom I have coached or worked with and who have experienced similar patterns of CEO transition.

The situation meant that his senior staff did have to think about them. Whichever courses of action they plumped for had started to acquire political stakes.

In relation to the aspiring candidates, call them P, Q and R, each week their colleagues took business decisions which had differing likelihoods of pleasing or upsetting P, Q or R. A change of accounting convention might change the apparent success of different parts of their business. Theresa had to think how much time and visibility to give to progressing a cross-company proposal on the environment which was enthusiastically backed by P and popular with the board, but thought unimportant by Q and a waste of time by R? Whatever the thought processes of P, Q and R, at most one of them would become CEO and quite possibly one or both of the others would leave the group thereafter.[2] The situation would be political even in a community of saints.

The Possibility of Discussion

A quick reality check before we move on. I have suggested that, once noticed, the near-complete[3] absence of power and politics from management writing on selection is surprising. But can we sketch from readily available experience something political with which selection writers might be expected to deal? If not, we may have overlooked something which makes the suggested kind of discussion impossible.

Quite readily, yes. An important power issue which arises routinely in senior appointments but is rarely discussed is loyalty. For example, S has served successfully as finance director of more impressive companies than T. Yet both are technically competent. However as chief executive you trust T implicitly: the two of you have worked together in several challenging situations, whereas S is a stranger. Good selection practice treats appointing T as cronyism and a mistake.

Often it would be. However, sometimes T's proven loyalty might be in the organisation's best interest. For example consider the situation of Henry in Chapter 4, who took on a CEO role in a reliably profitable company only to find most of the senior management team complicit in serious financial misrepresentation. If Henry had had any inkling of what he faced, he might

---

2   See for example the succession to Jack Welch at GE (Bower, 2007: 124–125).
3   A (rare) counter-example in the academic literature is Bozionelos (2005) who reconstructs an academic selection process as a political struggle.

have placed the existing finance director on gardening leave and brought in an urgent replacement. A cogent case could be made for T rather than S in the shareholders' interest. There are pros and cons which the selection literature could discuss but does not.

Power in Management Literature: The Icebergs

Politics – actions (often struggles) involving or affecting power, even if framed around a different issue – appear in two ways in management literature. Explicit texts on the subject are like the visible parts of icebergs, unusual and intriguing. Most of us are happy to visit the subject from a safe distance; a happy few plunge right in. We tend to worry about the few.

We should worry more about the invisible parts of icebergs. Management texts and good practices speak to us about power even when they are not explicit about doing so. This is no conspiracy but simply how an ecology of common sense ideas sustains itself in the background of our thoughts. We will examine both aspects of power and politics in management literature.

A prominent scholar of power in management today is Jeffrey Pfeffer. In his book *Power: Why Some People Have It – And Others Don't* (2010), this Stanford professor observes that politics is an inevitable part of managerial life. After all one way to understand management is as the allocation of scarce resources. He explores what impedes our noticing, understanding and acting in the light of this. For example he finds that a common expectation among younger managers – unsupported by reality – is the just-world hypothesis, which has been studied by social psychologists for some time. He finds a common belief that, in the long run, meritorious actions earn their deserved reward – in other words a 'just deserts' view. Those managers (the majority) who do not simply dive into politics may feel diffident, shameful or incompetent (because they are unpractised) at taking political actions. Pfeffer wants them to realise that they can learn political skill. They can learn to express themselves in appropriate and competent political ways just as they have learned many other things, but attention and effort are needed rather than denial. At its simplest we can picture Pfeffer saying, 'Grow up!'

We can compare Pfeffer with the author on power with the most influence among managers today – Machiavelli (2005). We will see why he is influential even on managers who have never read him.

Machiavelli's *The Prince* says this to would-be princes of today, which is no less relevant than it was in 1513. Whatever good you would wish to do, you will first need to obtain and maintain power. To obtain power but not credibly maintain it is to blight your country (or organisation) with fighting as others try to wrest it from you. Finally, observation of the world suggests that it is not possible to maintain power by remaining wholly good. To associate with Machiavelli the evangelically amoral or immoral tone which better fits Nietzsche is to ignore what he says. Machiavelli would be happy to see good government succeed and bring peace and prosperity to their lands. Indeed, far from being indifferent to tyranny, he was a committed republican. But his contribution to good government is to explain to leaders, which others will shy away from, that to govern well they will have to play dirty – and they had better think about how they do so. As Princeton Professor Maurizio Viroli writes:

> *A prince or a ruler must 'not depart from the good', as long as he can (potendo); but he 'should know how to enter into evil' forced by necessity (necessitato) (Ch. XVIII). (Macchiavelli, 2005: xxxiii)*

> *Contrary to the black legend of an atheistic or anti-religious Machiavelli, there is nothing in The Prince that goes against God or against what Machiavelli believed to be true Christian moral and political teaching. Without taking into account this aspect of Machiavelli's thinking, we cannot hope to grasp ... [what] makes The Prince such a unique and original work. (Macchiavelli, 2005: xxxix)*

On the face of it Pfeffer (2010) says little about what is good or ethical: neither of those terms nor morals or virtue appear in the index. In fact we will look more closely at this in the next chapter. But in explaining why individuals should overcome their distaste for power he argues that:

> *... power is part of leadership and is necessary to get things done – whether those things entail changing the US health-care system, transforming organizations so they are more humane places to work, or affecting dimensions of social policy and human welfare. (Pfeffer, 2010: 7)*

So allowing for a transition from mediaeval technicolour to contemporary managerial pastel, I take Pfeffer's stance to be similar to Machiavelli's. I think Pfeffer would be happy to see more good managers succeed. Like Machiavelli, he wishes to point out that adhering to the 'just deserts' view is not going to help them do that.

However the reason Machiavelli is so influential even among those who have not read him is that a vivid (and different) set of interpretations have entered our language in his name. These interpretations apply in scholarship and not just in casual thought. Furnham (2010) has a chapter on the Machiavellian leader and cites the work of psychologists such as Christie and Geis (1970) who developed the idea of a Machiavellian type ('the Mach').

> The Mach's salient characteristic is viewed as coolness and detachment. In pursuit of largely self-defined goals, he disregards both his own and others' affective states and therefore attacks the problem with all the logical ability that he possesses. He reads the situation in terms of perceived possibilities and then proceeds to act on the basis of what action will lead to what results. (Christie and Geis, 1970: 89–90)

Furnham himself introduces the term like this:

> To be described as Machiavellian is to be insulted – it means being duplicitous, egocentric and manipulative. The Machiavellian is exploitative, competitive and selfish.
>
> Machiavellians make, but break, alliances, promises and rules. They make misleading statements, are high on blame and low on forgiveness. They seem deeply cynical. They may do particularly well in many organizations. In a dog-eat-dog corporate culture Machiavellianism may be the only way to survive, let alone thrive. (Furnham, 2010: 140)

These quotations highlight the depth of what Machiavellianism has come to mean in our thought, as well as a shift in how we see 'the Mach'. Macchiavelli left the ethics and values of his prince open; the prince was not constrained to care only about selfish things or to think that other people did not matter. On his analysis, unselfishness will have to be compromised, but it does not *have* to turn into its unmitigated opposite. The wise prince will break an alliance when it is necessary but does not break alliances for the hell of it (in fact the latter is quite poor statecraft).

In our times, however, the quotations show how we have coloured the blank space in – 'largely self-defined goals', 'egocentric', 'selfish'. Under the hand of psychologists, 'the Mach' has a deceptive trait, and so many break alliances often. They may enjoy it. Psychologists have a purpose in doing this. If there are people with such dispositions, we may want to identify this before we choose them to lead us.

In specific cases colouring in the ruthless operator's values and drives in this way might be justified. For example I coloured in Adrian's motives in demolishing the senior management team which he inherited, because I interpreted them not only as ruthless but also as selfish. I suggested that he valued change which suited him in the short term above building the organisation's capacity in the long term.

The upshot of this way of perceiving Machiavellianism having become written into our thinking perhaps without our noticing, is that Machiavellianism becomes even more strongly something which our society avoids or explains away. Some people strongly reject the selfish values now read into it. Some, more sensitive to the social disapproval which it attracts, reject it for those reasons. Most 'Machs' also condemn it because being identified as Machiavellian makes winning harder (in the same way that being identified as a liar makes lying more difficult). So Machiavellian is indeed a universal no-no or insult, although for 'Machs' the insult is to their skills of camouflage.

Finally, part of how management thinking understands politics today derives from game theory and the study of evolution. Gigerenzer (2000) sets out the argument in these terms. Humans and other primates biologically close to us (for example chimpanzees) practise co-operation between genetically unrelated individuals, which is biologically unusual. Co-operation can be found in highly developed forms across human societies, from hunter–gatherers to the technologically advanced, and some evidence suggests that co-operation is extremely ancient. Finally, game theory allows us to show that co-operation has a place as a species strategy. In simulations 'always co-operate with others' does not work as a strategy for the species, because more selfish species might well wipe the always co-operative species out. However other, conditionally co-operative, strategies such as 'tit for tat' – start by co-operating but continue only if the other party co-operates – can be shown to work.

Evidence for this can be found in the field.

A vampire bat, for instance, will die if it fails to find food for two consecutive nights, and there is high variance in food-gathering success. Food sharing allows the bats to reduce this variance, and the best predictor of whether a bat, having foraged successfully, will share its food with a hungry nonrelative is whether the nonrelative has shared food with the bat in the past.

... Co-operation between two or more individuals for their mutual benefit is a solution to a class of important adaptive problems ... (Gigerenzer, 2000: 213–214)

Contemporary work of this kind provides new grounds for rejecting (or qualifying) Machiavellianism.

Power in Management Literature: The Seas in Between

The stance towards power and politics implicit in most management literature, including selection literature, is that politics and interpersonal conflict within organisations are dysfunctional or negative, and to be overcome. Professor Jo Silvester at City University London (2008) summarises the dominant perspective in this way:

Politics is associated with the 'dark side' of workplace behaviour and researchers have described political behaviour as inherently divisive, stressful, and a cause of dissent and reduced performance. (Silvester, 2008: 107)

She goes on to point out that higher levels of perceived politics inside organisations are associated with lower job satisfaction, morale and organisational commitment, and higher intentions to quit. A wealth of additional clues point in this direction.

Few business schools advertise courses which teach political skill – a four-day course in power and influence at the Cranfield School of Management is a notable British exception – although many management coaches find the subject regularly comes up in the privacy of those relationships.

Models of team-building, for example 'forming, storming, norming and performing' (Tuckman, 1965), teach that conflict is something we want to emerge from.

Take out the scale against which the performance of managers in your own organisation is judged. Count the references to integrity, delivering on one's promises, building relationships, offering and obtaining co-operation, and aligning with the values and goals of the whole organisation. Then count the references to outmanoeuvring colleagues, picking fights and winning them, fulfilling promises only when expedient to do so, and remaining detached from organisational values.

Commonly we take for granted in organisations today, both as an ideal and as something which we work hard to realise in practice, that everyone should be aligned and co-operate on the basis of goals, strategies and values which they may have helped to create but which top management have a particular responsibility to shape. This is so even in (self-described) progressive models of organisation which value bottom-up innovation, such as the 'vanguard' companies which Rosabeth Moss Kanter identifies as emerging from the global financial crisis (Kanter, 2009).

Consistent with this, challenging basic strategy outside the board room is dangerous. Furnham cites research from the Center for Creative Leadership which identifies as one of six warning signs of future executive derailment '[the executive] disagrees with higher management about how the business should be run' (Furnham, 2010: 34–39).[4]

At this point we might scratch our heads. Of course there is challenge outside the board room, although managers are encouraged to categorise it as inertia, resistance to change or vested interests rather than perceptive critique. Successful management has to overcome this resistance. So are political skills being practised outside the board room, but under another name – under a guise which does not describe itself as political (let alone Machiavellian)?

Consider a book on strategy which I much admire, by INSEAD professors W. Chan Kim and Renée Mauborgne (2005). They provide a stirring picture of how even organisations in unpromising, declining industries can reinvent themselves radically and profitably. They start with the circus industry and consider Cirque du Soleil. One attractive feature of their analysis is that they do not imagine that radical strategy can rest on making bold strokes with a pen on

---

4   Yet one conclusion drawn by a number of distinguished authorities from the global financial crisis is that it demonstrated lack of challenge to banks' basic strategies within the board room (Board, 2010b).

a flip-chart: they tackle the change management problem. Radical reinvention of an organisation and its marketplace will encounter resistance – conflict.

To address this they stipulate that a key part of successful radical strategy is a fair, open thinking process, in which employees are encouraged to articulate and refute ideas – especially management's. In other words, conflict is legitimated and (so far as possible) de-politicised. Central to this is creating a playing field accepted by staff as reasonably level in which certain pre-determined ideas do not automatically win.

By organising the strategy formulation process around the principles of fair process, you can build execution into strategy making from the start. With fair process, people tend to be committed to support the resulting strategy even when it is viewed as not favourable or at odds with their perception of what is strategically correct for their unit (Kim and Mauborgne, 2005: 184).

How hearteningly different from strategy as a 'black box' process developed confidentially by a small group supported by an expensive consultancy, whose large resources then provide the intellectual 'shock and awe' to support the strategy when it is unveiled! It means sharing information (which itself is power). It is participative. It stresses fairness. What could be less Machiavellian?

Except that elsewhere in the same book they address the same question differently. They praise at length a vigorous form of 'tipping point leadership' in which leaders propel through their organisations 'a fast change in mindset that is *internally driven of people's own accord*' (Kim and Mauborgne, 2005: 152). That is, internally driven towards what the leaders have chosen in advance. What about the possibility that the strength of the arguments for a contrary point of view reaches a tipping point (a critical mass) among the leadership, who 'rapidly and of their own accord' dump their announced goals for a new way of thinking? Having stressed the crucial importance of a level playing field of ideas, under the guise of leadership or change management we find ourselves groping for the rapid manipulation of others' consent. This is certainly political and possibly Machiavellian – in an uplifting book about strategy which is not overtly about politics.

I'm not suggesting that Kim and Mauborgne are being deceptive or deliberately inconsistent, or that they have failed to grasp what management is. On the contrary, I think they are sincere, insightful and well worth reading. Precisely because of this they illuminate particularly clearly two points which can be found (though not always so clearly) in a wide range of management literature. Firstly, that power and politics are part of the stuff of management – for example change management – and may be being addressed even without our (or an author's) knowledge. The icebergs and the seas in between are made of the same stuff: water. Secondly, politics is distasteful to most of us, and, in their own logical interests, those who disagree with this judgement will tend to fake it. So as a society we may be trying very hard to teach ourselves that good management (including personnel selection) is apolitical when this might be an impossibility.

The Inescapability of Politics at High Organisational Altitudes

We are starting to float the possibility that politics both exists and (through the interaction of all of us) is frequently painted out of the picture quite pervasively in organisations. This is potentially a large suggestion which needs more work. In particular, most of the thinking we can draw on about power and politics has been done outside management studies – in political science, sociology and philosophy. But we can nail now a simpler point, which brings us back to the theme of this part: in what way senior jobs differ from those at the front line and in middle management.

Politics exists at high organisational altitudes. At its simplest, senior jobs are senior because many of the decisions which have to be made cannot be settled by an appeal to overarching rational principles. Mostly, if they could have been settled earlier, they would have been.

Consider an organisation in which all the executives share the most seemingly narrow, objective goal – for example a management buy-out in which the managers are the shareholders. Imagine that the managers were similarly educated at business school, such that they like making decisions by eating up large quantities of analytical data and they see the sole objective of business as maximising shareholder value (in this case making themselves rich). Even here, the problems coming to the board will not have one right answer. If they have net present value calculations attached – calculations which reduce the whole of the future to a single cash value – there will be arguments of interpretation as well as calculation which at bottom reflect what Chapter 4 emphasised – the future's deep complexity and uncertainty.

Is escape possible if one considers organisations (such as some religious groups) in which loyalty is sworn not only to a claimed absolute value but to the person of a supreme interpreter? Possibly, for a period of time: but eventually if nothing else the question will arise of the interpreter's successor. Certainly the largest faith traditions within which monarchical interpretation has been attempted – Christianity and Islam – have seen major conflict and splits.

Pizza Recipes Revisited

The young managers whom Pfeffer teaches at Stanford are not fools, nor are they short on ambition. If politics is a pervasive part of reality, why is the 'just deserts' view so strong? Recalling how we began this chapter, can we – even speculatively – tell any remotely plausible story of an intelligent, scientifically-minded society which ends up with a collection of pizza recipe books none of which mention dough?

Let's try. The institutional experience of talented young people is dominated by school and university. Part of the *raison d'être* of schools and universities – especially the good schools and universities attended by many future leaders – is an intense, institution-wide effort to encourage students' efforts and to give those efforts (whether academic or sporting or artistic) their just deserts. Breaches of this code are treated as grave, whether plagiarism by students or favouritism or inappropriate relationships on the part of teachers. Of course, at the same time as the students experience the formative law of the institution they continue to experience (referring back to Chapter 1) outside institutionally-sanctioned activities the formative law of the playground, where there are all kinds of power plays and unjust rewards. Life is a dual experience in which institutional practice is scraped clean of the practices of the playground (true even if at university the student chooses to study what goes on in playgrounds rather than subatomic particles).

If working life takes them into 'blue chip' private or public sector institutions, while still in reasonably junior roles they will be taught good management practices. These present themselves as, and encourage young managers to be, meritocractic, apolitical, indeed scientific. Our young managers are beginners. Applying these practices helps them get better results than having no idea. Knowing some techniques which their staff do not know also helps (a bit) answer the question, in their own minds as well as their staff's, why they are in the manager's job. Showing commitment as a young manager to practising 'just deserts' in giving recognition and rewards to staff also helps. Finally, in blue chip organisations applying good practices will be rewarded in its own right as showing a commitment to learning.

At the same time there is still life in the playground, and from time to time that erupts in the workplace. But those are aberrations. By the time our young manager from a good school and university is 30, she has spent half her life learning to live in the dual world of quality institution and playground, in which the language and practice of the first continues to be scraped clean of the second. By now it comes naturally. And, at this level, the unavoidable political content of her jobs is still low.

According to this chapter, as she climbs the pyramid this changes. Who knows what happens next: she has a mentor, she goes to Professor Pfeffer's MBA class, she figures it out for herself, or she takes some quite other direction. But the following is logical. If she becomes both senior and politically self-aware, then she will be no less aware of the political advantages of seeming apolitical. In any case decades of dual-experience habit – the institution and the playground – together with any distaste which she actually has for politics all pull in the same direction. While acting politically when she has to, or wants to, it will be either more expedient or more agreeable to continue to keep the language and practice of the institution seemingly free of contamination by the playground.

The story is a speculative one but it suggests a better analogy than a world of pizza recipes with no reference to dough. We live in a world of thousands of detailed car manuals none of which explain how to drive. The books make sense in a limited, self-contained way, but only make a wider sense for readers who have a skill which none of the books try to explain.

From the relatively sheltered waters of personnel selection and management studies we have now found ourselves swept out to sea. However help may be at hand. In other academic disciplines, power and politics have been studied by some of the most capable minds that have ever lived.

6

A Deeper Crisis

Our Two Tasks

In Part I we noticed a stuckness in personnel selection and selection research, whereby the major changes brought about in choosing people for front-line and middle management roles over the past 30 years – driven by science – have left senior selection relatively untouched.

Part II explored some ways senior roles are different. Chapter 4 presented some differences summarised under the themes of complexity, humility and responsibility. The chapter's main task was to present arguments and evidence which enabled us to deepen our existing insights and to organise them more clearly. The ideas that senior roles involve more unpredictability over longer timescales, pose a risk of hubris and involve accepting large responsibilities did not come out of the blue.

Chapter 5 suggested another difference, the inescapable involvement of senior roles in power and politics, but the argument made did claim surprise. The chapter suggested that although power and politics are central to senior appointments, in books, articles and training in senior selection the theme is absent. The chapter suggested a widespread discomfort with politics which affects both how managers go about their jobs and how that activity is thought about in management literature. Explicit treatment of politics is rare. Where politics becomes explicit, located either in ideas such as Machiavelli's thought, or in people such as 'high Machs' as a personality type, we are prone to distort and demonise both.

We now have two tasks. Firstly we need to re-assess the stuckness of senior selection in the light of these arguments. Secondly we need to test further Chapter 5's claims, drawing on the much wider scholarship on power and politics which exists outside of management literature. The two tasks turn out to be closely connected. They are the work of this chapter.

Stuckness Reconsidered (I)

Based on Chapter 4, the prospects for improving senior selection do not look too bleak. There are (on this analysis) real differences between senior roles and middle or junior ones: we are not living on planet Delusio. It is no surprise that selection research has concentrated on middle and junior roles. At those levels larger numbers, less complex tasks and fewer barriers such as sensitive confidentiality all make scientific study easier. Therefore changes in selection procedure would take time to climb the peaks of organisations, needing in all likelihood some modifications to take into account the differing job contents. Research into senior selection may have lost momentum, but this could be rectified, with the targeted use of research funds. Coupling a revival of research with continuing efforts to improve senior selection by forward-thinking and influential HR directors, any stuckness should dissolve. Indeed good progress could be made using research available now – for example the BIOSS tools for levels of complexity, or, as Furnham advocates, psychological assessments to select out candidates with undue levels of narcissism or other weaknesses which may be exacerbated by too much seniority.

From this perspective science will continue to be the engine of progress and to speak of crisis is unjustified. Whether a happy future for society with better selected leaders in senior roles is achieved in reality will depend on scientists doing good science, selectors doing good selection and good candidates coming forward. But whether that happy future would be *possible* depends only on one thing: whether science can crack the problem in Chapter 5 – power and politics.

How Science Appears in Our Story So Far

Science (including social science) is embedded in our story so far in more ways than we might at first notice. Firstly, and most obviously, there is the explicit research which underpinned all the progress in Part I – everything from studies of how quickly interview impressions solidify (in Chapter 1), to Boyatzis' studies of 2,000 managers in 12 organisations (in Chapter 2), to Hollenbeck's reflections on working in selection as a psychologist (in Chapter 3), to give only three examples.

Secondly, in a more pervasive and tacit way the scientific mindset shapes the common sense actions of practical selectors who have no interest in science or research as such. The influence is there in the way the selection problem has been framed as a measurement problem, even if there is nothing remotely scientific about the way particular selectors make their selection judgements. The influence of science is deep and wide, coming through half-remembered books and training courses and the advice of HR specialists.

Thus in contemporary good practice we begin by specifying as objectively as we can what are the attributes (KSAOs) for which we are looking. That done, the task of the selectors is to try to measure the candidates as accurately as possible, even if most of the 'measuring' is not quantitatively expressed. For example, two key criteria in the example specification at the end of Chapter 13 are 'leadership of innovation' and 'sensitive, tactful, persuasive with a wide range of people': the invitation to the interviewers is to say which of the candidates in front of them have more of these qualities than others. We treat the candidate Hamid as an object whose leadership of innovation and sensitivity, tact and persuasiveness with people are relatively stable abilities, even if hard to express in simple numbers. Of course when psychometric instruments are used then the measuring process is explicit, with results often expressed in percentiles – for example a candidate's numerical reasoning is in the top 5 per cent of the adult population but their emotional stability is about average.

This is not the end of it. Ideas about how the world can be grasped scientifically, and what it means so to grasp it, are part of our contemporary culture and common sense. We do not usually notice or speak about these things because they go deep and seem obvious. To see how deep this goes, let us revisit the book on power by Jeffrey Pfeffer (2010) which we explored in Chapter 5, and look more carefully at what he is saying from the perspective of ethics and values. Of course, Pfeffer is a professor and social scientist, but I will also be pointing out things which only work because they strike us, his readers, non-scientific as well as scientific, as common sense.

Recall that the historical Machiavelli favoured good over evil. His point was that for leaders, doing evil (and preferably doing it decisively and skilfully) was a necessary part of doing good. However in our time to be Machiavellian has come to suggest being immoral or amoral – either not recognising virtue or despising it. I suggested that Pfeffer's stance was similar to that of the historical Machiavelli. But let us look more closely.

a)   The index to Pfeffer's book has more than 800 entries. None of 'ethics', 'morality', 'virtue', 'good', 'evil', 'wrong' appear even once.

b)   Pfeffer explains why his readers should want power. They may live longer and have less stress, they can make more money and they can do things like reform health care. Also, some people enjoy power for its own sake (these readers he does not need to persuade).

c)   Pfeffer's predominant stance is that he is explaining objective realities, facts and techniques. By implication the ethical questions lie with how the reader uses them:

> How you behave and what you should do needs to fit your particular circumstances – the organizational situation and also your own personal values and objectives. (Pfeffer, 2010: 15).

However in a closing chapter Pfeffer does address ethical questions. He asks whether power dynamics are good for organisations and individuals. He repeats research which suggests that human affairs are unavoidably political – in other words politics is a fact, get over it and get yourself skilled. He points out that if a 'non-political' organisation were possible, the most plausible structure would be a strict hierarchy which has its own significant disadvantages. In these respects his stance towards us is as a values-free scientist reporting on objective realities. But the largest part of this chapter takes an explicit and selfish ethical position:

> So don't worry about how your efforts to build your path to power are affecting your employer, because your employer is probably not worrying about you. Neither are your co-workers or 'partners', if you happen to have any – they are undoubtedly thinking about your usefulness to them, and you will be gone, if they can manage it, when you are no longer of use. You need to take care of yourself and use whatever means you have to do so – after all, that has been the message of companies and business pundits for years. Take those admonitions seriously. (Pfeffer, 2010: 217–218) (emphases added)

Why does the logic of (a), (b) and (c) – indeed the overall logic of Pfeffer's stance – make sense? It makes sense because he expects us, non-scientists as much as scientists, to recognise that he is engaged in an apolitical, ethically neutral activity which provides understanding about an objective world.

This scientific enterprise is values-free. Splitting the atom is ethically neutral: what we do with that knowledge is something else. So learning techniques to cope with a political world is also ethically neutral. What Pfeffer's readers do with those techniques is a matter for their 'personal values'. This not only makes sense: for most of us it is common sense. We know it in our bones and share this with Pfeffer.

By contrast the paragraph beginning 'So don't worry' makes an argument which is, from the perspective of the book as a whole, an aberration. The scientific stance is abandoned (Pfeffer cannot know 'undoubtedly' that all his readers' co-workers are ruthless as well as selfish). Ethical neutrality is also abandoned in favour of taking the ethical position (familiar to gangsters) called 'getting your revenge in first'. Here Pfeffer is expressing amorality or immorality rather than historical Machiavellianism.[1]

The main point of the foregoing discussion is to illustrate how deeply our thinking is shot through with what we think about science. Not only does science shape *how we research choosing leaders* (explicit science), and *the activity of choosing leaders itself* (we think we are measuring people), it is shaping *what we accept or take as obvious in the process of trying to reason our way out of our present position* (witness what Pfeffer expects which we grant without noticing it). To return to Chapter 3's image: the scientific mindset, noticed and unnoticed, is critical not only to the car stuck in the big ditch (stuck senior selection) and the tractor with the broken axle (stuck senior selection research), but also in how we construct, visualise and discuss the whole scene. Now we return to the task of extending our insights into power and politics with the help of wider scholarship.

Extending our Account of Power

How to think productively about power and politics has exercised some of the most acute minds in every century and many disciplines, including philosophy, political science and sociology. The result is a large and bewildering forest of arguments and ideas. If we had to capture all of this and reflect on it, plainly our task would be impossible. But because power and politics has only been

---

1   Nevertheless in Chapter 5 I put the two thinkers together, because this particular argument of Pfeffer's is an aberration. The book as a whole offers strong indications that Pfeffer favours workplaces becoming more humane and ethical. Nothing in it suggests that, for example, Pfeffer regards Enron or Madoff as cool businesses which simply ran out of imaginative puff.

treated within management literature to a limited (and almost always scientific) extent, even a little help from new sources can greatly increase our illumination and understanding.

We will start our walk in the forest by extending the scientific account of power. Then we will take some other tracks. As we go we will try to notice two things: firstly, the extent to which the basis of our thinking is independent individuals or minds (I will call this atomism) versus more social perspectives; and secondly, the changing way of understanding science (for which I will borrow the label post-modernism). The two themes connect and capture important developments in thought which took place during the twentieth century and the decades immediately adjacent to it.

There is common ground in much of the analysis of power in neighbouring academic disciplines such as sociology, social psychology, economics and game theory. Atomic individuals interact and exert influence on each other. For example, citing an American sociologist Robert Dahl (1957), the Oxford and Florence academic Steven Lukes (1974) starts with the proposition that:

> *A has power over B to the extent that he can get B to do something that*
> *B would not otherwise do. (Lukes, 1974: 11–12)*

Sophistication is added to this basic concept in several ways, for example to embrace interacting groups of individuals or to reflect the fact that the exercise of power may entail costs. Thus the economist's idea of 'opportunity costs' (what has to be foregone in order to carry out the chosen option) is picked up in a refinement discussed by Dahl (1986) in which the opportunity cost to *A* of attempting to influence *B* becomes the cost of *A*'s power, while the opportunity cost to *B* of refusing to comply becomes the strength of *A*'s power. But the overall feel remains slightly mathematical, with individuals rather like balls on a magical snooker table exerting influence over each other: we count how much influence in each direction. They influence each other because they want different things, and what each individual wants is a matter entirely for that individual. In that sense the individuals are independent.

Game theory works with individuals similarly, for example in the well-known Prisoners' Dilemma. Two members of a group are caught and imprisoned separately. They face differing outcomes if both remain silent, if one confesses or if both confess. The problem is usually structured so that, for each prisoner separately, the rational course is to confess, even though if both remained silent, both would walk free. One can then play artificial but interesting games and see how in some circumstances sacrificing power could increase it. Making credible commitments to silence (for example group members pledging to take a lie-detector test every time they are released from arrest or imprisonment, with refusal to test or discovery of confession being punished severely) could give up freedom to increase it.

An aspect of power which is obvious if one thinks in game-theoretic and similar ways is the distinction between loud power and soft power. Deterrent effects mean that some kinds of power are enhanced by being exercised as loudly as possible (for example punishing looters publicly) while other kinds of power work best if their exercise is not noticed (for example intercepting someone's telephone calls). Let us simply note that some kinds of power do depend upon not being noticed.

Of a similar era but coming from a social psychological perspective is the analysis of French and Raven (1959), considered further in Raven (1992). French and Raven take the perspective of a person, P, acted on by another person O.[2] They define the strength of O's power over P as the maximum potential ability of O to produce a change in the whole system of behaviour, attitudes, goals, needs or values of P. Their division of the sources of social power into reward, coercion, legitimacy, expertise, reference and information is well known. For example, if one of the brightest consultants in a firm is appointed chief executive, that can be described as an increase of power combined with some conversion from power based on expertise to power based on legitimated authority.

As we should expect, psychological insight opens up the snooker ball. Our atomic individuals acquire internal structure, with behaviours, needs, values and so on – not unlike atoms if we picture them as electrons orbiting a nucleus. A psychologically complex picture foregrounds the possibility that someone might be changed (be subject to an exercise of power in French and Raven's terms) without realising it – for example by subliminal advertising's contemporary cousin, behavioural nudging. Thaler and Sunstein's 'Nudge' (2008) holds out the promise of all manner of beneficial outcomes, from schoolkids eating healthier lunches to all of us making more adequate pension provision, to the work of 'choice architects' working to alter beneath our conscious awareness the choices we are likely to make.

---

2   While French and Raven stipulate that P must be a person, they allow that O might be a group or for example a social norm. However we will not take that up here.

French and Raven still define power in terms of an action of *O* which produces a change in *P*. Steven Lukes (1974) argues that this, and similar ways of thinking such as Dahl's, is not enough to capture power's subtle range. He argues that we need to move to what he calls a three-dimensional view of power.

Imagine examining the possibility of unfairness in a refereed football match. According to Lukes, taking a one-dimensional focus we would look at the referee's actions, when he blew his whistle and stopped play (or not): we examine actions and decisions. Taking a two-dimensional view, we realise that the referee's non-decisions (not seeing a bad tackle in the fifty-third minute) are also possible sites for bias. Here, even though there is no decision, our attention can be caught by a conflict – the two sides probably did not view the tackle in the same way. In taking a three-dimensional view, Lukes argues that even when there is no conflict – even when the two sides agree – there may still have been unfairness. The playing field may not have been level.

> ... Is it not the supreme exercise of power to get another or others to have the desires you want them to have – that is, to secure their compliance by controlling their thoughts and desires? ... Is it not the supreme and most insidious exercise of power to prevent people, to whatever degree, from having grievances by shaping their perceptions, cognitions and preferences in such a way that they accept their role in the existing order of things. ... To assume that the absence of grievance equals genuine consensus is simply to rule out the possibility of false or manipulated consensus by definitional fiat. (Lukes, 1974: 23–24)

The conclusion which Lukes draws is that the workings of power must be detected not only by paying attention to inaction as well as action, but also questioning apparent agreement. The consent of smokers and gamblers to being advertised and sold what is objectively injurious to them is a case in point. So Lukes advocates that:

> A exercises power over B when A affects B in a manner contrary to B's interests. (Lukes, 1974: 34)

Now we can see both sides of a difficult argument. If we hold that individuals are authoritative about their own interests, we will certainly miss some important exercises of power. Yet if we follow Lukes, we make the agent subject to another power, namely ours (or that of experts) to determine in an over-riding way what is in the agent's interests.

Yet it is still the case that individuals remain at the centre of Lukes' stage, and are atomic in the sense that each has her own (on Lukes' view) objectively identifiable interests. When we introduce one of the twentieth century's most influential thinkers on power, Michel Foucault (1984; 1986) we see several shifts of emphasis. For one thing Foucault does not find it helpful to be captivated by questions about individual agents, who are much more porous to shifting social currents than they can realise. He wants to approach questions of power like this:

> Let us not, therefore, ask why certain people want to dominate, what they seek, what is their overall strategy. Let us ask, instead, how things work at the level of on-going subjugation, at the level of those continuous and uninterrupted processes which subject our bodies, govern our gestures, dictate our behaviours, etc. (Foucault, 1986: 233)

An example of a pattern or process which Foucault thought it fruitful to study, and which (over periods of decades or centuries) could illuminate changes in a wide pattern of subjugation affecting us all, was bio-power, or the increasing emphasis on defining average or desired human behaviour and measuring deviations from it. Foucault explored such patterns on a large canvas, taking up subjects such as sex or mental health; but such a theme can put such things as the growth of psychometrics, psychological typologies and competencies backed by measured benchmarks into a different context.

> Another consequence of this development of bio-power was the growing importance assumed by the action of the norm ... Such a power has to qualify, measure, appraise and hierarchize ... [and] is increasingly incorporated into a continuum of apparatuses (medical, administrative and so on) whose functions are for the most part regulatory. (Foucault, 1984: 266)

For Foucault, patterns of power were intimately connected with ways of defining truth, and both cannot be explored properly without noticing what is not said (and cannot be said) as well as utterances – a point which could not be more relevant to our discussion of the silence on power and politics in Chapter 5:

We are subjected to the production of truth through power and we cannot exercise power except through the production of truth. (Foucault, 1986: 229–230)

I would like to put forward a few 'propositions' – not firm assertions, but simply suggestions to be further tested and evaluated.

'Truth' is to be understood as a system of ordered procedures for the production, regulation, distribution, circulation, and operation of statements.

'Truth' is linked in a circular relation with systems of power which produce and sustain it, and to effects of power which it induces and which extends it. A 'regime' of truth. (Foucault, 1984: 74)

Silence itself – the things one declines to say, or is forbidden to name, the discretion that is required between different speakers – is less the absolute limit of discourse, the other side from which it is separated by a strict boundary, than an element which functions alongside the things said, with them and in relation to them within overall strategies. There is no binary division to be made between what one says and what one does not say; we must try to determine the different ways of not saying such things, how those who can and those who cannot speak of them are distributed, which type of discourse is authorized, or which form of discretion is required in either case. There is not one but many silences, and they are an integral part of the strategies that underlie and permeate discourses. (Foucault, 1984: 309–310)

A detailed analysis of organisational life which brings abstractions such as these compellingly to life is Bent Flyvbjerg's study (1998) of town planning in the town of Aalborg, the administrative and commercial centre for a Danish region of half a million people, over a period of nearly 20 years. We are taken into an account of cars, buses, businesses and politicians. On one level:

A typical medium-sized European city, Aalborg has a high-density historical centre several centuries old. When the case opens, the center has for decades had to adapt to an ever-increasing number of cars, which have transformed, and even destroyed, substantial parts of the city's historical center. Now city officials decide that the car will have to adapt to the city. They initiate what will become known as the 'Aalborg

> Project', an award-wining scheme that later will be recommended by the
> Organization for Economic Co-operation and Development (OECD) as a
> model for international adoption, on how to integrate environmental and
> social concerns into city politics and planning ... (Flyvbjerg, 1998: 3–4)

But on another level we explore the inseparability of power and politics from
the creation of supposedly objective knowledge and facts.

> 'In some remote corner of the universe,' begins Nietzsche in one of his
> early essays, 'there once was a star on which clever animals invented
> knowledge. That was the most arrogant and untruthful moment in
> 'world history'.' In this book I will take the reader to a remote corner
> of the universe ... [to] the Kingdom of Denmark, that is, nowhere
> and everywhere. Here, too, knowledge was invented. How, why, and
> the consequences of this knowledge constitute the tale of this book.
> (Flyvbjerg, 1998: 1)

In the last few pages we have been extending our account of power. We have
been walking for a short while into the forest of twentieth-century scholarship
on the subject outside the boundaries of management, stopping to look at a
few trees here and there. Yet we can already make with some force two points
which bear heavily on our subject of choosing leaders.

Firstly, the forest is vast and complex, representing decades of work by
thinkers in different disciplines and in different countries. With it in our minds
we can already see in a new and striking light how limited the discussion
of power and politics is in management literature (and even more so in
personnel selection literature) – limited in quantity and quality alike, because
of a predominant stance among managers and management researchers to
treat power and politics as marginal or dysfunctional, and because of the
predominance of scientific thinking in personnel selection research as the only
model of valuable thought.

Secondly, wherever we have turned within the forest, whether to
psychologists such as French and Raven, political scientists such as Lukes
or sociologically-oriented philosophers such as Foucault, at every turn the
connections between power and what must be kept quiet, what cannot be
spoken have multiplied. Returning to personnel selection, drawing from its
scientific roots the *sine qua non* of good contemporary selection practice is to
begin by getting everything 'out onto the table' – the organisation's goals,

its strengths and weaknesses, the threats and opportunities offered by the environment, and any other issues affecting the appointment – as the basis for attempting to produce an agreed and (so far as possible) objective person specification. Yet if power and politics are intrinsic to senior roles (both the doing of them and the filling of them), what we have noticed about power and silence this critical first step may be undo-able, or only do-able in unrealistic ways.

At the least we are given serious pause. Perhaps the vast forest in which we have started to walk is a garden of grotesque weeds tended by idle academics. But if it is not; if instead it is a clue to the tangled, subtle, tenacity of power and politics – ubiquitous and evasive at the same time – then we should *not* expect the stuckness described in Part I to succumb to some targeted research funding and a few more years' continued efforts by HR leaders.

However, we are not yet finished with the forest.

Extending our Account of Science

The twentieth century saw an explosion of scientific knowledge and its practical application like the sun, at once familiar to us yet virtually unimaginable. Relativity, quantum mechanics, nuclear power, lasers, DNA, stem cells; from the Wright brothers to a man on the moon; from Marconi's first radio signal to the mobile internet with satellite navigation as commonplace. Less well understood is that our understanding of what we are doing when we do science also changed fundamentally.

Something happened which was more than, as a matter of historical fact or intellectual fashion, a significant number of thinkers starting to talk about science in different terms – for example as a regime of truth, to use Foucault's expression. That something is an objective change in human thought, which we can summarise (and make more precise below) as the end of the possibility of a universal foundation for human thought, outside of the particularities of time and society.

> *37. Owing to three Errors. – Science has been furthered during recent centuries, partly because it was hoped that God's goodness and wisdom would be best understood therewith and thereby – the principal motive in the soul of great Englishmen (like Newton); partly because*

the absolute utility of knowledge was believed in, and especially the
most intimate connection of morality, knowledge, and happiness – the
principal motive in the soul of great Frenchmen (like Voltaire); and
partly because it was thought that in science there was something
unselfish, harmless, self-sufficing, lovable and truly innocent to be
had, in which the evil human impulses did not at all participate – the
principal motive in the soul of Spinoza, who felt himself divine, as a
knowing being; – it is consequently owing to three errors that science
has been furthered. (Nietzsche, 2006: 41–21)

Any selection of dates will be arbitrary, but earlier this chapter talked of 'the twentieth century and the decades immediately adjacent to it'. We can take as our starting point 1889, when the German philosopher Friedrich Nietzsche went insane, and prior to which, as the Cambridge scholar Michael Tanner (2000) suggests, his work was almost completely neglected. Since then Nietzsche's work has been seen as prescient in widely differing ways and his fame has increased. Nietzsche (2006) articulates the claim for which he is most famous outside philosophical circles, that 'God is dead' (Nietzsche, 2006: 81, 90–91, 155). But as the foregoing quotation from the same work *The Gay Science* demonstrates, God was by no means the only point of Nietzsche's attack.

I want to borrow from Nietzsche the idea of the death of God (in one precise sense) and in order to identify (in the same sense) the death of science. One crucial thing which an eternal monotheistic God provided within a society and an era in which most educated people were believers was an intellectual binding and foundation: a shared understanding of reality and procedures for judging things to be true, with important truths being valid for all people in all places at all times. Thus, taking up Nietzsche's comment on Newton above, belief in such a God not only provides Newton with a motivation for his work, and his peers with foundations for agreeing or disagreeing with it, it also makes it possible *to find intelligible the possibility of a 'law of gravity' valid for all people in all places at all times.* And in such a society it is possible for believers to claim, on the strength of intellectually competent arguments, that given time all right-thinking people should agree with them. The claim will probably not be successful – there will be intellectually competent disbelievers – but in itself the universal claim is not impossible or meaningless.

The meaning of 'God is dead' on which I wish to focus is not that belief is now impossible or meaningless. An intellectually competent defence of faith is possible, even if the arguments are no longer compelling for others. What has changed is that today it would be intellectually incompetent for me to claim that all right-thinking people should agree with me. The more I insist on such a claim, the more I cut myself off from recognition as someone who understands logic and argument.

In precisely that sense of the phrase, we should also understand Nietzsche as heralding the arrival of a century in which science (understood as the activity of grasping an objective reality with the aid of reasoning which is independent of time, place and society) also died. For science understood in that way provided for society, for a period, what an eternal monotheistic God had provided, namely an intellectual binding and foundation: a shared understanding of reality and procedures for judging things to be true, with important truths (scientific laws) being valid for all people in all places at all times. In such a society it is possible for scientists to claim, on the strength of intellectually competent arguments, that given time all right-thinking people should agree with them.

Today such a universal claim is intellectually incompetent. Belief in such a world is still possible. An intellectually competent defence can be made of the view that there is an objective reality which is appropriately grasped with the aid of reasoning which is independent of time, place and society; and that is the position of many (but not all) scientists. This view remains cogent and coherent. What is incoherent now which was not formerly so, is the idea that all right-thinking people should accept the same view.

In other words something of quite special importance comes to fruition during the twentieth century. The view that all human thought (including the most apparently timeless, abstract principles of logic or mathematics) is inextricably bound to places and times, histories and societies, and so also to power and politics, gains serious purchase. It does not conquer all, but it does not have to in order to defeat universals (whether called God or science) which would negate it.

The substance of so large a change does indeed require a forest of thinkers (on both, or all, sides of the argument), spanning for example the change in thinking between the early (1920s) and late (1950s) work of Wittgenstein – for one account see Pears (1971) – or Kuhn (1970) who introduced us to the idea of a paradigm shift. In Chapter 8 we shall study one of the trees in the forest, taking up some ideas of the French sociologist Pierre Bourdieu (2004). But now we should spell out the implications of this movement in twentieth-century thought for the business of choosing leaders.

Stuckness Reconsidered (II)

We can make this summary. Dealing with the distinctive features of senior roles proposed in Chapter 4, we reached a provisional conclusion which was not too gloomy. There were good reasons for changes in the way we select for senior roles to lag behind progress at front-line and middle management levels. It would be good for selection research to re-focus on this challenge but even without the fruits of this work, evidence-based tools are already available which recognise the challenges of complexity, humility and responsibility. This view suggests that we simply need to take up these tools and make more use of them. I went on to say:

> From this perspective science will continue to be the engine of progress and to speak of crisis is unjustified. Whether a happy future for society with better selected leaders in senior roles is achieved in reality will depend on scientists doing good science, selectors doing good selection and good candidates coming forward. But whether that happy future would be possible depends only on one thing: whether science can crack the problem in Chapter 5 – 'Power and Politics'.

Before moving on, we noted how deeply scientific thinking and suppositions about science are embedded in our thinking – influencing not only selection research, and senior selection practice, but how we think about the very situation of stuckness. For example we saw that Pfeffer's managerial analysis of power and politics makes sense only because we (and he) can take as common sense that science is apolitical and values-free.

Starting our journey into the forest, we were given pause by the fact that the analyses which we encountered multiplied the connections between power and silence, stealth, deception and self-deception. This was not encouraging since the premise of good selection practice is to get the situation of the organisation, of the job to be filled and all other relevant factors out into the open.

We then went further into the forest, taking a 'helicopter tour' of how the twentieth century has been significant for changes in the way wider scholarship understands science itself. These changes – associated with post-modernism – are very problematic for our subject because they can be described as the death of science as a uniquely authoritative, universally compelling perspective.

So to be specific, what this chapter has argued does *not* provide a basis for concluding that Pfeffer's stance (as I have interpreted it) is wrong; it *does* provide grounds for not accepting his unquestioning use of an apolitical scientific stance. Pfeffer expects his readers to take the apolitical scientific stance as obvious, and with it his own power as an expert, because otherwise (not least in a book about power and politics) he would raise the question himself. In writing as he does, and in reading him as he expects, he and we are both do what is par for the course in our society; but this should no longer be good enough.

At approximately the mid-point of the book, we find ourselves in the position of dwellers in an apartment (personnel selection) which a crack in the wall, noticeable if you look but not too alarming – we do not deal adequately with power and politics. On looking around the block in which we live (management studies), we see the crack is not in our apartment alone. But now we find our block is poised directly above one of the most significant fault lines in twentieth century thought (post-modernism). We are part of a deeper crisis.

Whether we can move beyond it is not obvious. Any movement has to involve re-thinking what we are doing in personnel selection in a fundamental way. Without throwing out the progress made in Part I, we have to shed its skin and grow a new one. We need both new freedoms and new discipline: new freedoms to re-imagine concepts like skill, and new disciplines to test what our re-thinking produces. That is our task in Part III.

Postscript

To pave the way for those steps, recall this invitation from earlier in this chapter:

> As we go we will try to notice two things: firstly, the extent to which the basis of our thinking is independent individuals or minds (I will call this atomism) versus more social perspectives; and secondly, the changing way of understanding science (for which I will borrow the label post-modernism).

We have discussed the latter changes at some length. Also apparent are some signs of the first shift (noticeable for example in Foucault). We will now go further in these directions.

PART III

Re-thinking Fundamentals

7

Skill and Intuition

Our Next Steps

One way to describe our next steps would be to say that, although looking outside the usual boundaries of personnel selection made our problem of stuckness worse, that 'outside' is a sprawling world of knowledge which we have hardly scratched. Continuing to look outside might bring us some movement. This is what we do in this chapter with intuition. In personnel selection, intuition is demonised since it leads, as Chapter 1 pointed out, to many awful results. We will look at whether the wider management literature on intuition says something different. Then, having introduced our three central themes (science, politics and intuition), we will set about the 're-thinking' which this Part promises. Hopefully our understanding of these themes or of how they relate to each other will change.

All this sounds relatively matter-of-fact and under control, and it does describe the path we will take. But let me put things in more personal terms. This book contains three personal 'Ahas!' – moments of insight which I wished I had gained earlier in my career as a headhunter. We have had the first, about the slippery pervasiveness of power and politics. This chapter presents the second: the Dreyfus conception of expertise, or a way of thinking about skill which embraces intuition and gives an entirely different interpretation of 'competence' to Boyatzis (Chapter 2). The third 'Aha!' will be the re-thinking of science in Chapter 8.

Yet even this, more personal, description is not good enough. We can gauge the scale of our task by comparing what we are looking for with science. Reverting to the car stuck in the ditch (senior selection practice) and the tractor unable to help (selection research), science is the principle of internal combustion which has powered both vehicles. To get out of our stuckness, we probably need a body of thought – a way of understanding ourselves and the world – as significant as science itself. How likely are we to find that? Historically humanity has waited centuries for shifts of thought on that scale. And if we do find something so fundamental, we can anticipate on the way some disorientation and unsettling which may be disagreeable. The disturbing of previously solid foundations may make us sea-sick. If so, that will be because we are not simply putting some new thoughts through our existing mental apparatus but trying to think in a different way about how we choose leaders.

But that is a matter for Chapter 8; let us return to intuition.

Intuition in Management

Outside of personnel selection, intuition is increasingly noted and studied as a feature of contemporary studies of organisational life. Eugene Sadler-Smith (2008) noted a study of senior managers in US businesses in which 59 per cent said that they used intuition often or very often in making decisions, and 89 per cent said they did so at least sometimes. Quoting a global study of more than 1,000 managers (Parikh, Neubauer and Lank, 1994), Sadler-Smith observed that:

> ... The three most popular accounts [of intuition] were: a perception of decision without recourse to logical or rational methods; an inexplicable comprehension that arrives as a feeling 'from within'; and an integration of accumulated knowledge and previous expertise. (Sadler-Smith, 2008: 499)

Sadler-Smith formulated intuition in this way:

> Intuitions are rapid, affectively charged judgements arrived at without conscious awareness of the reasoning processes involved ... Intuitive judgments based on nonconscious pattern recognition ... and somatic (bodily) state activation/awareness (commonly known as 'gut feeling' ...) are acknowledged as significant in human decision-making processes. (Sadler-Smith, 2008: 494)

When we speak like this, in effect we are using the word 'intuition' to point out that we think with our bodies and that the moving focus of our thinking is often ahead of what we are consciously aware. If and when those thoughts, or the impulse to act to which they point, arrives in consciousness, we experience this as an intuition.

That we think with our bodies and that our focus of thinking is often ahead of consciousness is what Malcolm Gladwell wrote about in *Blink* (2005). He cites an ingenious experiment conducted by Bechara, Damasio, Tranel and Damasio (1997) which demonstrates the point succinctly. People were invited to turn over cards from four decks, two red and two blue. The cards had different financial gains or penalties attached. Unknown to the players, taking from the red packs was disadvantageous. In the experiment, after turning over about 50 cards most players had a hunch that they should concentrate on the blue decks, and after about 80 cards most players could articulate what they were doing and why. But the experimenters, who had also been measuring the activity of the sweat glands in the palms of the players' hands, found the players' bodies had started reacting to the red cards as early as after ten cards, at which point their card-choosing behaviour had also begun to change.

Within the management literature on intuition a significant distinction is then drawn between first impression heuristics of the kind just described – the players did not have any prior 'expertise' in knowing what might lie inside the four red and blue decks – and the intuitions of those who have spent years developing a specialist expertise. We can follow this argument in the wide-ranging study of intuition in managerial decision-making by Erik Dane and Michael Pratt (2007). After reviewing 17 definitions of intuition from the psychologist Jung onwards, they adopt this formulation:

> ... We conceptualize intuition both by its process (which we refer to as intuiting), as well as its outcome (which we term intuitive judgments) ... Our review of the various literature on intuition has tended to converge on four characteristics that make up the core of the construct: intuition is a (1) non-conscious process (2) involving holistic associations (3) that are produced rapidly, which (4) result in affectively charged judgments. (Dane and Pratt, 2007: 36)

They note that there is a substantial body of research which suggests that intuitive judgements are inferior to rational decision-making. But they go on to this view:

> While the heuristic-based view of intuition has dominated research on intuition and problem solving, a growing body of research suggests that

> *'experts' can make highly accurate intuitive decisions ... We argue that*
> *the main differences between these bodies of research lies in the nature*
> *of the schemas of experts, which are (1) highly complex and (2) domain*
> *relevant ... [For example a 1973] study revealed that chess masters are*
> *able to recognize at least 50,000 different configurations of chess pieces*
> *on sight ... . (Dane and Pratt, 2007: 42)*

Now research has *not* provide unqualified backing for expert judgements, indeed a significant body of research argues that in a wide range of situations mechanical, algorithmic decision rules would be better: in other words that you would be better off consulting a computer instead of a human doctor, even one specialised in your condition. In Chapter 1 we had already referred to some of these debates within psychology (Spengler, Strohmer, Dixon and Shivy, 1995), and this argument about the quality of 'clinical' judgement processes, pitting one or more experienced individuals weighing up complex information about a unique case against the algorithmic precision and enormous memory capacity of modern computers, will be central in this chapter.

For the time being we can rest on the point that there is also a body of research which points to objective success being achieved by some deep experts, and that the 'thinking' which they do is, as Dane and Pratt, describe highly complex and specific to their field of knowledge. It is also thinking done with the body which may not be readily accessible to the conscious mind. Gladwell gives the example of Braden, a world-class tennis coach, who knew intuitively just before players on their second serve hit the ball whether they would double-fault. This unnerved him because in professional tennis double-faults are not common, yet Braden's intuition worked even when he saw someone play for the first time. In one tournament there were 17 double-faults in the matches which Braden attended, of which he predicted 16. What did that feel like?

> *'For a while it got so bad that I got scared,' Braden says. 'It literally*
> *scared me. I was getting twenty out of twenty right, and we're talking*
> *about guys who almost never double-fault.' ...*
>
> *'What did I see?' he says. 'I would lie in bed, thinking, How did I do*
> *this? I don't know. It drove me crazy. It tortured me. I'd go back and*
> *I'd go over the serve in my mind and I'd try to figure it out. Did they*
> *stumble? Did they take another step? Did they add a bounce to the*
> *ball – something that changed their motor program?' The evidence he*

used to draw his conclusions seemed to be buried somewhere in his
unconscious, and he could not dredge it up. (Gladwell, 2005: 49–50)

Intuition in Personnel Selection

My own experience as a search professional connected strongly with this research on intuition. I realised that intuition had become almost a taboo word in personnel selection 'good practice', because (as Chapter 1 showed) it produced so many truly awful results. There was also a rush of ego to the head from reading about the chasm of difference between expert intuition (which in my imagination was what I did) and first impression heuristics (which in my imagination all too many of my clients did). But, setting self-flattering fantasies aside, two questions loom large if we bring this thinking about intuition in a wider management context into personnel selection.

Firstly, because the research picture on expert judgement versus rules-based decision-making is so mixed, we must look more closely at the difference. We will not be able to reach a conclusive view but the work of Hubert Dreyfus and Stuart Dreyfus yields important insights.

Secondly, if doing something a lot makes a good proportion of people expert, why is the general standard of intuition which we develop in selecting people in the ordinary course of life and management as low as Chapter 1 suggests it is? After all, in the ordinary course of life (let alone management) we constantly make choices about people – witness the playground which also appeared in Chapter 1 – and often the consequences of those choices matter to us. We pick friends and who to spend time with in our personal lives, we elect politicians, and as managers we pick staff and put together teams, and all of those choices affect our happiness, our wealth and even our biological reproduction. Why can't we read people as accurately as bats read the night with echolocation? Why would evolution take such a foolish turning?

We can point to some important elements. Evolution has done well in enabling us to observe each other's physical characteristics, such as location and speed as well as shape and appearance, to make fast guesses about likely strength, and to react to potential physical attack – the equivalents of the problem to which echolocation is a remarkable resource for bats. However, what makes for good friends, good politicians and good team members is physically invisible to us. These things belong in the symbolic world of human meaning-making, in which however insightful and skilled we as a species become at interpreting our own behaviour, the same insights and skills are available to us to confuse, to pretend and to deceive, ourselves as well as others. We do not live in Pinocchio's world where morally and politically significant qualities have stable, objective, physical correlates.

So the evolution question becomes slightly less puzzling: evolved skill does not simply peter out but enters a new space in which it is constantly pitted against itself. In some dimensions of this new space, notably knowledge of the physical and biological worlds, the result of this competition against self (scientific theory competing with scientific theory) is a dramatic acceleration of development. Where – as in personnel selection – we ourselves are intrinsic to what we study, the results are more mixed and in some situations arguably there is no 'progress' at all. In these necessarily social sciences, personnel selection sits perhaps in the middle, alongside sociology, sandwiched between economics (greater signs of progress) and ethics and philosophy (fewer).

Reflecting on my direct experience of personnel selection suggests a second element. We all have many years' experience of choosing people, in ordinary life and in management, but the learning effects are weakened by several factors. Few of us give the choosing we do intense and consistent focus. Similarly, most of us have many years' experience of cooking meals, but that does not make us all chefs. Then, in organisations, choosing people is normally hierarchically organised: the more powerful choose the less powerful. A good proportion of the time when a hiring mistake is made, the hirer may not experience or notice the mistake, because the price of the error is either unseen (no-one in the organisation including the hirer is competent enough to know that their expensively hired strategy or technology director has come up with plans which are nuts) or picked up by others (subordinates of the person hired suffer in silence, compensate where they can or leave rather than go over the newcomer's head to tell her boss that she made a mistake). Next, some misjudgements about people can become self-fulfilling prophecies (my intuition that someone does not like me can quite quickly lead to body language to which they in turn react). Reinforcing all this, work by Einhorn and Hogarth (1978) modelling the effects of feedback upon decision makers' confidence showed how in a broad range of managerial situations like selection, where the nature of decision-making means that the true abilities of those judged less suitable (that is, not selected) will go unseen:

> *... good outcomes are quite likely even when judgmental ability is low.*
> *Furthermore, the learning model helps to explain how the concept, 'my*
> *judgement is accurate,' is both learned and maintained even though*
> *judgment may be invalid. (Einhorn and Hogarth, 1978: 414)*

Lastly this question is central for Gladwell (2005). He points to research which
shows us acting as if we were in Pinocchio's world, with fast and strong
associations giving all of us misleading 'intuitions' about a person's qualities
thanks to physical characteristics such as race, gender, way of speaking or, of
course, height. Chapter 1 introduced the Broadway Manufacturing Company:
it turns out that we all work there. Having polled half of the *Fortune* 500 list,
Gladwell (2005: 86–87) found that almost one-third of CEOs were six feet two
(1.88 m) or taller, compared with 3.9 per cent in the adult male population.

Intuition and Skill: The Dreyfus Model of Expertise

The book *Mind Over Machine* by Hubert and Stuart Dreyfus (1986), is the fruit
of an unusual pair of minds – brothers, a philosopher (Hubert) and a computer
scientist (Stuart). Stuart also captained his college chess team. Prompted in part
by increasing claims that machine intelligence either already had, or would
soon, outstrip what humans could do, they decided to strip their understanding
of skill acquisition *by adults* back to fundamentals. They studied how adults
learned to fly airplanes, play chess, drive cars and master a second language.
They emerged with a surprising five-stage process assessed by McPherson
(2005) as follows:

> *This account has been widely used, adapted, discussed and evaluated.*
> *It has had some influence on occupational or professional formation*
> *and training for nurses, schoolteachers, social workers, community*
> *education workers, social science researchers and others. (McPherson,*
> *2005: 708–709)*

The Dreyfus model is surprising if we contrast it with our experience of
learning or teaching children, who generally progress from the concrete to the
abstract. Learning the significance and use of a rule, for example the rules of
division in arithmetic, can be a slow process with many difficulties. By contrast
the Dreyfus brothers propose that the higher levels of skill move beyond what
can be captured in rules and in some ways are quite child-like.

They observe the following pattern of adult learning in all the activities which they studied, and which they laid out in five stages called novice, advanced beginner, competent, proficient and expert. They use learning to drive a car to illustrate the stages.

The *novice* is taught to focus on a few features of the situation and, based on these, to follow firm rules. Both the features and the rules are specified in advance, and for simplicity all context and nuance are stripped out. For example the novice driver may be told to notice her speed, and to change gears at predefined speeds regardless of context. The novice has little or no experience and what is taught corresponds to this.

The *advanced beginner* begins to recognise some contextual elements and to allow her use of rules to be influenced by this. For example, through experience and beginning to recognise similar situations the advanced beginner will start to change gear based on engine sounds as well as speed. The engine sounds are not just another data item categorised in advance like speed, but involve some complexity and judgement in perception, which grows with experience. The advanced beginner is not learning a more convoluted (but still pre-specified) rule based only on the engine's decibel level: or at least, if she is, she is still in Dreyfus' terms a novice.

The *competent* student has progressed to the point where she has her own goal in mind as she acts – for example she wishes to drive from here to there as quickly as possible. In the light of her goal she may make certain conscious choices, for example as to route, how closely to follow other cars or how much risk to run in overtaking. Or her action could be characterised as problem-solving: wrestling rationally with a small set of elements in the situation. But when those rational choices or judgements have been made, the competent performer will still be guided by rules. (An important point for Hubert and Stuart Dreyfus is that this defines the limit of skill which rule-based computer simulation can reach.)

At this point the term intuition is introduced:

> When we speak of intuition … we are referring to the understanding that effortlessly occurs upon seeing similarities with previous experiences … Intuition … as we understand it, is neither wild guessing nor supernatural inspiration, but the sort of ability we all use all the time as we go about our everyday tasks … (Dreyfus and Dreyfus, 1986: 28–29)

In the fourth stage of skill, the *proficient* performer recognises situations intuitively and holistically, rather than on the basis of rational consideration of a limited number of elements. However she then decides consciously how to respond. Thus a proficient driver, approaching a curve on a rainy day, may intuitively realise that she is going too fast. She then consciously decides whether to apply the brakes, remove her foot from the accelerator and how to steer.

In the final stage, *expertise,* the whole action from perception and interpretation of the situation through to action becomes seamless, fluid and intuitive. A stage of rational decision-making cannot be distinguished, which is not to say that the end product lacks rational quality – one could not become a chess master if one's actions reflected poor quality reasoning. The expert driver simply becomes one with her car, and she experiences herself simply as driving.

The foregoing is an abbreviated account of the Dreyfus categorisation, in which what matters for us is less the precise definition of each stage as the direction and pattern of travel between them. Some supplementary information is provided in Chapter 14 (see Table 14.1).

I quote an example in detail from a different source because it will repay further visits both in this chapter and the next. The Danish scholar Bent Flyvbjerg (2001) cites this description of group virtuosity from a Danish book *Football Angels* by Hans-Jørgen Nielsen:

> We get a free kick, just within the other team's penalty zone, just to the right of the goal, and I take it, self-assuredly waving the others off, with the seductive movement which means that I and no one else knows what needs to be done. The opponents stand up in a wall in front of me in order to block a shot aimed at the goal, as I perhaps also had first thought, but suddenly, Franke stands next to them, far to the right, like an extension of their wall. This has happened during my approach, while everything is focused on me, and I keep running toward the ball as if to kick directly. When I get to it, I instead kick it in a very flat arc, over the defensive wall, and the ball would have taken the turf a few meters behind it. In the same moment, Franke has made his way around and has rushed toward the place where it would have landed. It never does, he catches it in the air with his right leg, half-gliding it into the

goal with his left. No one else is able to grasp what has happened before he lifts his arms.

Soccer players tend to have this kind of thing with them from home, working on it over and over again during training. Franke and I have perhaps done something similar before, but never practiced it as something specific in this way, we don't exchange a word before I take the free-kick, not even a telling glance, everything happens during the run-up, completely natural, he just stands there where he stands, I just play him like he has to be played when he has positioned himself where he has suddenly positioned himself, the thought doesn't even become anything we are so aware of that it can become clear for us in advance. It is a shared knowledge, from the perspective of the body and the eyes, ready to become reality, and it is prior to our being able to speak about it as a language and an ego … (Flyvbjerg, 2001: 18)

Captured here with limpid clarity is expert action as a process which is physical as much as cerebral, intimately connected with intuition and hard to articulate. Not only *may* the expert not grasp consciously and be able to explain the action–conclusion which she reaches, but if the Dreyfus model is right, she *cannot*. Special efforts will be necessary to articulate what she does in rational, linear sentences and even these are likely to come up short. The skilled actor's intuition is a 'knowing what to do' accompanied by a feeling of assurance or confidence appropriate to action, which is different from the predictive or probabilistic confidence appropriate to science. In the passage just quoted, Nielsen kicks the ball with confidence of a kind distinct from knowing with high probability what will happen next or whether a goal will result.

Appraising the Dreyfus Framework

The simplicity of the Dreyfus framework of expertise is deceptive. McPherson (2005) notes the connection with the familiar suggestion that the learner moves from unconscious incompetence, to conscious incompetence, to conscious competence and finally to unconscious competence. Is the Dreyfus framework the same thing with added jargon?

A cursory answer might be yes. The two perspectives share an intuitive end-state reached through conscious, rule-based strivings which have to be transcended. But – and this is a clue to the punch which the Dreyfus framework packs – we might do better to argue that the two perspectives are opposites.

Obviously we do not always start in unconscious competence. The first reaction of most of us on looking at an aircraft is not to assume unconsciously that we can fly it (although many selectors and candidates do assume they can wing selection interviews). But the four-stage cycle beginning with unconscious incompetence makes sense if we think of a person possessing some level of a skill but ignorant of higher levels. For example I may walk or jog oblivious of the fact that with training I could strain my skeleton and musculature less and increase my stamina. So the four-stage cycle is a suggested pattern claiming to show how a learner moves up from one level of intuitive competence to another, and the pattern is through conscious reformation.

The Dreyfus model contradicts this, proposing instead that the path to the higher levels is not conscious reformation but more intuitive immersion. One could summarise this by saying that young children and adults with advanced skills can only learn by intuitive immersion, while older children or adults (having learned an intuitive grasp of rules) can learn intermediate levels of skill by immersion or by rules. We can assess the interplay of these things directly in our own experience of learning first and subsequent languages.

Another thing missed in the four-stage formulation which, by contrast, Dreyfus and Dreyfus emphasise is the shift of the learner from a stance of detachment to one of increasing involvement. This emerges as competence is reached and intensifies thereafter. At the stage of competence:

> *[The] combination of nonobjectivity and necessity introduces an important new type of relationship between the performer and his environment. Recall that the novice and advanced beginner recognize learned components and then apply learned rules and procedures. As a consequence, they feel little responsibility for the outcome of their acts. Assuming that they have made no mistakes, an unfortunate outcome is viewed as the result of inadequately specified elements or rules. The competent performer, on the other hand, after wrestling with the question of a choice of a plan, feels responsible for, and thus emotionally involved in, the product of his choice. While he both understands and decides in a detached manner, he finds himself intensely involved in what occurs thereafter. An outcome that is clearly successful is deeply satisfying and leaves a vivid memory of the plan chosen and of the*

situation as seen from the perspective of the plan. Disasters, likewise,
are not easily forgotten. (Dreyfus and Dreyfus, 1986: 26)

In this way, just as we begin to see skill acquisition more closely bound to context, we also edge towards finding it more closely bound to questions of human identity and emotion. According to Dreyfus, people put themselves at risk in trying to gain higher levels of skill. Shame, respect and self-esteem creep into the picture. We become more circumspect about any idea of a person 'having' skills like a player in a card game 'has' cards, not only transferable but detachable.

A further question which arises is reflexivity or self-awareness. Dreyfus and Dreyfus picture the expert usually, but not always, acting without reflection:

While most expert performance is ongoing and nonreflective, when
time permits and outcomes are crucial, an expert will deliberate before
acting. But … this deliberation does not require calculative problem
solving, but rather involves critically reflecting on one's intuitions.
(Dreyfus and Dreyfus, 1986: 31–32)

They illuminate what critical reflection involves by asking what a highly-skilled chess player (or manager or surgeon) spends time thinking about when many of their moves will come intuitively to mind? Firstly, few situations *exactly* replicate past ones, so the player will ponder the likely vulnerability of her intuitive move to the small differences. Secondly, she may probe whether her intuitive interpretation of the situation may be suffering from tunnel vision and risking catastrophic error. Mentally disturbing parts of the situation which seem unimportant may allow a completely different interpretation to come to mind. Thirdly, she will need to use calculation where her past experiences are not close to the current situation and her intuitions are hesitant (Dreyfus and Dreyfus 1986: 36–39).

Implicit in the Dreyfus model is that experts can outperform mechanical decision rules in a range of problems which will not yield to high speed, brute force computation This area is quite large. Even in a simple game of finite possibilities such as draughts or checkers, they quote an estimate that a computer which attempted to play by analysing all the possible moves and counter-moves to the end of the game and optimising among them would, even operating at the speed of light, would take ten[21] centuries to make the first move (Dreyfus and Dreyfus, 1986: 107). Therefore they also consider expert systems such as 'PUFF', which diagnoses lung disorders using 30 heuristic rules given to it by a leading specialist at the Pacific Medical Center in San Francisco. Despite the complexity of a 30-rule model, PUFF only agrees with the specialist 75 per cent of the time. Is it, however, the expert who is wrong in the remaining 25 per cent? This question was addressed in a scientific evaluation of a diagnostic programme for internal medicine, where the model's diagnoses on 19 individuals with multiple conditions were compared with those of clinicians at Massachusetts General Hospital and expert case discussants. Because of the multiplicity of conditions, the correct answer (as verified by *post mortem* pathology) was that between them the 19 individuals had 43 conditions. Of these the diagnostic program missed 18, the clinicians missed 15 and the discussants missed eight (Dreyfus and Dreyfus, 1986: 116).

These arguments provide no simple refutation of that body of research (referred to, for example, in Chapter 1) which finds situations in which clinical judgement is less reliable than decisions by formula. However the Dreyfus model does fruitfully open up the debate, inviting us to focus on whether the clinical judgement being used is competent rather than expert, and also alerting us to the possibility of misplaced transpositions of expertise. For example they point to a 1971 study which compared the results actually achieved by graduate students in a university psychology department with predictions made by the admissions committee of four professors and mathematical models which only used three data items: the candidates' scores in an examination for graduate admission, their undergraduate grade point averages and subjective assessments of the quality of the undergraduate schools which they had attended. The predictions of the models using such limited data correlated better with what happened than the professors' wisdom. However Dreyfus and Dreyfus point out that professors in such situations, while expert in their disciplines, do not have the intensity and repetition of experience to become expert in making admissions decisions. They make those decisions only once or twice a year, usually with little follow-up as to what actually happens.

Intuition and Interviewing

I now spend a significant part of my time offering careers advice to individuals who have achieved success in one or more fields but want to explore seriously a lateral or creative change (maslowsattic.com). If I was to work with you in this process which runs over several weeks, at its heart would be a three-hour session, longer and more intensive than any of the meetings which precede or follow it. It is also by some margin longer and more intensive than any of the interviews or one-to-one discussions which I had conducted in any of my previous work, including as a search professional. Yet when I was creating my careers advice business, I can remember today the idea of a three-hour session arriving as a sudden intuition, as if out of nowhere. Of course it could not have come out of nowhere. Pursuing this question as part of my doctoral work led me to focus on intuition and to encounter the Dreyfus framework.

For me it illuminated a great deal about my work. Intuition was not always wisdom's friend, because not all intuition is expert intuition, nor is expert intuition always right. But neither was intuition always wisdom's enemy, as I had been taught in my early training and as discussed in some detail in Chapters 1 and 2. Here are some of the things about selection which appeared differently, and clearer, to me in the light of the Dreyfus framework of expertise.

Thinking first of the expertise which selectors are looking for in candidates, the limitations of many conventional interviewing approaches became stark. I had already taken on board the foolishness of most hypothetical questions: it is hard for the candidate to avoid interpreting them as a selection game in which the task is to guess what the questioner thinks is the right answer, but even if candidates respond predictively, usually they have little clue as to what they would do in practice. But now the limitations of asking candidates what they did to achieve certain results – which seemed safer, although not safe, ground – were glaring. In general experts know little about what they are doing or why it works. Questioning of this kind would favour a combination of competent candidates with a few highly reflective experts, while at the same time generating quite a lot of misinformation about what produced success in the relevant activity – for example an activity as relentlessly pursued in interview Q&As as 'change management'.

And yet a fascinating experience in executive search was how, in certain circumstances, with no prior knowledge of a field, we could make progress and create genuine value in identifying expert candidates in that field. We might think of this as tone-deaf recruiters finding pitch-perfect performers whom leaders in that field did not already know about. How could we do that? In part there was a process of triangulation by external factors. Asked, for example, to construct a shortlist of the best first violinists in the world we would start by talking to violinists in the most famous orchestras. Soon, from these conversations a more subtle picture of truly elite institutions – elite in a way relevant to our search – would emerge. After some iterations of this one might sit down to interview 15 or 20 individuals, without hearing any of them play a note. Reflecting on what I had most commonly done as an interviewer, I realised that I had spent a lot of time listening to and probing the individual's career progression in a way which highlighted significant learning transitions. The correlation of these changes of gear with Dreyfus' levels of expertise was not exact, but certainly it was illuminating.

Expertise in Dreyfus' sense is highly context-dependent. Both the protagonist and the interviewer remain on highly speculative ground in trying to work out how expertise which is manifest in one field and organisational environment may play out in another. Transferability in the sense encouraged by competency-based thinking looked more in doubt. The expert does not know what all the cues are which prompt her judgements. For example consider Anthony Bolton, a fêted London-based investment fund manager whose specialist Fidelity UK fund produced over 28 years an annualised return of 19.5 per cent. He switched to investing in China raising a £460 million fund in 2010. He does not speak Mandarin but works through bilingual staff. A year later the results were not promising (Cookson, 2011). One year is not a sensible period for that judgement but the open question about the tension between expertise which is context-dependent and transferable skills is clear.

As significant as the implications of Dreyfus are for how interviews can appraise the skills of candidates, the implications for what is going on among the selectors is no less important. Let us clear up one point right away. Dreyfus does not imply that all experienced search consultants are, within the fields of their expertise, highly-skilled interviewers. In fact the conditions of survival and success in the search industry make experienced consultants much more likely to be experts at 'reading' clients and selling search; 'star' search consultants often delegate the interviewing of candidates to (in Dreyfus' sense of the phrase) competent juniors.

However a minority of individuals in search and in HR departments do immerse themselves in interviewing, seeking to stretch themselves, venturing courageous judgements and staying close to how those judgements turn out in practice. We can see that compared with such individuals, most line managers (even those who have made many significant personnel appointments) will not have had the opportunity to develop true expertise. Indeed the position of some line managers will be quite close to that of the professors on the graduate admission committee: in relation to selection they will look experienced, and their standing as line managers may be senior, but their actual skill level at interviewing may be low.

These individuals abound in the experience of HR specialists including search consultants. It is they whom the HR specialists have in mind when they advance on a senior selection process bearing rules and uniform procedures. And, if the selectors' skill at selection is (in Dreyfus' sense) competent or worse, then wisely chosen rules would help them. But often the rules and procedures are put forward by the HR specialist in a way which does not recognise that advanced skill cannot be rule-bound and is difficult to articulate. This creates the likelihood of the rules being rejected, or only being paid lip service, before the process has even begun. For the selectors involved in a senior selection probably have, and certainly believe they have, advanced skills; they know they are looking for candidates with advanced skills; they know that such judgements must have intuitive elements which are not bound to standard procedures or easy to spell out; and they experience being asked to 'dumb down' in order to conform to HR bureaucracy.

Those involved in senior selection experience this being enacted daily. It is not confined to the public and non-profit sectors but can be enacted there with particular intensity. There – although fortunately only once – did I have the experience of having to present the same set of candidates twice, in the meantime leaving the office and appearing to arrive again an hour later at the same time as the HR powers-that-be, so concerned was the client that the procedures which HR would enforce would empty what we had to say about the candidates of all useful content.

The Dreyfus framework would make this an obvious question at the start of any senior selection process: how much experience – roughly how many hours over (say) the past ten years – does each selector have of interviewing what sort of individuals? Among selectors I would include any search professionals or HR specialists. I have never heard the question asked. It feels gauche and embarrassing.

We can imagine what the results would be like if patients were operated on by teams composed of individuals with a mixture of impressively senior and relevantly specialist job titles, but whose actual experience of anaesthetising and cutting up people might vary from profound to negligible, and could not be questioned. Those may well be the results that we currently have in the stuck practice of senior selection, yielding – to recall the examples which opened Chapter 1 – no shortage of fired Jack Griffins, resigned David Sokols, or charity heads who spend $3.8 million building a school without even acquiring the land on which to build it.

Conclusion

The Dreyfus framework of expertise is one attempt to describe how we think and act. In this chapter I have suggested that it is one which illuminates senior selection, and particularly the place of intuition, well. The framework is certainly not perfect. Indeed, given the work which we did in Part II to identify power and politics as central to senior selection, an important warning light in our minds should be that, for all the insight offered, this chapter has again constructed an account of the world in which power and politics disappear. In fact it is another pizza recipe which manages to avoid mentioning dough, or another car manual which is silent about driving. Therefore we will have more work to do in the next chapter.

Commenting on the framework, McPherson (2005) warns us against a common misunderstanding, which is that Hubert and Stuart Dreyfus extol the intuitive and reject the analytical. In fact they stress:

> *Experienced intuitive managers do not attempt to understand familiar problems and opportunities in purely analytic terms using calculative rationality, but realize that detached deliberation about the validity of intuitions will improve decision-making. Common as it is, little has been written about that conscious deliberative buttressing of nonconscious intuitive understanding, probably because detached deliberation is often incorrectly seen as an alternative to intuition …*

> *Aware that his current clear perception may well be the result of a chain of perspectives with one or more weak or questionable links and so might harbour the dangers of tunnel vision, the wise intuitive manager will attempt to dislodge his current understanding. He will do so by rethinking the chain of events that led him to see things the way he does, and at each stage he will intentionally focus upon elements not originally seen as important to see if there is an alternative intuitive interpretation. (Dreyfus and Dreyfus, 1986: 164–165)*

It is worth recalling Hubert's background as a distinguished academic philosopher, and Stuart's as a computer scientist. These are occupations demanding formidable analytic capability in which intuition alone will sink without trace. In whatever capacity, whether as line manager or specialist, to practise senior selection as a professional discipline demands cultivating the ability to do what several times in this chapter has been described as difficult: to articulate the substance of one's intuitions, so that others (and indeed oneself) can be persuaded by or challenge them.

Academically I started as a pure mathematician. I breathed logic, formulae and context-independent symbols. Later, when asked why, having found headhunting, I had stayed in it, I frequently answered, 'Because it makes the two halves of my brain talk to each other' – meaning by that colloquialism that it was an activity impossible to do without intuition, but also impossible to do to the highest standards by intuition alone. In terms of understanding my own professional vocation, coming across the Dreyfus framework was like, having spent much time swimming around in a darkened shipwreck, accidentally hitting a switch and watching lights come on everywhere.

8

Games, Skill and Belonging

Introduction

The previous chapter offered an enriched understanding of skill which foregrounded intuition. Both skill and intuition are salient concepts when we select people. However in making this gain we lost sight of politics, which does not obviously fit into the Dreyfus conception of expertise. The purpose of this chapter is to introduce the thought of a twentieth-century French sociologist, Pierre Bourdieu, who understood human action which brings intuition and politics together. As we shall see, his thought accomplishes a lot more than this, but for now this will suffice.

In approaching Bourdieu's thought, we will take a particular path which touches some key developments in twentieth-century philosophy. The journey will not be a 'proof' or a comprehensive account. A great deal will be left out, and even among what is included, other paths (including contradictory ones) could be traced. But equally the exploration is not whimsical. The features of twentieth-century thought with which we will engage are central ones, and the connections we will make between them are not idiosyncratic. We will follow steps taken and argued by academic philosophers. In particular I will not only be quoting but drawing heavily on the arguments of José Medina (2003) and Charles Taylor (1997) – without, of course, making them responsible for the way I put or illustrate their points.

In sum, an appropriate way to engage with this chapter and the next will be as a serious 'what if?'. What if the way of thinking about human action which unfolds was worth taking seriously? What insights would follow?

The Split Cartesian World

When René Descartes (1994) formulated in 1637 the argument 'I think, therefore I am', he was searching for a foundation on which to base his understanding of the world. He used doubt as his tool, his spade with which to dig. Appearances, no matter how obvious, were perilous. Instead he would doubt whatever he could, until he found something which he could not doubt. When his spade hit what could not be doubted, he reasoned, he would have reached a firm foundation from which he could reason. He found himself unable to doubt the fact that his doubting was itself an activity of thought. Here the spade of doubt hit rock which it could not turn, so here Descartes found his foundation.

As we follow his argument, our eye and ear are drawn to the cutting edge of his argument, where his spade hits the earth, and we are inclined to ask ourselves whether we agree. We are less likely to notice the way in which the argument imports and reinforces a particular way of conceiving of our being in the world, namely as a mind contemplating whether the world exists. This is no invention of Descartes; indeed it traces its roots at least as far back as the ancient Greeks and the invention of philosophy, to the point that, for many of us in the West, it is part of our intellectual lifeblood. Indeed, unless we make strenuous efforts, it is likely to sit in our intellectual 'blind spot' – an aspect of how we see the world which we cannot ourselves notice.

Implicit in making the Cartesian argument is a splitting. What is doing the thinking asserted in 'I think' has a disembodied quality, not unlike some kind of spirit or pure energy, but quite unlike the world of material objects (including my own body as well as other people's bodies, as well as tables and chairs) whose existence the mind is doubting or affirming.

Without attempting here to make the argument in a rigorous way, this splitting which we make without (typically) noticing that we are doing – of which the splitting in Descartes' argument is simply one prominent and potent example – then crops up like a weed whenever we try to think about the world. For example, think back to the measurement of the skills of senior management candidates in a *Fortune* 50 company which opened Chapter 2, in which taped interviews lasting between four and eight and a half hours were rated by five individuals. This is an attempt to assess skills from the outside, measuring the candidates as if they were (particularly complex parts of) an objective material world. By contrast the Dreyfus framework differentiates levels of skill according to how the individual's way of understanding and acting in the world – is it rule-bound or intuitive, is it involved or detached? The Dreyfus framework makes distinctions coming from the inside of the agent's subjectivity.

In fact this should raise a warning flag in our mind, because, were the Dreyfus account a sufficient framework on its own, we could, simply by inspecting our own way of thinking and acting, know our level of expertise at an activity. Now, in part we do know this – it is a very reasonable surmise that my standard of French or Italian is poor because I find myself struggling to remember rules (such as how verbs change, how adjectives agree and in what order words should come) just to produce basic fragments of speech. But we do not have to work in personnel selection to know that people who believe they are competent are not automatically so. Nor is it safe to get into a car simply because the driver is highly intuitive, steering and accelerating in an effortless flow which supersedes rules. Indeed, when we stop to think about it, skilled action is produced through the collision of experienced agents and the world, and therefore we should hope to produce an account of it which embraces both the subjective and the objective. However the splitting of human action in the world into subjective and objective poles is buried so deep in most of our thought that it becomes difficult to imagine how else we might proceed.

Conflating several different philosophical strands, most of us have come to take the Cartesian mind split off from the world to a particular extreme – a mind which is solitary, disembodied (not limited to any one place, time or society and detached from selfish bodily impulses) and seeks to conform itself to principles of thinking which are eternal – such as the laws of logic or mathematics. While this representation is a simplification and Western philosophy has always contained contrary currents, this idea of mind and of thought remains extremely potent, indeed foundational, in modern society. It is the kind of mind and thought epitomised by science, which seeks to construct descriptions and explanations which are not limited to any one place, time or society nor contaminated by selfish interests, and which reflect universal laws (such as general relativity or the conservation of mass-energy, which require but go beyond the laws of logic and mathematics).

No very advanced philosophy is needed to run our finger down the crack in the split Cartesian world. We can take, as Medina does, simple arithmetic: what shall we say is going on when we competently calculate 'What is 2 + 2?' Taking the subjective perspective, the perspective of the agent, we might say that we have free will, and having invested the effort needed to understand the principles of arithmetic, we choose to perform the calculation in accordance with those principles, and if we do so skilfully, we produce the answer '4'. We are then very likely to start treating '2' and '4' and the laws of logic and arithmetic as abstractions which exist beyond time and place, and to argue (quite vehemently) that the truth of 2 + 2 = 4 is not and cannot be dependent on the results obtained by any particular humans attempting to perform the calculation at particular times. At this point we have invoked the existence of universal entities independent of time, place and ourselves. Well, it may be so: but it is a large supposition to conjure out of thin air. Can we get to the necessary results with more frugal assumptions?

Taking the objective perspective, treating the agent as part of the material world, the producing of the answer '4' corresponds to a particular vocalisation of sounds or movement of fingers over a piece of paper or a keyboard. Here we are likely to say that this physical effect must have physical causes, which in this case correspond to the fact that the person's brain has been trained to follow a rule – in effect to mimic a calculating machine.

Now, we can easily agree that it is no answer – or at least no part of mathematics – simply to produce something such as a parrot which always produces the answer '4'. But as Medina points out, nor is it sufficient to produce a calculating machine which has been programmed always to produce '4' when presented with '2 + 2'. To qualify as a piece of mathematics, the production of the answer needs to comprehend a principle.

> The import of saying that someone is following the rules of addition is not that she will or would (under the appropriate conditions) answer '4' to the question 'What's 2 + 2?', but rather, that she ought to give that answer. (Medina, 2003: 300)

So, even taking a very basic skilled action, the split in our Cartesian intellectual foundations leads to an awkward dichotomy: on the one hand a realm of ideals populated by which can only with great difficulty be said to have existed before someone started to think about them, and yet are timeless universals, and on the other, limited objective explanations which struggle to give an adequate account of what is involved even in the very act of offering explanations.

Can we take another turning? If, contemplating our own thinking, we want to say something different from 'I think, therefore I am', what might that be?

Rediscovering Common Sense

One important movement within philosophy in the twentieth-century which Charles Taylor particularly associates with Ludwig Wittgenstein, Martin Heidegger and Maurice Merleau-Ponty (Taylor, 1997: 20–33) develops a very different set of ways of thinking about human thought and action in the world. Heidegger (1962) particularly challenged the idea of detachment, suggesting that a better description of human existence was that we find ourselves thrown into a world in which we always already have stakes and commitments. Merleau-Ponty (2002) focussed particularly on the bodily nature of perception and thought. But for our present purposes we shall focus on how Medina and Taylor interpret a fundamental contribution of Wittgenstein to the exploration.

To most commentators the philosophy of Ludwig Wittgenstein (1889–1951) has two movements which contrast sharply – his early work congruent with the split Cartesian world, followed by the proposal of something quite different. Medina suggests that a central thread running through both halves is Wittgenstein's concern with the limits of sense. Not unlike Descartes, Wittgenstein keeps digging at the foundations of our statements and our reasoning until he hits bedrock – until he can challenge and dig no more (Medina, 2003: 304–306). Unlike Descartes, Wittgenstein proposes a bedrock which is not universal, eternal and independent of us, but rather that all human meaning-making rests not on theories or ideals but on actions, on practices, on things we do together, and on a common sense – common in the sense of 'shared', and 'common sense' in the sense of obvious, taken for granted – without which the activity makes no sense.

This thought may well strike us as strange, indeed off-putting, and shortly we will note why this might be so. But since the point is so unfamiliar, we would first do well to look at it again. The claim is going to be that the foundations of all meaning-making (including the rules of logic) rest on the practical activities that we carry out in groups, and in particular on the shared sense (the common sense) belonging at a place and time to that activity, and without which the activity would be pointless. Medina again:

> It is not because we have laid down certain propositions as unmovable normative foundations that we are able to engage in certain activities. It is because we engage in the activities that we do that certain propositions take up a normative role and are held fast ...

As Meredith Williams (1999) puts it: 'Because we do history, because we make claims about the past, because we celebrate past events, because we hold grudges, because we give birthday parties, because we are sad when an anniversary is forgotten – because of all these particular activities and many others, it is certain that the world has existed since long before my birth.' (1999: 74) Everything we say and do forces us to hold fast that the world has existed for many years. But this is not a knowledge claim with absolute certainty or some special kind of truth. It is, rather, a normative presupposition that our judgments and actions do not leave room to doubt, something so deeply buried in the normative background of our practices that we accept nothing as counting against it. (Medina, 2003: 307)

Or, recalling Descartes' quest for the indubitable, Wittgenstein is proposing that our search for foundations should take us to practices – embodied actions carried out with others which strike us as meaningful. Each practice rests, in any particular place and time, on a common sense among the participants as to what is obvious, what is interesting and what is nonsense – what cannot be doubted (without bringing the activity to a shuddering halt).

Through the Looking-glass

We will not make much progress with this suggestion unless we allow ourselves to experience its strangeness. We may experience it as infantilising and uninformative.

For to suggest that the bedrock which holds arithmetic fast is not eternal truths but the counting of apples and oranges to fill up or share out a picnic basket, in other words the games through which as near-infants we were taught to count, flies in the face of our intellectual sensibilities. We have turned from searching in a columned temple for the key to the universe (an activity which, even if we stood at some sceptical distance, took place in a fitting environment) to scrabbling around in a sand-pit. Not only is this infantilising but (we are likely to think) uninformative to boot. We learned all we need to know about child's play some time ago. While it is very kind of Professor Wittgenstein to offer us his musings, our inclination may be to return them to their sender, whose need of them seems to be greater than ours.

But – what if?

For the kind of mind that strays easily, starting to notice that every activity (and every set of rules) only makes sense within an unspoken common sense is not so hard. Actually it is part of Wittgenstein's argument that, however cleverly written, rules can only make sense within the common sense of a practice (Medina, 2003: 299), as witness the signs in London which say 'Dogs must be carried on the Underground'. I do not have a dog but fortunately so far I have been able to roam the tube freely.

Or, notice the role which an invisible common sense played as we studied the Dreyfus framework of expertise in the previous chapter (see the summary table on p. 229 in Chapter 14). The framework is insightful only if it is applied to actions which, in a common sense way, we already start to recognise as skilful. If we drop this requirement, which we may not have noticed as we read Chapter 7 because it was part of our background common sense, then we see that the Dreyfus framework describes equally well someone getting more drunk.

Wittgenstein's claim that understanding a rule requires understanding something much less tangible – its background common sense – already adds some complexity to the Dreyfus framework, because rule-following is now not quite as simple as it may have appeared. Even in a beginner's very earliest steps some halting seepage of the common sense of the activity into her being is needed, to enable even the simplest rules to be interpreted adequately. Witness learning to cook from a recipe – but the same is true of algebra.

Well, perhaps. But is this reminder of childish things getting us anywhere? José Medina (2003) and Charles Taylor (1997: 171) point to the work of the sociologist Pierre Bourdieu to take us forward.

The Grammar of Games

The work of Pierre Bourdieu (1930–2002) overlapped philosophy, anthropology and sociology, culminating in his appointment as Professor of Sociology at the Collège de France. He was particularly interested in finding an adequate way to describe what goes on in the games we all play, but in a markedly different way from either the rational constructions of 'game theory' (such as the well-known Prisoners' Dilemma) or the emotional–psychological constructions of transactional analysis (parent–adult–child interactions). He was particularly interested in what we approached in Chapter 7 under the heading of advanced, intuitive levels of skill. We can see the connection if we compare Hans-Jørgen

Nielsen's description of a free-kick on page 115 with an iconic passage in which Bourdieu (1990) captures the essence of what he is trying to study:

> *A player who is involved and caught up in the game adjusts not to what he sees but to what he fore-sees, sees in advance in the directly perceived present; he passes the ball not to the spot where his team-mate is but to the spot he will reach – before his opponent – a moment later, anticipating the anticipations of others and, as when 'selling a dummy', seeking to confound them. He decides in terms of objective probabilities, that is, in response to an overall, instantaneous assessment of the whole set of his opponents and the whole set of his team-mates, seen not as they are but in their impending positions. And he does so 'on the spot', 'in the twinkling of an eye', 'in the heat of the moment', that is, in conditions which exclude distance, perspective, detachment and reflexion. (Bourdieu, 1990: 81)[1]*

What Bourdieu proposes I shall describe as a grammar of games. By 'games' we will include very disparate kinds of repeated human interaction, from chess to skateboarding, from courtly etiquette to how to speak a language. By analogy with the grammar of sentences, the first time someone advances on us with the idea of subjects, verbs and objects, as already fluent speakers we may find the terminology artificial. However if we decide to study sentences or to compare languages, we may come to find the pattern illuminating. The labels 'subject', 'verb' and 'object' do not exist for their own sakes but to help us notice more about the work which is going on in any particular sentence. Similarly with Bourdieu's framework, in which he distinguishes these interlocking concepts: *illusio, habitus*, field, symbolic capital (or power) and misrecognition. He does not see these as valuable in their own right but as an interlocking set of tools which may help us understand games better.

The first feature of a game is that it has stakes which matter to those who are drawn in to play. If we remain outside the game, what matters about the game may well remain impenetrable to us.

> *When you read, in Saint-Simon, about the quarrel of hats (who should bow first), if you were not born in a court society, if you do not possess the habitus of a person of the court, if the structures of the game are not also in your mind, the quarrel will seem futile and ridiculous to you.*

---

1   I owe to Professor Cliff Oswick the suggestion that Bourdieu's ideas were formed through playing rugby.

If, on the other hand, your mind is structured according to the structures of the world in which you play, everything will seem obvious and the question of knowing if the game 'is worth the candle' will not even be asked. (Bourdieu, 1998: 77)

Bourdieu calls the enchanted relationship to a game in which its stakes matter to you, viscerally, *illusio*. It is the appetite to play.

Every social field, whether the scientific field, the artistic field, the bureaucratic field, or the political field, tends to require those entering it to have the relationship to the field that I call illusio. They may want to overturn the relations of force within the field, but, for that very reason, they grant recognition to the stakes, they are not indifferent. (Bourdieu, 1998: 78)

The close inter-relationship of Bourdieu's concepts is pointed to by the fact that these quotations have already introduced the terms *habitus* and field. In a well-developed game, these form a matching pair. As the game progresses historically, if it is one which embeds itself deeply into a society, then progressively the shared common sense of the game inscribes itself ever deeper into the minds and bodies of the players and into the arrangement of institutions and structures, objects and locations in which (or around which) they play. In Bourdieu's conception, a single social reality creates both. That which is internal to the players he calls *habitus*, that which is external the field.

Social reality exists, so to speak, twice, in things and in minds, in fields and in habitus, outside and inside of agents. (Bourdieu and Wacquant, 1992: 127)

This sounds convoluted, so let us take the ideas back to the game of football (association or rugby) which has already given us two descriptions of fast, skilled, intuitive play. By *habitus* Bourdieu wants to suggest several things which for him are connected. Firstly, the result of much playing means that what the player 'sees' is already loaded with values, interpretation and anticipation: in Bourdieu's description above the holistic grasp of the situation of the two teams already pregnant with anticipations of how each might change in response to each other. The experienced player sees what is important and does not see what is not (nor is he in a position rationally to describe, let alone explain, what this is). If we could stop time and insert into the experienced player's place a novice with the same build, with his body in the same position, his head happening to look in the same way as the expert, the two would not see the same thing at all.

But secondly, for Bourdieu *habitus* is generative, creative. The experienced player does not simply see a scene, he intuits a shortlist of possibilities of action (or possibly only one); whereas the novice's attempted rational consideration of a myriad of possibilities is defeated before it begins. (I write this having just spent two hours trying to tack in a particular way on a windsurfing board. At a certain point in the turn, with the wind rocking the water and the board, I get lost. I see innumerable possibilities for where to put my feet, most of which dump me promptly in the water. When I am more skilled I will only see something like a shortlist of the foot positions which are viable in the rapidly changing circumstances.) Indeed – and this is partly why Bourdieu is at pains to stress that *habitus* is written on the whole body, not only the mind – in a fast-moving game such as boxing or dancing, the body may have started to move well before the mind. Some of the possibilities presented may never have been seen before, called into life by the unique exigencies of the present situation. This intuitive reduction to a shortlist of possibilities from an overwhelming and potentially chaotic world of sense-data and potential moves does not suffocate choice and free will, it is the precondition for it. Otherwise time and again the world would simply leave us flabbergasted.

What Bourdieu wants to suggest by *habitus* is, then, intimately connected with habit and repetition, but because it contains creative possibilities and supports the scope to make new choices Bourdieu is not talking about conditioning or unintelligent biological programming.

All the foregoing aspects of *habitus* match Dreyfus's account of experts such as chess masters, but with a crucial distinction. *Habitus* is part of a social process, in which different players in differing parts of the field have different power. *Habitus* is not some souped-up piece of brain software which, if we could buy it (that is, buy the benefit of years of experience), could give us accelerated solutions to technical problems; *habitus* is highly sensitive to our place in the order of power, and presents us with accelerated solutions to political problems – including political problems of which we may be unconscious:

> *In short, being the product of a particular class of objective regularities, the habitus tends to generate all the 'reasonable', 'common-sense' behaviours (and only these) which are possible within the limits of the regularities, and which are likely to be positively sanctioned because*

they are objectively adjusted to the logic characteristic of a particular
field, whose objective future they anticipate. At the same time, 'without
violence, art or argument' it tends to exclude all 'extravagances' ('not
for the likes of us'), that is, all behaviours that would be negatively
sanctioned because they are incompatible with the objective conditions.
(Bourdieu, 1990: 55–56)

The logic of a particular field – what does this mean? To grasp this, let us start
with the actual field of play in a football game: a marked space with different
actions permitted to different players at different locations (such as handling
the ball by the goal-keeper within the permitted area). Even a player of limited
experience will start to carry an intuitive sense of where he is in the field of
play, not always needing in the press of action to find the nearest white lines;
and as our two quotations describe, the more skilled player will carry this sense
not only in respect of the static field, but also the dynamic field populated by
moving team-mates and opponents. The field corresponds to the shifting world
of positions and possibilities in which the player plays, subject to regularities
and unpredictabilities. For a highly experienced player, the game's evolving
demands have shaped both the field of possibilities (outside his skin) and his
habitus (inside it), so that his reading of the situation is expert, immediately and
intuitively focussed on a small number of the most advantageous possibilities
given his position in the field.

However to grasp more adequately what Bourdieu is saying we need to
add in that the social game of football does not end with the referee's whistle.
It continues into the changing room, the bar, the home and onto the internet.
The social game continues because the final whistle does not normally put an
end to the importance of the game's stakes – whether for the players concerned
those stakes happen to be winning, overcoming daunting odds, delighting the
crowd or athletic prowess. There are decisions to be reached as to who will play
next week, and who will be dropped. The regularities and unpredictabilities
of the social flow continue and the interlocking of *habitus* and field continue
(Bourdieu suggests) to do their work, achieving the result that even in the
most self-consciously egalitarian team, an intricate and politically astute co-
ordination of the so-called simplest acts is unfolding all the time. Such as, for
example, whether to buy a round of drinks – an act which will reflect differently
(and not always positively) on its initiator depending upon his standing in the
group, his part in the course of the game, how many drinks have been bought
already, and so on. For a skilled participant in the game – when *habitus* and
field match each other closely – possibilities which would represent a *faux pas*

for the agent will simply not arise for him as intuitive possibilities for action, any more than he would have thought to handle the ball outside permitted circumstances.

For Bourdieu a field:

> ... is a space of relations which is just as real as a geographical space. In which movements have to be paid for by labour, by effort and especially by time (to move upwards is to raise oneself, to climb and to bear the traces or the stigmata of that effort). (Bourdieu, 1991: 232)

An example of how the field of possibilities is not equally open to all players is given by Bourdieu (who described his own origins as very provincial) recalls a newspaper report of how moved an audience was in Béarn, provincial south-west France, when the mayor honoured a local poet by giving an official speech in Béarnais (the mother tongue of the mayor and his audience) (Bourdieu, 1991: 67–69). The mayor's standing with them rose because he defied the national convention to use French. However Bourdieu suggests that this was only possible because the mayor was a professor from a large town, putting beyond question his ability to speak immaculate French. The same speech given by a Béarnais lacking commensurate standing, and open therefore to the interpretation that Béarnais had been the resort of a mayor whose French was not equal to the task, would have had quite different consequences.

In effect we have already introduced one of the two remaining terms in Bourdieu's grammar of games, symbolic capital (or power). This is his term for what is at stake in the game, for the honour or respect that can be won (or lost) by playing, the importance of which is more a matter of heart than head. If after some initiatory experiences you do not see the point of football, philosophy or skateboarding – if you do not start to become enchanted – then the game will remain for you futile; not least because, lacking that appreciation that the game's importance is obvious which is the starting point of *habitus*, you will either not be invited to play, or alternatively offered an ironically diluted version of the game 'for foreigners'. Symbolic capital – at bottom, an increase in socially conferred capacity to act – is what the mayor gains by his speech, or a footballer gains by scoring a hat-trick, or (in some teams) by rising above an opponent's provocative foul, or (in other teams) by being sent off for punching the opponent's lights out.

These variations underline that symbolic capital means something more complex, creative and contested than economists mean when they use terms such as 'utility', which they picture us as maximising. Whether it is dignity or violence which raises your stock in a particular sporting community is not determined by any fixed principles, but is part of what the members of the community struggle over – in the same way that the arguments, actions and responses of members of an academic or religious community, or the management of a commercial company, determine at any point in time what range of interpretations of research quality, virtue or shareholder value command what degree of respect in that community. The person who understands a game's symbolic capital in the economist's singular, linear way is barely more knowledgeable about the game than the person to whom the whole affair is an empty mystery. His body does not see the game's artistry and conflict, and has no response to them.

Which leads us, finally, to misrecognition. This is Bourdieu's term for the consequence of the preceding point, that no-one can fully grasp the truth of a practice. What the game offers is only graspable if you play; the outside observer must miss, or misunderstand, the significance of a great deal. But the price of playing is to experience as obvious those things without which the game is pointless. We return to Wittgenstein's point. Thinking of every kind is a social practice – or what I have been calling a game – which is only possible given a sufficiently common (shared) sense of what is important, what is interesting, what is obvious and what is nonsense – in other words an appropriate *illusio*, *habitus* and an idea of symbolic capital, all dependent on players, place and time. With these we will always find, on Bourdieu's suggestion, a politically contoured field of possibilities and misrecognition of what is going on, by those who play and those who observe alike.

Preliminary Conclusions

Now is a useful point at which to recall that what this chapter offered was a journey taking one particular path through twentieth-century philosophy. Comprehensiveness was not on offer, nor the claim that the interpretations offered (of Wittgenstein and Bourdieu) are flawless or unique. What was offered was that the territory we have tried to explore, namely the underpinnings of human thought and action, is territory central to twentieth-century philosophy and that the path we have taken has been carved out and found worthwhile by a number of scholarly thinkers.

At bottom, what Bourdieu offers, distilled from decades of study of human society and action ranging from the Kabyle people to the French social and intellectual elite – he abhorred social theorisation in the abstract[2] – is not a rather convoluted way of describing football, but an alternative to Descartes's solitary mind contemplating a material world. Instead we are invited to explore the way we are in the world, and whatever we are doing, including thinking, in terms of being in play with others, in politically contoured fields of possibility, where the full truth of what we are doing lies always outside our grasp, whether we immerse ourselves in the game or stand aloof.

In offering this picture, Bourdieu offers a way of understanding the world which is not split in the Cartesian way; thought is not severed from action but deeply dependent upon it; mind is not severed from body; person is not severed from person; and subjectivity is not severed from objectivity, but both are required in an unending effort to produce more insightful accounts of what we do together.

If we take up this account, how does our picture of skill change? A thorough response needs to be deferred until the next chapter. However we can see that Bourdieu's account not only maintains (or intensifies) the relation between skill and intuition to which Dreyfus pointed, but also fuses to it both an inextricably political account of human action, as well as the beginnings of an explanation (misrecognition) as to why, if politics is ubiquitous, we often fail to see this. But we have only integrated two of our trilogy. To do justice to personnel selection we need a handle on all three of science, politics and intuition. It is a measure of Bourdieu's thought that what we have done in this chapter equips us to integrate science in the next.

Without attempting that fuller response, what we can remark now is how the path suggested in this chapter deepens the connections between skills, belonging and identity. In practical applications of competency thinking we readily think of people having or not having skills, as they might have or not have been dealt particular cards in poker or bridge. Dreyfus nudged us away from this by suggesting that higher levels of skill required the player's involvement, not detachment. But Bourdieu takes this movement much further. To be recognised as having a high level of skill now implies several things at once. The *habitus* of the relevant game is written deeply in our flesh; what we care about has exacted a price; we are no blank slate. We are recognised by others as occupying a particular place in the community (or contest),

---

2   For example Bourdieu 1993; 2000b: 15.

as belonging. We see the world in a particular way which reflects both our place and our trajectory. And our 'highly-skilled acts' – for example Nielsen's free-kick, let alone (say) the successful launch of a radical new product from within a conservative matrix management structure – will, if they were truly highly skilled and not simply luck, have reflected an intricate, subconscious interplay between positions, movements and histories of different team-mates and opponents, which we are in no position fully to recall.

Exposed as part of this perspective on skill is its relationship to the belonging of individuals to communities of practice. Do you get what this game is about? Have you paid the price of commitment? Do you see the world the way we see the world? Are you one of us? – these questions emerge as part of a decision about admitting someone to a position of standing in a field. And yet, in terms of contemporary selection good practice, these are unclean, unsuitable questions. If we admit them, are we simply revalidating the worst, self-interested, task-blind, exclusionary practices of elites, described repeatedly in Part I and captured in Fanthorpe's poem (p. v)?

As yet the headache of personnel selection which grew during the first two Parts of this book has not lifted. Should we get Nielsen in for an interview (of what kind) about his 'transferable skills', or ask scientists to construct from video footage computer models of his kicks, in order to determine what price we should pay to bring him to an unfamiliar club, situation and ethos? It is scarcely credible that the selection task would be any easier for the commercial executive whose success in innovation we want to bring into a very different company.

Surfing Soweto is an award-winning documentary made between 2006 and 2010 by South African film-maker Sara Blecher. She tells the story of three teenage South African boys, Prince, Mzembe and Lefa, who live in the sprawling township of Soweto. Despite all post-apartheid efforts, young black male unemployment is 75 per cent and educational provision remains a serious problem. One scene in the movie shows a few kids in an otherwise empty concrete classroom. An administrator comes by and asks them to make sure that, if the teacher shows up, she signs the attendance register.

In this unpromising landscape (in this chapter we have spoken of 'fields of possibilities': what possibilities?) the young people create a game: the sport and art of train surfing. They climb on, and under, the commuter trains which run to Johannesburg. They hang at impossible angles. They ride on top of the train carriages. Looking the wrong way, they duck to avoid being electrocuted or decapitated by overhead pylons.

Here a game is created in front of our eyes. It has no pre-formed rules, it conforms to no design. Different 'moves' are tried out, different reactions obtained. Is the symbolic capital in the game pure lethality, the risk of injury and death? (Lefa dies during the course of the film.) Yes, but it is not only that; there is emergent artistry and athleticism, and the *habitus* of a train surfer. As well as a politically contoured field: Prince is acknowledged and admired by the other two as the most adroit, and as a result has more possibilities to act, influence and evaluate. And the game remains pointless and opaque unless something in your experience enables you to step inside it.

> *One of the most unequal of all distributions, and probably, in any case, the most cruel, is the distribution of symbolic capital, that is, of social importance and of reasons for living. (Bourdieu, 2000b: 241)*

Personnel selection decisions, and no less decisions about whether to offer ourselves for particular roles, are not simply problems in matching objective skills and requirements, or indeed in filling positions of power fairly in the interests of social justice (Walzer, 1983), but decisions which are necessarily creative or obstructive of possibilities of human flourishing and identity.

9

Re-thinking Science and Leader Selection

Trojan Horse or Occam's Razor?

Does the intellectual strategy of the last chapter owe something to the idea of the Trojan horse? We focused on games, for which Bourdieu proposes an interplay of elements inseparably interlocked: a stance of deepening commitment to the game's stakes (*illusio*); progressive adjustment of the body and mind (*habitus*) to the pattern of the game which surrounds and is external to the actor or agent (the field); a field which is a site of struggle for the stakes which matter in the game (symbolic capital); and the resulting ensemble of activity disclosing its full meaning neither to individuals involved in the game nor to individuals who try to stand outside the game's common sense in order to study it in a detached way (misrecognition). When *habitus* and field mesh very well the stage is set for skilled actions which move too fast for rational construction or explanation, which the agent might describe as intuition or flow.

Having brought this somewhat cumbersome wooden horse into our mental compound, with the suggestion that it might relate to a particular class of activity called games, the invitation was made to see it as describing the grammar of all human meaning-making. In other words to explore thinking about all we do as games, as social activities with a Bourdieusian structure: the games of thinking, of science, of leadership, and of selection, and not least the game of being a person – of having a human, and not merely animal, existence. To dig up the many places in our edifices of thought where the idea of the solitary, disembodied Cartesian mind was built in as part of the foundations and to substitute the idea of the Bourdieusian game. The strategy is not so much the Trojan horse as Occam's razor: if a game is fruitful account of one kind of human activity, let us pause before inventing other, different kinds – because we may not need to.

What we shall do in this chapter is begin by taking up Bourdieu's account of what is going on when we 'do' science, a game which was of major importance for him. Science matters to our inquiry because of its pivotal role in personnel selection and dominating personnel selection research, producing much progress but then – at senior levels – falling prey to stuckness. Then we will seek to illuminate Bourdieu's thought by exploring three critiques or suggested limitations. In the last of these we will make a comparison with ideas about human meaning-making under the pressure of action developed by the American organisational psychologist Karl Weick. We will conclude by borrowing some elements from both thinkers to sketch a new picture of what is going on in leader selection.

In Part IV of this book we ask 'So what?' – taking in turn the candidate's and the selector's perspective, what does this new account lead us to notice or to suggest? Has engaging with scholarly concepts and debates far removed from classical personnel selection research enabled us to shift our stuckness? Are the possibilities of action which open up not just different from the present but better?

Re-thinking Science

Having set out to inquire into the choosing of leaders, we now confront one of the fundamental challenges of post-modernism. Indeed the philosopher Hubert Dreyfus (whose concept of expertise developed with his brother we drew on in Chapter 7) writes:

> Pierre Bourdieu has developed one of the most analytically powerful and heuristically promising approaches to human reality on the current scene. As opposed to the other two plausible living contenders, Jürgen Habermas and Jacques Derrida, Bourdieu has continued and enriched the line of modern thought that runs from Durkheim and Weber through Heidegger to Merleau-Ponty and Foucault. (Dreyfus and Rabinow, 1993: 35)

This quotation comes from a critique of Bourdieu which Dreyfus and Rabinow offer which will be one of two taken up later in this chapter. But first let us locate how Bourdieu understands science within these wider currents of twentieth-century thought.

We can do so with the help of a twenty-first floor New York apartment occupied in 1996 by Alan Sokal, the noted hoaxer and Professor of Physics at New York University.

Ways of understanding science and ways of understanding post-modernism are multiple, so what follows has to be a simplification. But its simplicity singles out something which remains important even if the complexity of this discussion were to be multiplied one hundred fold.

A way of understanding science which we commonly encounter (quite possibly within ourselves) is that, at least at scales intermediate between the subatomic and super-galactic, we experience a single, physical, objective reality. This is a world of facts which may yield to discovery or which may remain hidden, but which exists independently of any social, historical or political currents and is not changed or constructed by acts of interpretation. This reality is what science explores, in the interest of discovering truths (such as scientific laws like the constancy of the speed of light) which remain true whoever, wherever and whenever you are living. Any specific formulation of a law (like the laws of gravity) is likely to turn out to be provisional, because scientific discovery may replace it with a more accurate or insightful version; but what each provisional law is groping towards is a reality of a universal kind. By contrast the philosophical journey described in Chapter 8 proceeds from understanding all human meaning-making and resting on a shared social context – a local and temporal 'common sense' as to what is obvious and beyond refutation. We can call views tending towards the former 'modern' and the latter 'post-modern'.

Sokal, a physicist, famously wrote an academic paper parodying the latter position – 'Transgressing the Boundaries: Toward a Transformative Hermeneutic of Quantum Gravity' (1996a) which appeared in the journal *Social Text*. The paper opened like this:

> *There are many natural scientists, and especially physicists, who ...*
> *cling to the dogma imposed by the long post-Enlightenment hegemony*
> *over the Western intellectual outlook, which can be summarized briefly*
> *as follows: that there exists an external world, whose properties are*
> *independent of any individual human being and indeed of humanity as*
> *a whole; that these properties are encoded in 'eternal' physical laws; and*
> *that human beings can obtain reliable, albeit imperfect and tentative,*

knowledge of these laws by hewing to the 'objective' procedures and epistemological strictures prescribed by the (so-called) scientific method.

But deep conceptual shifts within twentieth-century science have undermined this Cartesian-Newtonian metaphysics; revisionist studies in the history and philosophy of science have cast further doubt on its credibility; and, most recently, feminist and poststructuralist critiques have demystified the substantive content of mainstream Western scientific practice, revealing the ideology of domination concealed behind the façade of 'objectivity'. It has thus become increasingly apparent that physical 'reality', no less than social 'reality', is at bottom a social and linguistic construct; that scientific 'knowledge', far from being objective, reflects and encodes the dominant ideologies and power relations of the culture that produced it … (Sokal, 1996a: 217)

After Sokal revealed to the glee of scientists and public alike that the article was a satire full of jokes and nonsenses which any physicist would have recognised (1996b), he went on to discuss his reasons for doing this (1996c). In part he wished to underline the importance of academic rigour – by design the original article was so bereft of coherent reasoning and disciplined thought, as opposed to fashionable post-modern genuflections, that (in Sokal's view) the editors of *Social Text* should have thrown it out, regardless of their knowledge or ignorance of physics. But in part he wished to assert the view of reality set out above:

… I'm a stodgy old scientist who believes, naïvely, that there exists an external world, that there exist objective truths about that world, and that my job is to discover some of them. (If science were merely a negotiation of social conventions about what is agreed to be 'true', why would I bother devoting a large fraction of my all-too-short life to it? I don't aspire to be the Emily Post[1] of quantum field theory.) (Sokal, 1996c: 94)

Note 3 in the paper encapsulates his point tersely:

By the way, anyone who believes that the laws of physics are mere social conventions is invited to try transgressing those conventions from the windows of my apartment. I live on the twenty-first floor … the fall from

---

1   An American society journalist and adviser on etiquette.

my window to the pavement will take approximately 2.5 seconds ...
(Sokal, 1996c: 98)

The arguments between modernism and post-modernism can be conducted at as many intellectual levels as there are floors in Sokal's building. We will not follow them (although we might take the lift from the ground floor and turn up at Sokal's apartment claiming to have jumped from his window while he was out: determining the 'truth' of the claim would ultimately be a matter for social convention). Instead the value of the episode to us is to provide a canvas of vivid clarity on which to locate Bourdieu's (2004) understanding of science:

> *[I reject] both the naïve realist vision in which scientific discourse is a direct reflection of reality, a pure recording, and the relativist-constructivist vision, in which scientific discourse is the product of a construction, oriented by interests and cognitive structures, which produces multiple visions of the world, underdetermined by that world ... Science is a construction which brings out a discovery ... (Bourdieu, 2004: 76–77)*

Bourdieu (2004) argues that we must look to features which combine, especially in the physical sciences, to give the game its particular characteristics. For reasons such as the level of mathematical skill needed to gain access to the game in modern times, the physical sciences have evolved as games with relatively high walls, so that its rules (such as experimental rigour) are more consistently and vigorously applied than those of more corruptible fields (such as social science or art or history, which games of money-making or national politics can affect more easily). The game's stakes – the search for fundamental truths about the universe – motivate scientists to exceptional vigilance and challenge of each other's work. The relative stability of the physical world enables increasingly accurate and valuable predictions, which attracts more (and more talented) people to play the game.

Science's autonomy is neither perfect nor guaranteed to last. It was won with some permanence from religion but suffers some continuing encroachment from politics and business, as witness the history of pharmaceutical companies not reporting adverse experimental results. But overall, science has evolved defences against corruption which are manifestly stronger than that of the social sciences, which are more vulnerable not only to the ulterior purposes of business and politics, but to the hegemony of the physical sciences themselves (such as the 'physics envy' which is characteristic of much economics).

From this vulnerability no wand can provide an escape. What we study in the social sciences is ourselves, unstable objects unlike material ones in which unpredictable change can be induced by a wide range of factors, not least any insight into ourselves which our study yields. Nevertheless (argues Bourdieu) those involved in social inquiry need to aim high and commit themselves, no less than physical scientists, to rigorous and disciplined challenge of interpretations and arguments, backed by what he calls reflexivity.

To summarise, a physicist like Sokal may think that he is not shaped and held by a game or social convention, but is making direct discoveries about a physical world. Bourdieu disagrees. But to be a game is not 'merely' to be a game, and because of the nature of physics, Bourdieu holds that in playing the game the physicist may well make real discoveries. Like any other game player, the physicist cannot grasp the full truth of what she is doing (this is what he calls misrecognition); but the end-product is not meaningless.

What we can now re-state is the significance of the philosophical path taken in Chapter 8. We took a post-modern path in which the truths of science are, like all human truths, shown to have feet of clay but are not, in consequence, tossed out simply as whimsical opinions or oppressive ideologies. And that is fundamental to moving forward in a field – executive selection – deeply concerned with human, political behaviour which science cannot fully grasp, but where we do not wish simply to toss out in like manner the hard-won improvements in selection which science has made possible.

Now we address some challenges to Bourdieu – not least because that is precisely the discipline for which he argues.

The Challenge of Misrecognition

The first challenge is put by Dreyfus and Rabinow (1993) and also by Sayer (1999). Quite simply, according to Bourdieu being involved in games is our way of being in the world. As a consequence we all misrecognise what we do. Therefore this must be true of Bourdieu's work itself. How can it be that what he studies (people) are, at least in part, deluded about what they do without the one who studies them (Bourdieu) being no less deluded?

Sayer puts a similar challenge with wry elegance:

As an admirer of the work of Pierre Bourdieu I sometimes wonder why I appreciate it. Is it because of my habitus – those deeply engrained dispositions towards other people, objects and practices in the social field, which orient what I think or do? Am I just swayed by Bourdieu's educational capital? Is my appreciation actually an unconscious strategy of distinction, a way of ingratiating myself with academic colleagues? (Sayer, 1999: 403–404)

Bourdieu's answer retraces what we have just discussed in the case of science. Let us recall what misrecognition is. The full truth of a practice cannot be grasped from the outside, by an observer for whom the stakes in the game do not matter. If the stakes in the game do not engage you, you cannot understand them. In this way the detached observer is fated to misrecognise what she observes. But if you become a player – if you acquire not just a superficial, intellectual understanding of the game but its *habitus* becomes part of you – then you also misrecognise your practice. The price of becoming a player is an intuitive obviousness of what the game is about, in particular why the stakes matter.

In my interpretation, what misrecognition entails is that no agent can command the whole truth of what she does: there is always something more to be said. It *may* be, as in Bourdieu's interpretation of the mayor's speech in Béarnais in Chapter 8, that the new understanding which the agents have missed (that the speech and their response to it serve to perpetuate the dominance of French) so undercuts the agent's own understanding that one might say that the agent is in the grip of an illusion, or fooled. But the *necessary* burden of misrecognition is that the agent's understanding is incomplete, not negated. Hence Bourdieu (1998) insists that the 'somewhat disenchanted' nature of the gaze which he seeks in research is 'not sniggering or cynical' (1998: 75).

So games such as science – and with greater difficulty social science – can produce knowledge but it is never complete. The incompleteness is not of the (for present purposes) rather trivial kind, that there remain things (fish in the sea, planets, scientific laws, human phenomena) as yet undiscovered – that incompleteness is akin to saying that the game is not yet finished. The incompleteness indicated by misrecognition says that even if we had infinite time to find all the fish in an infinite sea, there remains a different, more creative, never-ending task: that of establishing hitherto unexpected ways of thinking about what we do as we fish which may qualify, challenge or upset our existing understandings, without rendering them meaningless. Bourdieu's analysis is self-consistent: he holds his contribution to knowledge to be of the same kind as any other, radically incomplete and in need of challenge.

The Challenge of Symbolic Capital

In developing their critiques, both Dreyfus and Rabinow (1993) and Sayer (1999) question the idea of symbolic capital, but from opposite directions. According to Dreyfus and Rabinow, the concept is flawed because it can explain anything; according to Sayer, it is flawed because it cannot explain morality and unselfish action.

This is the first argument:

> *Everything from accumulating monetary capital to praise for being burned at the stake automatically counts as symbolic capital. To say that whatever people do they do for social profit does not tell us anything if profit is defined as whatever people pursue in a given society. (Dreyfus and Rabinow, 1993: 42)*

Sayer's contrary suggestion is that morality and unbiased, unselfish action are an important part of social life and that Bourdieu's world is too flat and selfish, too similar to economists' worlds of agents who maximise 'utility', to account for this. He sees this as a contradiction because he sees moral commitment as implicit in Bourdieu's world, surfacing from time to time in the use of terms such as domination.

Opposing the first argument, symbolic capital cannot explain everything. It has a radically social grammar, which can form some kinds of explanation but not others. In particular it could not explain human action if we were isolated Cartesian individuals, each pursuing private goods which are meaningless to anyone else – such as a world in which I am attracted only to starlight, you to plainsong and she to whole numbers divisible by three.

Bourdieu sets out his position on the second argument in a lecture 'Is a Disinterested Act Possible?' (1998). Important disinterested practices can and do develop, such as being a parent, a judge, a scientist, a bodyguard or a suicide bomber. The content and purity of the disinterestedness varies over time and place according to the principles embodied in each specific game, and contingent factors (already discussed in the case of science) which shape how vigorously transgressions of those principles become unthinkable in the flesh of those who play.

Again, misrecognition is (I argue) necessary incompleteness, not necessary negation or cynicism. Suppose last year I took vows as selfless as you please; I also join a monastic order which studies such vows deeply and punishes infractions severely. Today I express those vows in an act as unselfish as anyone in the community can conceive. Perhaps I give up my main meal so that a dying stranger may be fed: the more I go hungry, the longer the stranger lives, and vice versa. Misrecognition does not render my act greedy: it exposes that there will always be something more to say. That 'something more' could be like:

> ... [the] sculpture found at the Auch cathedral, in the Gers, which represents two monks struggling over the prior's staff ... (Bourdieu, 1998: 78);

Perhaps my ego was caught up in making the community's most famous sacrifice. But something which shows my act to have been even more selfless than hitherto imagined may also come to light. In Bourdieu's world action is fated to be complex, with feet of clay, but not to lack generosity or virtue.

Revisiting Delusio and the Playground

At the heart of Bourdieu's potential to shift the stuckness in the way we carry out and research selection to senior roles is the way in which, seeing human meaning-making as arising as social processes or games with the aspects to which he has pointed, opens up in a profound way some puzzling juxtapositions which we noticed in the course of Parts I and II. I will focus on Delusio and the playground.

At the beginning of Part II, in Chapter 4, we began our examination of whether (and if so in what way) senior roles differed from junior and middle ones. To sharpen our critical faculties we asked, are senior jobs different or just better paid? To flesh this out we considered whether we might be living on a planet which I called Delusio, described like this:

> On the planet Delusio there is a pyramid of increasingly well-paid jobs. Delusians believe that the better-paid jobs are harder, requiring high levels of skill as well as the training which comes from working up the

pyramid from one level of difficulty to the next. As the economy grows
and vacancies arise, they are filled by senior individuals choosing from
those who have shown promise at the level below. But the opportunities
are few and this makes it tough for ordinary Delusians to have a go at a
top job. However, if they could, they would find it no more difficult than
the job they are doing already. That is what distinguishes the planet
from its neighbour, Earth, where there is a similar structure but the top
jobs are in fact more difficult. (p. 58)

The conclusion which that chapter offered was that Earth was not Delusio
yet the resemblance was close enough to be uncomfortable. It was not easy to
account for the closeness of the similarity. But seen through Bourdieu's eyes,
it is of clay like this – the selfish pursuit of stakes in which we cannot but be
somewhat deluded as to what we are doing – that all human meaning is made,
and what is made has the potential to include ethics, virtue and knowledge. On
this account, that the pattern on Earth has significant similarities to Delusio is
not surprising.

We can approach the same point in another way. The accounts of personnel
selection and job analysis given in Parts I and II can be seen as a struggle
between two voices, which we might call the Scientist and the Cynic.

The Scientist strives to build a meritocratic world in which jobs and people
are measured and matched. Jobs require honest endeavour. Some people prove
more skilled than others. The Scientist helps us understand these things better,
to measure them and as a result to make better decisions. Among the jobs
which require honest endeavour is the Scientist's own.

The Cynic sees a self-serving world of misinformation, kept away from the
public gaze. (Leaders are not kept away from the public gaze, but the reasons
for their selection usually are.) Elites readily convince themselves that they
have special talents, which can only be spotted in others by themselves, and
this only happens rarely. The in-breeding of this world facilitates extremely
generous pay (thanks to the interplay of supply and demand, but with a
very limited supply). The only professionals who gain much access to this
environment link their remuneration to that of their clients through percentage
formulae, in return for which – according to Khurana's research – they do not
do much of what they are ostensibly there to do, namely to find talent and
assess it carefully.

In reality, both the Scientist and the Cynic have valid points, but both offer pictures which are inadequate – incomplete in a way which is inhospitable to additional or complementary perspectives. Bourdieu offers a different way of thinking about the underlying activity which leads naturally to necessarily incomplete contrasting perspectives, in which professional (and scientific) activities – like all human activities – invariably have feet of clay, yet that is not to say knowledge can never be produced nor good created. What Bourdieu argues that we need to do, in trying to produce the best accounts that we can of human action, is to acknowledge necessary incompleteness (misrecognition) and not to tire of taking the reflexive steps which re-think the activity in a radical way, accepting that there will be no terminus.

We can understand the journey of this book in those terms. We started with human selection in the raw, called variously the playground or the Dark Ages. Science provided the means and some of the impetus to re-think this activity in a new way. Broadly speaking society has taken this step, at least in the sense of acknowledging standards if not always living up to them, in relation to junior and middle-level positions, but selection and research into senior selection has remained stuck. The perspective of the Cynic is a further, critical re-thinking, post-modern in its debunking of meritocracy. But it is a step which (broadly speaking) society has not taken – it is deeply uncomfortable, contrary to the interests and self-image of those in power and potentially anarchic in its effects. If the only choice available is Scientist or Cynic, we can see why we are stuck with the Scientist.

Bourdieu's account can help us see further. If we understand what we are doing in terms of Bourdieu's grammar of games, we know we are following one path which was created as parts of the movement of thought in twentieth-century philosophy. If we do this, we see the perspective of the Cynic as also a misrecognition, also necessarily incomplete, and – while a fierce challenge – not something which forces the collapse of our professional and moral worlds. It also gives us resources to see questions of power and politics as central to human activity, without which attempts to 'improve' the choosing of leaders are likely to remain stuck.

Going back even further, Chapter 1 claimed that:

A microcosm of human selection can be found in the school playground.
(p. 5)

Perhaps this too is unsurprising if we take seriously the game as a pattern as diverse as, and fundamental to, all human meaning-making.

Bourdieu and Weick

At the beginning of this Part of the book, in the opening section of Chapter 7, we paused at the daunting challenge involved in re-thinking science. That Bourdieu opens a way of doing this, and of integrating science, politics and intuition in a single account of human meaning-making, points to the scale of his achievement. That achievement is underlined rather than undermined by having limitations. Part of Bourdieu's own account is that no single gaze can swallow the world; necessarily and endlessly, something is always left out, taken for granted, misrecognised.

When Bourdieu's thought has been taken up by thinkers about gender and identity, many have found value in it.[2] However they have noticed a limitation which arises from the intensity of his focus on situations in which agent and environment, in the form of *habitus* and field, fit seamlessly. Life is not always like that. One situation which is not like that is the contemporary situation in which a leader or executive formed in one field is selected and placed in another – such as the appointment of a business person to run a prison service or a university.[3] It is useful, then, to compare Bourdieu's ideas with the contrasting but overlapping framework (known as sensemaking) particularly developed by the American organisational psychologist Karl Weick.

Having in common some of the twentieth-century philosophical influences (such as Heidegger) indicated earlier in this chapter, Bourdieu and Weick worked on opposite sides of the Atlantic to develop accounts of human action and decision-making in practice – that is in conditions of complexity, uncertainty, time pressure and involvement. In Weick's case one study which caught his eye early in his career was a study by Harold Garfinkel of how jurors reached their decisions. In place of the Cartesian *I observe – I think – I act*, a more accurate

---

2   See the notes on this chapter in Chapter 14.
3   Such as (taking examples of business executives from my own experience) the media executive Derek Lewis becoming Director General of the British Prison Service from 1992 to 1995 or the New Zealand businessman John Hood becoming vice-chancellor of Auckland and then Oxford Universities between 1998 and 2009. Lewis (1997) is an autobiographical account of the former. An example of multiple sectoral jumps (with which I had no professional connection) is Adam Crozier, who moved from advertising to being chief executive of the English Football Association from 2000 to 2002, to being chief executive of the Royal Mail from 2003 to 2010.

(even if disturbing) account appeared to be that the jurors reached conclusions first. Afterwards they constructed accounts of why their conclusions were correct ones. (Recall from Chapter 8 that Bourdieu also rejects what we called there the split Cartesian world.) This pattern of action and thought led Weick (1995; 2001; 2009) to make a lifelong focus on sensemaking, the term which he used to capture our attempts to act intelligently in a confusing world and to make sense of what we have done.

That (to borrow Bourdieu's term) we misrecognise the relationship between thought and action is captured in a story of soldiers lost in a snowstorm to which Weick returned many times.

> *The young lieutenant of a small Hungarian detachment in the Alps sent a reconnaissance unit into the icy wilderness. It began to snow immediately, snowed for two days, and the unit did not return. The lieutenant suffered, fearing that he had dispatched his own people to death. But the third day the unit came back. Where had they been? How had they made their way? Yes, they said, we considered ourselves lost and waited for the end. And then one of us found a map in his pocket. That calmed us down. We pitched camp, lasted out the snowstorm, and then with the map we discovered our bearings. And here we are. The lieutenant borrowed this remarkable map and had a good look at it. He discovered to his astonishment that it was not a map of the Alps, but a map of the Pyrénées. (Weick, 2001: 345–346)*

In the story, Weick's suggestion is that the significance of the map is that it had plausibility as a means of understanding a threatening situation. Plausibility, rather than exact accuracy, mattered because it enabled calmer thinking and intelligent action. The action produced new data to interpret and the motivation to study the data closely. The repeated combination of all these things saved the soldiers' lives. Extending this to the organisational context, Weick argues:

> *Strategic plans are a lot like maps. They animate people and they orient people. Once people begin to act, they generate tangible outcomes in some context, and this helps them discover what is occurring, what needs to be explained, and what should be done next. Managers keep forgetting that it is what they do, not what they plan that explains their success. They keep giving credit to the wrong thing – namely the plan – and having made this error, they then spend more time planning and*

less time acting. They are astonished when more planning improves
nothing. (Weick, 2001: 346)

The picture of the world which Weick paints differs in several respects from
that of Bourdieu. Bourdieu particularly focuses on the work accomplished
unnoticed in habitual, accustomed actions. By contrast for Weick:

Discrepancies, surprise, the unexpected, the dissonant, are implied as
the occasion that stirs thought – which is partly why my work seems
to contain so little mention of routine/habit/automatic action. (Weick,
2001: x)

Weick's agents live in relatively malleable worlds in which strong, committed
actions are more likely to create sense than the indefinite wait for a chaotic
environment to resolve itself into clarity. Bourdieu's agents are more
constrained than they realise by *habitus* and field, social structures which can
and do change but not easily.

There are other important differences between the two frameworks,[4] among
them that power and politics are not inextricably embedded into sensemaking
in the way they are into Bourdieu's understanding of games. For reasons which
by now have been argued at length, this omission of Weick's strikes me as
a significant weakness. Conversely, whereas Bourdieu has relatively little to
say to a senior executive put into a leadership role in a radically unfamiliar
environment, Weick's emphasis on early sensemaking actions strikes many
chords, witnessed to by the common focus on a new leader's 'first 100 days'.

One way of understanding sensemaking is to grasp the insight of the
suggestion that, rather than picturing ourselves looking and striding forward
into the future, we might picture ourselves striding forwards but looking
backwards. This picture emphasises that everything we see is in the past, it has
already happened. Our rational thought is preoccupied with making sense of
what has happened, including (as in the example of the jurors) what we have
decided and done. Out of observing the past we can, of course, spot patterns
which we can use to predict the future – as when we see the sky has darkened
and therefore we predict rain – but on this account we do not (and rationally
cannot) see the future directly.

---

4   See also Chapter 14 and Board (2011).

The account given by this picture covers not only individuals but also organisations: we think of all the time-lags in the information flowing in monthly and other reports to the organisation's decision centres. But if we take it at an individual level, then there is the possibility of putting forward a synthesis of Bourdieu and Weick which enables us to complete the re-thinking of the fundamentals of selection which has been the objective of this Part.

Instead of the disembodied Cartesian mind, observing and rational, I invite you to think of the human agent as a kind of centaur: a forward-looking, intuitive, fast Bourdieusian horse fused with a slower, backward-looking, rationalising, Weickian rider. The human agent reads the politically contoured game in which she is involved. If it is a game of which she has had a lot of experience, then *habitus* and field match. What to do next – either one action or a short list of alternative actions, conjured out of the infinitely many which would be possible – appears immediately, intuitively and without a rational explanation. This intuitive thinking process (which is also social and political) may produce highly rational results – think of the intuitions of a chess-master or an advanced mathematician – but these are the fruit of profound immersion in a highly rational (but still also social and political) game. When *habitus* and field match, when the horse recognises the field in which it is placed, it already begins to jump even as the thinking continues.

Even as the horse jumps, the backward-looking Weickian rider sees what has happened, including what she has decided or done. Because no gaze can swallow the world, her ability to notice anything is shaped by her ability to make sense of what is going on. She has some sense of what is going on – a story she is telling herself, or a map which she is constructing – and this leads her to identify certain changes and actions as significant. This may lead her to change her sensemaking, and consciously to make certain action choices.

If she finds herself in an unfamiliar field, the bulk of her actions and decisions will become slow, awkward and perhaps rule-following, the majority of calls (whether to jump or not, and if so how) coming from her slower, Weickian rider. She might, in Dreyfus's terms, exhibit the early stages of learning a skill. Or, especially if she is conscious of having a powerful position, she may make a few decisive and apparently confident bold flourishes, confident not in the expert sense, but in the Weickian sense that her job is to help others make sense of chaotic situations, and bold plausibility may easily trump timid accuracy. Or, in addition to any of the above, there may be false starts where she responds to situations intuitively, because she spots a pattern in the new field which resembles one in the old. If the fields have similar structures (in Bourdieu's term are homologous), her intuitive grasp of the new field will be accelerated. If the fields are structurally dissimilar, then her instincts will betray her and she will stumble and fall.

Now let us re-tell the story of this book, of choosing leaders, in these terms. For according to this story, we need to grapple with the interplay of intuition and rationality, sensemaking and perception, suggested by the centaur figure not only in the candidates but also in the selectors.

Re-thinking Senior Selection

This book is about the selection of individuals to fill positions at high organisational altitude – for example to run an organisation A. Therefore the candidates will be individuals who have achieved some apparent level of success and expertise in their chosen field or organisation B.

The first problem we confront is weighing up what we make of the candidate's apparent success in B. We will face variable challenges in determining whether the candidate really has been as successful as they claim in B, but suppose these can be set aside – for example because both A and B are divisions of a larger organisation C, in which there are reasonably accurate records of personal and business performance which can be shared with us. Let us further simplify and suppose that the candidate from B wants to co-operate with the selection process: she herself wants the selection process to choose well, because she would like to move to A if she will succeed in it, and not if not. We remove these complications from the stage in order to leave more starkly and clearly on stage some of the consequences which flow from our re-thinking of fundamentals.

What the centaur-figure makes apparent is that the candidate from B does not herself know the full truth of what she did at B which was successful, or all the aspects of the situation in B (information resources, corporate culture, relationships, subconscious cues) which shaped and sustained her own actions. We know she is very likely to have a story which she tells herself about these things, which forms part of her sensemaking, but we do not know how insightful that story will be. Following Bourdieu's lead, that does not mean we adopt a sneering or cynical stance in which the agent's own thoughts are thought to be those of a dupe. Indeed, especially if the world of B is not our own world, we need her insight. But it is apparent that the complications in interviewing *B* are of a different order to those imagined by naïve, self-taught interviewers; by the writers of most interviewing handbooks; or even by the scientific perspective. And this is so even after supposing that our candidate has no motive other than to co-operate with us.

Continuing to follow Bourdieu's lead, while we will understand more if we can supplement the official records and her account with accounts from others involved in *B*, we now notice that we cannot avoid all such accounts and records treating variously as obvious, or important, or beneath notice those things which are part of the *habitus* of that activity.

We should hope for further insights if we can subject the candidate and her record to scientific study, but now let us now be more careful about what this might mean. Minimally it would mean interrogating the candidate according to the rules of a discipline (a game) which has rigour – for example which searches for evidence which disconfirms as well as reinforces its initial hypotheses. But we would have at the foreground of our minds that the 'skills' we seek to 'measure' are all inescapably defined with social and political contexts, and we would think very carefully about how much use our 'science' might be in the face of political and expert phenomena, both of which are likely to show deviations from 'good practice' rules. The greater the capacity of our 'science' to interpret political phenomena, the more subjective or disputable the likely results; the more objective the conclusions or measurements, the more potentially simplistic what was measured. Consider again in this context the five raters each assessing transcripts of interviews lasting between four and 8.5 hours which were described in the selection process of the *Fortune* 50 company described at the beginning of Chapter 2.

We can try to assess not only records or recollections of past behaviour but also actual, present behaviour. The more our understanding of the complexity of action has grown – in other words the greater the likely gap between what our centaur-figure candidate might do in an actual situation and what she might, quite sincerely, opine that she would do in a hypothetical described situation – the more attractive this becomes. But at the same time the more difficult it becomes to achieve. Consider, for example, the complexity of creating a role-playing scenario in which each candidate in turn acts as chair of a budget-setting meeting and actors play the parts of the 'barons' around the table. One could create (quite expensively) a detailed intellectual scenario, but the unspoken social and political contouring and body language of a real meeting with real stakes and real histories of interaction between all the parties would be impossible to capture in its detail in the slapstick of some briefly rehearsed actors. But we are now taking seriously the idea that 'skilled at getting principled outcomes out of disagreements' may not be a transferable skill living somewhere beneath the candidate's skin, but may be nurtured, stimulated or made possible by social, historical or political ties which to a significant degree are unconscious.

Having somehow overcome these difficulties to form some assessment of what our candidate's success in B might mean, we would then have to address the question of 'transferability' to A. The centaur-figure enables us to break this question down in a new way. The transferability judgement becomes a composite of judgements on several different facets: how similar are the underlying structures (in social and political as well as technical terms) of the activities in A and B? This inquiry needs to go beyond superficialities – for example A and B are both highly sales-driven activities – and even beyond market structure arguments – for example A and B both have the second-largest share of markets dominated by a giant – to embrace all the things, unspecifiable in advance, which might turn out to shape the *habitus* of highly-skilled players in each activity: star players or team cohesion; 24/7 responsiveness or careful reflection; 'work hard/play hard' versus family friendly; social snobbery; racism; and so on.

The more dissimilar the structure of the fields which define A and B seem, the more the transferability judgement will need to turn on the resilience of the individual's self-confidence, when the feeling not only of at-homeness but recognisable expertise is withdrawn as a result of transplantation to somewhere unfamiliar; her likelihood of being able to give, and of her new colleagues positively responding to, early, bold, sensemaking actions outside of their familiarity; the line-up of political forces seeking her success and her failure; all things open to thoughtful exploration but not to transparent or simple resolution, since it is never possible to grasp all the political factors in a situation and bring them out into the open.

What the centaur-figure crucially brings home is that the same image applies to the individuals taking part in the process as selectors. Quite apart from any involvement they may have in the games of A or B, they are involved in a game of selection in which in most cases their intuitive horses will start jumping well before their rational minds start making sense of what they have done as well as what they have seen. We then have a brutal set of further quandaries to confront.

As described in Part I, science (taken up by HR good practice) has attempted to tie down or blinker the horses, asking their riders to interview according to rules. But rule-bound behaviour cannot be expert, and the judgements needed in filling senior positions demand the best expertise which collectively we can summon.

What expertise? Expertise in the extremely problematic task of making judgements about candidates in situations such as the one just described. Yet, in most selection situations it is not clear whether (or where) any such expertise exists. Typically all the parties to the process collude in the face-saving (political) judgement that they all have expertise. In most senior recruitment situations it would be an explosive act to ask those present to account for and be quizzed on the depth and quality of their selection experience.

Few senior managers – indeed, relatively few senior HR managers – concentrate on the repeated, intensive making of selection decisions with consequences judged over several years, which would be necessary (but not sufficient) to support such a claim; while many of those who pass themselves off as having that focus (notably search professionals) do not actually do much interviewing. The expertise which they are economically rewarded for developing is selling – selling their own services, selling candidates to organisations and organisations to candidates. Of course there are exceptions, but the collusive silence about interviewing experience makes identifying them difficult. Psychologists concentrating on individual assessments of senior executives are probably the professionals best placed to bring expertise to bear. But to succeed at senior level they need to make politically insightful readings of clients as well candidates, which means accepting some reduction in scientific objectivity (and being given sufficient access to the politics of the client situation).

The latter point underlines that it is not only search professionals but also hiring executives or board members whose actions in the hiring process may not be aligned with the 'best interests of the organisation'. Indeed, the latter is, and has to be, a political construction – because the position being filled is senior.

In this Part we have explored the possibility of thinking differently about skill and expertise, science and intuition, power and politics, in a way far removed from the dominant thinking and good practice in personnel selection, but connected to some important developments within twentieth-century thought. From my perspective, the account developed in this Part – which is not a unique, best or right account – is insightful. It illuminates powerfully years of experience while never losing sight of the limitations of its own (or any single) perspective. But so what? Does the journey we have made open up in the way of new possibilities for action for candidates and selectors? Is it possible to move forward how we choose leaders in professional situations which not only unsticks what has become stuck, but offers us the chance to make these decisions better?

Part IV of this book will claim 'yes'.

PART IV
So What?

10

The Candidate's Perspective

Introduction

Having traversed a high mountain pass, we drop downwards and welcome the prospect of air that is easier to breathe. What has our effort gained us?

In Parts I to III of this book we have identified a stuckness in the way senior selection decisions are made. It is a stuckness which science alone is not equipped to shift. To get a different purchase on the problem, and drawing on advances in thought in the last century beyond science, we have outlined a different view of human activity and expertise. In it science, politics and intuition are woven inseparably together. Now we ask, what difference does this re-thinking of senior selection make?

In Chapters 10 and 11 the book's argument draws to a close, considering first the candidate's perspective and then that of the selector and society. Maintaining the connection with reason and theory, I venture some practical conclusions. A key purpose of this book has been to point to a large intellectual terrain not so as to 'deduce' recipes for action from it, but to provide a backcloth which guides me in offering suggestions based on my professional experience and enhances your ability to assess those suggestions critically.

Chapters 10 and 11 look at the scene with a longer focus and a wider angle than the single selection process. Chapter 10 considers the length of a whole career, and the position of successful managers who sense they could rise further. Some may be sure of how far they want to go, but others are not. Chapter 11 enlarges the selector's perspective to consider the good of society at large. Specifically, it looks back from our mountain climb to the car stuck in the ditch (senior selection practice) with no prospect of help from the nearby tractor (senior selection research).

Chapters 12 and 13 drill down to detailed practical advice in single selection situations. Our arguments have applied to senior roles in organisations large or small, regardless of sector. But detailed practical advice has to be particular. So Chapter 12 looks at a candidate competing for her first chief executive role, while Chapter 13 picks out a lonely and difficult selection task – that of the board of a small or medium-sized organisation needing to appoint a chief executive. The scale of such an organisation makes all of the following likely: that external candidates must be attracted and considered; that internal candidates, important to the organisation in their current roles, may be disappointed by the selection outcome and leave; that the internal HR function (if any) lacks experience at this senior level; that external help looks very expensive; and the board dynamics pose challenges (which may be grave, recalling for example Patrick, the never-quite-departing chief executive in Chapter 1).

Chapters 12 and 13 are 'field notes', practical advice stripped for action and uncluttered by theory. Chapter 14 is the obverse: notes for academic readers on the preceding chapters, adding detail or critique to the arguments made.

Good Selection Decisions are Not a Zero-sum Game

Exploring the implications for candidates and potential candidates as well as selectors is fundamental. There is no shortage of literature which suggests tricks, tips or 'best practices' for one group at the expense of the other – for example 'killer' interview questions or answers, according to taste. In a tight spot these may be of some help, but more broadly they seem to me misconceived. Selection at any level, and especially at senior level, is not a zero-sum, cat-and-mouse game. If genuine insight is to be had into the complexity of matching individuals to leadership roles, that insight should be helpful to potential candidates as well as to selectors.

On planet Delusio champagne bottles may be cracked open regularly by individuals promoted regardless of their talents to roles in which they are paid more for doing less. But on planet Earth, becoming an over-promoted matador risks a gory ending. In large cosseted structures the over-promoted can survive for a while, but even the largest human structures can rupture without warning, unceremoniously confronting the individuals within them with alarming challenges. In 2011 examples of those challenges included the tsunami and subsequent nuclear accidents in Japan, the threats to the Euro and, in Britain, the interlocking scandals of News Corporation and the Metropolitan Police.

Thinking beyond Transferable Skills

We start with two observations connected with intuition and follow that with observations linked to science and politics.

In Chapter 2 we explored the impact of competencies. While in their original form competencies were multi-faceted concepts, they have proliferated in simpler forms which approximate to the idea of transferable skill. We have been encouraged to suppose that there are general skills in (for example) setting targets, managing performance or getting colleagues aligned around a common vision, and these can be can be separated intelligibly from the local, specific or technical knowledge needed in particular contexts. Thus Chapter 7 gave the example of Anthony Bolton, a fêted investment fund manager who had specialised in the UK for over 28 years, switching to manage a Chinese fund working through bilingual local staff who (on this perspective) will have the local, specific or technical knowledge which Bolton lacks.

Chapter 2 speculated that part of what gave competencies a transformational impact was the offer of win-win-win gains to line managers, HR departments and employees. The gain to the latter included a mobility passport: doing one job competently demonstrated transferable skills. (Chapter 2 noted that the gain was in part illusory, since the same increase in mobility meant more people could compete for any new role.)

The view of skill emerging from Part III, at least at the advanced levels which Dreyfus and Dreyfus called proficiency and expertise, is much stickier to context – caught up in an invisible, situational, spider's web of understanding which the individual experiences as intuition. It is an elusive but logically unavoidable web of ways of seeing the world and of doing things; of formal and informal structures of power, respect and challenge; of, fundamentally, a background 'common sense' shared with similarly able practitioners as to what is important, obvious and so forth.

This view has multiple implications for managers, for example when they contemplate 'delayering' an organisation in a way which will lose much organisational memory. But from a candidate's perspective, what does it imply about mobility?

The shift is not absolute. We can make an analogy between the promise of portable skills and Mastercard or Visa's promise of portable credit. The shift in our perspective does not mean that in a distant country plastic becomes useless, rather that using it becomes complicated. The card may still buy you something but only after more effort to find a place to use it, and more local haggling, than advertisements of instant financial relief portray.

To shift from emphasising transferable skills to emphasising expertise and context is to sharpen the significance for candidates of two linked issues: expert focus and career mobility. What is my career equipping me to do, not merely competently but at an advanced level? And is my career mobility (or immobility) supporting this cultivation of expertise, leveraging it or impeding it?

Context-sticky skills make mobility both more difficult and more important: to stay indefinitely in one 'place' (meaning organisation or activity as much as location) means becoming captured by its common sense, social networks and props of status, to an extent beyond any capacity for self-knowledge. Conversely, never to stay in one 'place' may mean not developing any expertise.

Quite naturally, most careers show diversity in some ways but not in others – in different divisions but within one company; in different companies but in one country; or in different countries but within one industry. No-one can be everywhere. Fortunately, the context-stickiness of skills means that succeeding in a small number of very different contexts counts for a lot. If you manage successfully front-line operations in New York night clubs and on the Indian railway, and if your expertise is in short supply, most people will give you the chance to prove yourself in something very different – perhaps managing a charity mountain climb or the customer service operations of an internet service provider. Something analogous applies if your skill is being a turn-around general manager, or a finance or sales director.

However do too many disparate things without sticking at any, so that your success is unclear, and the likely conclusion will be the opposite. The whole of a career can be more than the sum of its parts, or less. The extent to which success and expertise is convincingly demonstrated is a critical differentiator between the two.

Which Expertise?

The question 'what is my career equipping me to do, not merely competently but at an advanced level?' is worth taking more deeply.

The bar for expertise is set much higher than for competence – recall the Dreyfus framework (Chapter 7). Expertise takes years to acquire. In all probability we will only become expert at a handful of things – certainly fewer than the range of competencies in a typical annual appraisal form. We might imagine that we can be sure what our own most advanced skills are, even if our achievements still fall some way short of world-class. After all I know I have been working on the perfect roast chicken for 20 years; Dame Kiri Te Kanawa knew her own expertise as a lyric soprano.

Can we be sure? We certainly know which skills we have been spending years trying to improve, which is what those examples demonstrate. The experience of my career advice work with clients, certainly in mid-career and onwards, is that there is exploratory work to be done with individuals to identify unnoticed advanced skills.

The way of understanding skill which we have built up in this book gives us at least three reasons for this. Firstly, the exercise of advanced skill feels easy and intuitive; if we have not had to create the expertise out of blood, sweat and tears we may not know we have it. Perhaps no-one has pointed it out to us (or they have but we have belittled the point as politeness or exaggeration – after all everybody can make strangers feel at ease or pull out the three key questions from a long memo, can't they?).

Secondly, some kinds of political skill are likely to go unmentioned for the reasons discussed in Chapter 5. Management is full of discussions of pizza-making which do not mention making the dough. In the era of employment for life, one sometimes met executives of mediocre competence whose primary (perhaps only) expertise was climbing the promotion ladder in their large corporation. On those occasions, not only were their résumés silent on the point, but also the individuals did not understand this about themselves.

Thirdly, the web of human meaning is creative. If a central statistical office somewhere dreams of possessing one day a complete index of skills, with every crevice between 'scuba diving' and 'sculpture (ceramic)' filled, they will be disappointed. Bourdieu's focus on the game as the template for human meaning-making highlights that new games constantly arise. So arise new skills. Let us not miss the breadth of this point. Suppose a new game emerges (say skateboarding), so now the list of things which I cannot do today but which in theory I could learn, is now one longer. But we are saying more than this. Something I already can do may be newly recognised as a skill. In fact an incompetence becoming recognised as an expertise is a common, often entrepreneurial, business story: Angela's extreme inability to follow procedure (which was the good reason to fire her from my business) *is* the ability which makes her wacky new business the hottest show in town. Skills may have an objective dimension but their foundation is social.

Given the subject of this book, one expertise in particular stands out as capable of making a significant difference to most senior careers, and a dramatic difference to some, and yet mostly overlooked – not recognised as an advanced skill – in early and mid-career: skill at choosing people. Choosing (and removing) people becomes one of the most direct levers a senior person possesses to influence outcomes, yet few have invested the time to develop their skill. For reasons explored in Chapter 7, most of us rapidly persuade ourselves of our competence, or indeed expertise. We confuse the intuitions of first impressions with the intuition of expertise. Or we are led by basic, scientifically grounded training into thinking that intuition has no place in good selection and so progress to competence with little inkling of what lies beyond.

Is advanced skill in choosing people likely to help you in your career and, if so, is your career equipping you accordingly? This is not an outlandish plea for everyone to do a spell in an HR role such as resourcing or talent management, or as a headhunter. It might mean re-thinking how you spend your time within your existing role; volunteering to assist in difficult, time-consuming selection decisions; and asking yourself who you know from whom you might learn. Above all it would mean nourishing an insatiable curiosity to discover what actually happened after selection decisions – your own and colleagues', some months later and some years later – looking hard for the uncomfortable truths.

What Gets Measured Gets Cocky

A major thesis of this book has been to point to the central role of science both in improving personnel selection and in leaving it stuck at senior levels. We take the scientific stance unconsciously when we confront something – in the case of selection, a candidate – and decide to measure her. Our third observation springs from this.

It's likely that if you are to be a candidate for senior roles you are managing operations, and your success in doing so will significantly affect how high you rise. You will know well, and perhaps use, the hardy management mantra 'what gets measured gets done'. What is certainly the case is that what gets measured gets treated as a scientific object, something with sufficiently stable and relevant objective dimensions – such as IQ in the case of a candidate – to be worth measuring. In the context of management more broadly, 'what gets measured' (for example an average customer waiting time) is usually a dimension of a human process (for example in a fast food restaurant or a hospital) much more complex than the output of a single individual.

The argument of this book, touching at bottom the philosophy of science and the nature of human meaning-making, is that the scientific stance may well produce valuable improvements. However the nature of human activity is messy. It will always both overspill measurement and react to it. If an organisation focuses attention and reward on managing measures which (due to unforeseen consequences) increasingly come adrift from the common sense of the relevant activity, then the measure is likely to become distorted or sabotaged. And – if the path which we have taken through twentieth-century thought carries weight – that will not ultimately prove fixable by altering or multiplying the targets, increasing the penalties for misbehaviour or replacing managers and staff.

The point is not that measurement is pointless. It can be valuable, indeed essential. The point is that any initial success tends to obscure its limitations. What gets measured may well get done, but it also gets cocky.

Skilled and Ethical Politics: How Individuals Can Learn

In addition to coaching individuals on career change I coach a number of executives on their leadership impact within their own organisations. Commonly these executives have delivered excellent performance in business units or functions which they have been able to align around shared goals. The individuals say in their own language what they want out of coaching, but in signing off their coaching requests their line or HR managers tend to repeat certain phrases: according to them, the individuals need to 'network more successfully with peers' and 'influence upwards' more effectively. Sometimes, but not often, someone will state directly that they want the executive to become more politically skilled. The idea of networking also comes up in the context of advancing one's career, which we will take up in our final observation, but for now let us keep our attention on political skill as part of effective and ethical performance in a senior role.

The problem is a shortage of visible role models. The perspective developed in this book suggests why this may be so, and why this shortage persists despite politics as a universal element in human meaning-making. Let us briefly recall some of the points made from Chapter 5 onwards.

One starting point is that while some power benefits from visibility (flexing the bully's muscles produces deterrent effects), other power needs invisibility (for example influencing an agenda so that an issue is not noticed or discussed). By definition we will struggle to find visible role models for the invisible.

Another starting point is Bourdieu's concept of misrecognition. None of us can grasp, or construct, the full truth of what we do. We pursue the stakes of a game which absorbs us; even if those stakes are unselfish, we struggle (Bourdieu suggests) in a way we cannot fully recognise for the standing and power which that game confers. If we do not recognise important aspects of what we do, we cannot *consciously* pass them on, even if we wanted to.

Or we may reflect on the maturation of the educated young manager in our society described in the final section of Chapter 5. She learns to separate the unpleasantness of the playground from the ideal of meritocracy, and, knowingly or unknowingly, participates in and sustains a social shame about the former. The consequence we described as a world of pizza recipes with no mention of how to make dough.

These are all ways of elaborating the first half of the problem, namely the shortage of visible role models as sources of learning. But of course the shortage cannot be total. If we have pizzas, dough-making must have been learned, just as a society which refuses any conscious discussion of sexual reproduction must still find a way of teaching it. Reflecting on how I may have learned political skill, I am struck by the role played by one-on-one apprenticeship. A classic feature of the fast-stream career in the British Civil Service was serving as the private secretary to a minister or senior civil servant. In the search firm which I joined, we emphasised consultants carrying out assignments in pairs (typically with differing levels of experience). Later we introduced 'executive assistant' roles with a strong apprenticeship function. That the learning 'curve' or opportunity in such roles is enormous is no new observation, but with hindsight I would highlight the tacit, often subconscious, learning which took place in the situation so produced – which at the time was masked by the torrent of explicit learning which was happening at the same time.

At its most effective, the one-on-one apprentice goes almost everywhere the senior executive goes, especially into as many of the more sensitive as well as apparently unimportant conversations as the situation permits. Immersion allows some unconscious spreading of expertise. In a live context, small details (which, if anyone could remember them, would look too unimportant to reproduce in a lecture, case study or autobiography) can get picked up alongside large ones. And if the relationship of professional intimacy works, the two individuals may come to discuss the shameful.

The suggestion that intimate apprenticeship is the only way political skill is taught in our society would be fanciful. In many cases it is learned simply by needing to fight political battles early, away from the more sheltered path suggested above for our educated rising manager. But having explored what about intimate apprenticeship may make it work, we can see some of the opportunities and challenges which other learning channels may face.

Coaching relationships come in many styles and formalities, but many share something of the intimate privacy (and so something of the learning possibilities) just described. Mentoring relationships, in which the rising executive gets regular opportunities to meet with someone senior, can also be valuable but also risk missing a lot. Unconscious action to shape or respond to a context may not be remembered, and vital small details may seem too trivial to be worth a senior person's time. The mentee can be encouraged to be bold enough to broach the possibly shameful, but the senior executive's insecurity or lack of self-curiosity may limit her answers.

Skilled and Ethical Politics: What Management Thinkers Can Contribute

As Chapter 6 pointed out, it isn't the case that there are no in-depth management books or courses on power and politics; simply that they are few and far between. That scarcity (or lack of learning opportunity) is what we have been describing as the first half of the problem of lack of visible role models. The second half is the lack of visible role models of *ethical* skilled politics. Here there is more that can be done for the aspiring manager beyond encouraging her to take whatever opportunities she may get to explore political struggle, compromise and partial truth-telling with leaders whom she considers ethical.

In one respect our aspiring manager remains poorly served by many of the management treatments of power and politics which are available (such as Pfeffer's, discussed in Chapter 6). They simply do not go deeply enough into the philosophical basis of the relationship between politics and ethics. Politics and political tactics may be treated as ethically neutral techniques, with ethics left undiscussed (by implication ethics becomes a separate subject to do with the purposes and effects of using those techniques in concrete situations). Chapter 6 described this as the dominant stance in Pfeffer (2010). It is also typical of the treatment in change management literature, with a diagram showing forces in support of change counter-acted by forces opposed, an approach derived from Lewin (1947). Unsurprisingly the change manager is encouraged to strengthen one set of forces and weaken the other but with little or no ethical exploration. An example in Chapter 6 of a text which suggests in more depth how to shift these forces but remains ethically ambiguous was Kim and Mauborgne (2005). Or an ethical stance may be taken without contest – *this* is what it means to be ethical, for example the humanistic ethics in Moss Kanter (2010) – or leak out, as I argue in Chapter 6 an unchallenged selfish stance does in Pfeffer (and is also assumed, wrongly, to be the case with Machiavelli).

More management writers are needed to rise to the challenge of addressing ethics with the depth needed in a post-modern society, in which it is less work to assume either that the subject is dead or that its contents are purely private and relativistic. Some contrary examples from the management side are Griffin (2002) and Steare (2006). The interpretation of Bourdieu taken up in this book is that we have the potential to bring ethics to life by what, contesting politically together, we give value to in practices and about practices. Standards do not drop from the sky, nor are they dead, but we make them as part of our struggles with each other in human meaning-making; or, to borrow a thought from the philosopher Charles Taylor (1989), as part of the intrinsically human quest for standards by which we are content to be judged. Out of selfish, political struggle – and, on this view, only out of this – can morality emerge. A world without struggle would be a world without values, because we would have judged nothing worth struggling over. If we glimpse the possibility of a vital, generative connection between politics and ethics then we do something to repair the lack of visible role models of skilful and ethical political action.

What Do I Want? – Recapitulating Radical Sociality

Fundamental to the work I now do, exploring with individuals the relevance of career change, is helping them to discover what they want. The goal is not (and could not) be to fix 'what they want' – and by extension fix 'them' – into something which cannot change further. Rather, in some combination of discovery, acceptance and creativity, we find some ground which is sufficiently stable and challenging that life has more energy and meaning. In business terms I put it more prosaically: to help my clients feel clear about where they want to put their energies in terms of career development (and whatever other life changes may be caught up in that) over the next couple of years. To have the possibility of that sense of energy over the next couple of years involves taking some account of what may unfold over the next ten or 15 years.

Implicit in the foregoing is that at some times it is not self-evident to us what we want. It is worth noticing how the perspective developed in Part III intensifies and colours this lack of self-evidence compared with perspectives which are more familiar. One quite widely grasped way of noticing and understanding our lack of self-evidence to ourselves is through the idea of the subconscious. This tends to suggest that the journey to greater clarity is inward, probing into unknowns inside us. Another is to understand ourselves as a philosopher like Charles Taylor does. We are a kind of animal whose wants include not only goods (food, company, and so forth) but also (in Taylor's term) strong goods, or standards by which our other wants fall under judgement. Not only are we the confused ape capable of both wanting something (say alcohol) and wanting not to want it, but also some of these 'confusions' have a central place in what we think life is about. The path towards greater clarity suggested by this perspective is some form of reflection, whether analytical, meditative or spiritual.

A central feature of Chapter 8 was to develop a different understanding of self which opens another door. In it we stressed the distinction between the most common view of society in the West (both practically and academically) which we called atomic, and a radically social perspective (of which we took Bourdieu's *habitus* and field as an example). In an atomic perspective society, like the school physics understanding of a gas or liquid, is a complex interaction of basic particles which we take as indivisible. What an individual wants, or ought to want, may be a matter for exploration in ways like those in the preceding paragraph, but the distinction between an authentic versus an oppressive or manipulative expression of these wants is the respectful observance of the individual's atomism. Commonly we would speak about the individual's integrity, but atomism underlines that this integrity draws a clear boundary between that individual and the competing selves (ourselves included) which encompass her. In a radically social perspective individuality is something social which emerges from the wider pattern of interaction. Going back to a school physics perspective, an individual becomes more like a wave than a particle, pervading space and creating boundaries which exist, but only exist by virtue of interacting waves which do not respect them. A trivial instance may help, such as sitting down with someone to order a meal. Sometimes we are unable to order until they have chosen, even though there is no perceptible rational, emotional or even nonsensical connection between what they choose and what we then say we want. Sometimes other individuals do not confine us or compete with us, but are the condition of possibility without which our own individuality collapses into nothing.

If we take such a perspective, then an important challenge is to explore what replaces the boundary-driven idea of an individual's integrity which typically provides an ethical pole star in an atomic perspective. An example of a scholar who is shaping this intellectual landscape is Axel Honneth (1995; 2007). But in the terms of this discussion of individuals thinking about what they want in the context of their careers, what is underlined is the importance of a balance between introspection on the one hand, and action and interaction with others on the other, as the path to greater self-discovery. There are important things about ourselves which will only emerge – in other words be both created and discovered by ourselves with others – through action, or through the double nuance in 'finding ourselves in new situations'.

What Do I Want? – Practical Suggestions

Here are three suggestions. As described in the opening of this chapter, the discussion of ideas summarised above not only guides me in choosing which suggestions to offer based on my professional experience, but also aims to help you make your own assessment of those suggestions, at a deeper level than if they were offered simply as 'expert advice'.

Firstly, pay attention to sustaining throughout your working decades a small number of friends with whom (whether in twos or larger numbers) a progressively deeper sharing opens up of how careers are going, and whether each of you wants the present activities and future opportunities which are your present lot. It is a habit worth catching in one's twenties. Introversion is neither a bar to doing this (introverts may bring a lot to the depth of conversation sought here) nor does extroversion make the effort unnecessary. Everyone's path is different but many people who had plenty of friends to have this kind of conversation with in their twenties find an astonishing rate of attrition in their thirties and forties. Work (especially international work) may absorb or dislodge private life; the beginning and ending of intimate relationships and having (or not having) children can have dramatic effects on friendship networks; some early friendships will survive and thrive on the friends' increasing separation of work activities and seniority but others will wither; the natural supply in one's mid-twenties to mid-thirties of friendships with one's work colleagues (or other business counterparts) may dwindle as one's responsibilities become more senior, lonelier and perhaps more competitive; sport, hobbies and political or religious commitments do not automatically survive to, or get replaced in, later life. A radically social perspective means that our identities are more rooted in our relationships than we may have supposed. For many of us the ability to have generative, intimate conversations, undergirded by a degree of professional respect and in which relevant aspects of our lives are deeply known, will be more important than we realise to knowing better what we want in mid-career onwards.

Secondly, the same principle may encourage us to adjust our attitude towards the much-repeated advice to 'network' more as part of doing (and getting) senior roles. I referred to this in the previous section when discussing common requests for coaching for rising executives. While some of these relationships will deepen into friendships, it is a rare (and happy) thing when one deepens into the kind of friendship discussed immediately above: on the whole they remain at a professional plane. Some individuals appear born to network but many of us find it an expectation thrust upon us. In my experience common inhibitors to networking include doubt that one has something valuable to offer, a strongly rational task focus combined with a daunting in-tray, and distaste for colleagues whose influencing and climbing skills appear unaccompanied either by the delivery of results or a sense of ethics; but alongside any or all of these there is often the realisation that networking efforts often backfire if they are experienced as either manipulative or insincere. But for the beginning networker, the invitation to have coffee with a colleague with whom she does not normally do this may impale her on a dilemma. If she is experienced as manipulative, she will fail, and if she covers up her manipulation, she will be experienced as insincere. The whole exercise seems doomed to failure.

The understanding of human meaning-making which we have explored in this book opens another way forward. It suggests that we have underestimated the extent to which we need to interact with and understand others in order to know ourselves. It encourages us to take seriously that our own best and truest thoughts need conversations with diverse others in order to emerge (and similarly for those others). We do not have to understand ourselves as atoms with an already fixed, private agenda merely manipulating and being manipulated by other such atoms. To the extent that we can bring a sincere curiosity to understand both others and ourselves better (because we have come to sense the inseparability of these two tasks) we can bring a motivation to networking which is less crass than 'manipulative' or 'phony'. Bourdieu's understanding of unselfish acts necessarily being made out of, and keeping some of the character of selfish clay, may make less immobilising the realisation of our own mixed motives.

Thirdly, the majority of individuals in the senior ranks of organisations are individuals who have aspired to those positions from relatively early in their careers. Our society seems to tilt increasingly in that direction: the level of ambition needed to have a credible run at being president or prime minister seems high and rising, and in that respect moving in the same direction as the level of ambition required in many organisations or sectors to be (say) a chief executive. From society's perspective this seems to me problematic, for the reasons to do with humility and narcissism discussed in Chapter 4, but sticking here to the candidate's perspective, we may observe two consequences. We are continually reproducing significant numbers (far greater than the successful ambitious) of the disappointed ambitious and the disenfranchised less-ambitious.

A greater awareness that often we do not know what we want until we try would encourage more individuals who are told they have high potential, but are not sure that they would actually enjoy more senior leadership roles, to offer themselves as candidates. Hopefully they may do this without feeling trapped into trying until they succeed, or that they have to keep pursuing more such roles if they do succeed but do not find the result appealing. By the same token some of the 'driven-anointed' may decide to take more seriously – in other words, less self-evidently – the question of whether they actually want, and if so for how long, to do what they are doing. The meaning of the word 'intoxicating' explains why the question applies with no less force if they find their experiences at the top of that kind.

11

The Selector's and Society's Perspective

Ways Forward

This book has argued that the games most commonly played when we select people for senior executive roles are stuck and that science alone cannot unstick them. In this chapter, the culmination of our argument, we identify three ways to move forward. None of the steps are difficult to understand or require lavish resources. None require the agreement of large numbers of people. It seems unlikely, then, that they can measure up to the task; except perhaps for this. If the changes have the quality of seeming now as plain as day, almost obvious, and yet we can also see why they lacked that quality before, then our intellectual journey has paid off. We will have already started to create a new common sense to bring to the task of executive selection. The car will be out of the ditch.

Three themes which recurred throughout our journey have been science, politics and intuition (the latter intimately connected with skill). All three themes animate all three proposals but each takes the leading part in one. The proposals concern, respectively, research, the selection decision and merit.

Selection Research

If there is one thing which this book tries to show beyond reasonable doubt it is that executive selection is too important to be studied, overwhelmingly, as a specialist sub-discipline within behavioural and cognitive psychology. The range of potentially relevant scholarship (scientific and non-scientific) is enormous – a forest of trees within which we have only scratched a few trunks. Power and politics, ethics, sociology, decision science, game theory and understanding the nature of science itself have central and vital contributions to make.

To the extent that this is now obvious, why was it not before? We are living with the consequences of science's great success, including its impact in addressing selection at front-line and middle management levels. Recall from Chapter 1 the discussion of 'spotty faced' Chadwick in 1973. If rashly we attempt an historical perspective the scene resembles a knowledge surge. Science has covered most of the ground. Relatively few jobs are at senior management level; the prospects of getting access to data in those contexts are slim; draw a line and call it a win for science.

Viewing the question practically, it did not occur to me as a headhunter that research could be relevant either to the challenges with which I personally was engaged or to society more broadly. In the first place there is very little research into *senior* selection, and secondly the tenor of senior selection work is urgent, difficult and messy, with triumphs and disasters threatening in rapid succession. It is also intensely private and competitive. None of these things favour senior managers or relevant specialists reflecting slowly on what is going on. As practitioners we are too busy to notice either that research is not offering us productive new ways to engage with our problems, or that the practical skill of which we are proud is itself the prisoner of a research mentality (that candidates are objects and we should measure them). Psychologists are the players in the game most likely to notice the lack of critical thinking, but (see Hollenbeck in Chapter 3) too often they are left on the periphery of senior selection processes.

Who can sow the seeds of a multi-disciplinary approach to senior selection? Firstly, psychologists, as the predominant research discipline in selection, if some are willing to nurture cross-disciplinary dialogue through conferences and special issues of journals, and ask for (or produce themselves) relevant narrative material. Secondly, practitioners in senior selection and their professional bodies, if they are willing to write and collect anonymous narratives of senior selection in practice. Typically science has not asked for narrative material because its research methods are not adapted to it. And thirdly, those universities and research funders which see potentially significant impact from work in senior selection which crosses social sciences and humanities.

We do not need to wait for the results of new research to have reasons for acting differently. We can get the car out of the ditch without the tractor (see below). But a working tractor will help us learn more, faster – as well as helping us with the next ditch.

The Selection Decision

I owe to psychologist Ralph Mortensen the phrase 'opinion karate' which vividly describes how, so often, the crucial decision-making phase in senior selection goes wrong. It comes towards the end of a senior selection process. Interviews (maybe many interviews) have been carried out. Maybe a psychologist has been brought in to report some test results (and sent out again). The decision-making group is tired – quite possibly physically tired after a day of interviewing, or running out of patience in a broader sense (the process has dragged on, the position has been vacant too long and the line manager is tired of doing two jobs or worried about the business going awry) – and one of them needs to catch a train or a plane. An 'obvious' front-runner may or may not have emerged, with all the dangers such as the halo effect referred to in Chapter 1. The exact pattern of circumstances varies. But in my experience what can be guaranteed is that no-one has timetabled a significant period of quality time (an hour or more, with the selectors' minds fresh and prepared) for the decision itself.

They gather in that thin, ragged, interval of tired time like a group huddled on a narrow pebble beach. Behind them is land – the apparently solid certainties of a known organisation, full of problems, personalities, politics and meetings stretching as far as the eye can see. In front of them the candidates have come in like waves, in appearance predictably and unpredictably tame and daunting, drenching (or barely holding the attention of) the selectors in the interview experience, and then retreating. Depending upon the process they may have left seaweed behind on the beach – psychometric reports, references or some other data.

In this uncomfortable margin, after the last wave, opinion karate is a game which works extremely well. Opinions are delivered as short, loud, data-free blows. Of course there is a lot of evidence, but we are all experts, aren't we? 'X is quite hopeless. No idea about leadership at all' 'Y's the one – you can see it a mile off.' 'Z's not quite there yet – maybe next time.' 'Will you have time to catch your train?' 'Just about, thanks. I'll get the new budget figures to your people in the morning.'

Opinion karate is the unholy offspring of a triple conjunction: a taken-for-granted measurement mindset, a business-like executive style and the uncomfortableness of the beach of unknowing.

In the measurement mindset (operating subconsciously), we might size candidates up quickly or painstakingly, according to how tricky we think the measurement process is.[1] But once we have measured them, the judgement which follows is straightforward: which fit is closest, and is it close enough? This mindset is frequently complicit in the misallocation of time. If (subconsciously) I think I am Prince Charming hunting for Cinderella, it is quite clear that any spare hour is better spent seeing another possible candidate rather than debating how well the shoe fitted earlier candidates.

The business-like executive style shows itself by decisiveness. The complexity of the information has not defeated me: I have a clear view which I state strongly. Having brought scientific and business-like hammers, we define the selection decision to be a nail. But we are bringing the wrong discipline to the task.

Again wider scholarship than science can help us. Advanced study in the humanities has its own rigour. Unable to defer its judgements of better and worse simply to data (as in science's experiments) or to logic, it fosters disciplines of attentive and critical listening, attention to detail, the weighing of alternative interpretations and openness to challenge. The quality of discussion of different perspectives is key: the antithesis of opinion karate.

More than this, selecting people is not objective measurement. The environment into which they are selected, and we (the selectors) as part of it, is not fixed – we ourselves can make choices which will affect the success or otherwise of our choice.

So here is an alternative template for the selection decision. From the outset an hour (or more, if there are many candidates) is timetabled for it, at a time when the selectors have had time to reflect on the material gathered – perhaps on the following morning, or at least after a break outside the selection room. For each candidate, other than any on which swift (but reasoned) unanimity

---

1   Chapter 13 includes practical suggestions for capturing in a useable way the complexity of the 'measurements' made of candidates. But here we focus on what lies beyond any such tool – the selection decision.

proposes that they not be considered further, the selectors listen to and discuss two evidence-led scenarios, in these terms:

> *Suppose we appoint candidate X and things go reasonably well for her. She performs towards the upper end of her strengths and some important events turn out well. Paint a picture of how this might go, linking it back to the evidence in front of us.*

Similarly for the second scenario with 'badly' taking the place of 'well'. Call these respectively optimistic and pessimistic scenarios. Responsibility for leading the selectors towards a majority consensus in each scenario would be shared out between the selectors.[2] When all the candidates have been discussed, the result will be a range of scenarios for the organisation's future. If the scenarios are ranked on a scale from 1 (disastrous) to 10 (inspirational), then each candidate would be represented by the range – say (5, 7) – defined by their two pessimistic and optimistic scenarios. The final decision would then be made, with the panel having worked to achieve the highest quality of discussion (according to the principles summarised above) it can.

What does an approach of this kind accomplish? Firstly, while any executive selection process should be informed by some candidate 'measurement', more fundamentally the decision is an attempt – however problematic – to assess how things may go for the organisation if the person in question is appointed. In particular the phrase 'some important events turn out well/badly' invites the selectors to think widely. For example, will a candidate with an unusual background be accepted into a hide-bound organisation? Constructing the optimistic scenario invites us to think concretely about what we and others might do (as well as the candidate, and as well as luck) to give birth to success. How might it go that, if the selectors met again in two years' time, they could laud the decision as inspired? And the obverse, of course, with the pessimistic scenario.

Secondly, the use of a range of outcomes with an optimistic end and a pessimistic end – an intuitive equivalent of a probabilistic range – keeps uncertainty in front of us instead of masking it as a single judgement, mark or karate-style opinion.

---

2   If there is only a solo selector, then this template can still be followed if she invites a colleague (for example a peer or an HR professional) to act as a conversation partner, listening to and challenging the scenarios which she paints before she makes a final decision.

Thirdly, the use of a range highlights that the choice between candidates should be influenced by the organisation's risk appetite[3] in relation to that particular appointment. Whether (5, 7) is a better candidate than (3, 9) needs a situational judgement, not more candidate measurement. There is no reason why the risk appetite should be the same when filling different roles, or when filling the same role but at different times. On this view person specifications for senior roles need to include an assessment of risk appetite, which is a tricky judgement needing discussion at an early stage. (This aspect is developed further in the discussion of merit.)

Fourthly, simple techniques can help break the declaration of opinions karate-style and encourage a searching discussion. For example, a rule that after the initial scenario presentation, anyone can ask questions or cite evidence but opinions are only allowed in response to a different selector's question. Of course no tool will be universally appropriate to all selection groups.

Fifthly, the framing of the scenarios welcomes intuitive judgement. Future scenarios cannot be constructed purely deductively. But this is done in a way which is subject to elucidation and challenge.

Sixthly, a discussion with shared roles and structured imaginative tasks, at which the most experienced and most powerful in the group may not be the most adept, does not eliminate politics – the thrust of this book is that such a thing is impossible – but has some chance of creating a higher-quality discussion with braver speaking and more attentive listening, doing more justice to the importance and complexity of the decision.

However more important than any one person's suggestions for new actions should be a sense of opening up possibilities and making more use of the intuition and creativity of disciplined practitioners. Senior appointments are different and difficult. Science, and HR departments, have encouraged certain fixed perspectives, the alternative to which has seemed the chaos of the Dark Ages (Chapter 1). Moving forward, we propose firstly that intuition is a necessary part of expertise but secondly that it needs constructive challenge at

---

3 The idea of risk appetite is borrowed from investment practice to emphasise that risk is not purely a negative to be minimised. It emphasises the degree of openness of the organisation in making that appointment at that time to the unknown. A high risk appetite does not mean a desire to appoint candidates out of the blue, but rather candidates with skills and achievements relevant to the person specification, who may achieve significantly more success (and have a worse failure if the appointment fails) than a safer appointment: for example the decision in some circumstances to 'leap a generation' in filling a top role.

every level, since the 'expertise' which many people think they have in judging others is self-delusion and since politics is unavoidable.

One way of thinking about the change in practice which this book addresses is to borrow the Dreyfus framework[4] to describe our collective skill, inserting a level zero – the Dark Ages – before novice. This book is about raising our collective aspirations and recommended ways of working together in choosing leaders from competency to proficiency (expertise being some way off). A benefit of that analogy is its reminder that there is a ladder of progression. Those whose track record in making senior appointments shows them at home in the Dark Ages need to get to grips with the idea of disciplined process before making suggestions for new ways of doing things.

Merit

To follow the argument of this book is to emerge into a world in which merit loses some of its objective purity. It becomes messier, social and contestable. How much this messiness bothers us depends on the context. Few of us need to believe that the choice of a Poet Laureate by the Queen is, or can be, objective. It is different when it comes to races against the Olympic clock, or picking the winner of millions in a lottery. The Nobel Prize for physics or the latest television talent show come somewhere in between, hopefully not too close together. And yet (so this book argues) even winning the Olympic 100 metres is messy, social and contestable: for example how much financial support athletes receive or are allowed to receive, or the segregation of competitors into different events based on gender rather than, say, height.

In other words we are dealing all the time with messy standards – but messy does not have to mean blunt. Standards cut, separating the acceptable from the unacceptable, with consequences which matter and hurt: whether the standard of reasonable doubt as judged by a jury in a trial, the judging of a flower show, weighing the evidence required to publish a news story, or deciding the behaviour expected from a publicly quoted company.

In relation to appointing people to roles, the drive in recent decades to objectify standards (to treat messiness as something which can and should be removed) has had advantages and disadvantages. The progress exemplified in Chapter 2 has benefitted millions of people. People have secured employment

---

4   See the notes on Chapter 7 in Chapter 14, p. 229.

opportunities (for example in police forces) which prejudice would have denied them. We as users who depend on those services, and as citizens of a society founded in part on fairness, have also benefitted.

However, especially but not only in senior cases, losing sight of the intrinsic messiness of standards also has disadvantages. Take for example the contemporary debate on gender diversity on major UK corporate boards, on which Davies (2011) represents a milestone: unless of their own volition such boards achieve a better balance, the invitation is on the table for a government to legislate, perhaps imposing a quota. The word 'quota' is often enough on its own to transport our debates into a world of deeply misleading clarity, in which here stand the 'objectively qualified' candidates and there some would-be queue-jumpers whose selection would reduce standards, be tokenistic, represent political interference, and be insulting or long overdue, according to choice.

The debate which such issues need is on multiple levels, including values, pragmatism (the 'business case' for one side or the other) and whether the standards accepted to date are in fact being correctly applied. For example, in its simplest terms, if two candidates for a job are equal in achievement, but the difficulty of that achievement was greater for one than the other because of poverty, low societal expectations or other factors, then it is not positive discrimination to give the position to the more impressive achiever, it is only logic. A job is different in this sense from a pure recognition of past work (such as a class of degree or an Oscar). Selecting for any job is forward-looking, it is to predict success on the evidence available. That is the end to which the candidates' experience and achievements need to be judged; in selection we should not count experience in the same way as air miles.

What the argument of this book does to such debates on merit is two things: to underline the need for debate on yet another level, and to offer something much needed which could make the discussion of merit slightly less explosive than sometimes it has been.

The level of debate which can be lost in the noisy clash of values, pragmatism and whether existing standards are in fact being correctly applied, is whether – on the far side of several global financial crises, several generations of more universal education and several decades of fresh research into how organisations, markets and regulation work – our necessarily messy standards for board leadership can now be improved, or whether the stuckness of our standards is a good thing and evidence of their effectiveness. That level of debate is present, for example in relation to gender diversity on boards over whether gender diversity might reduce group-think or hubris, but the argument of this book strengthens its importance, and underlines that the discussion needed comprises an informed social choice and not simply the search for scientific evidence. (Of course, arguing that something is a choice does not argue which choice should be made.)

What we also realise, however, if we follow this book's argument, is that it is no accident that the motifs of the playground from Chapter 1 occur everywhere but are nearly always buried. The proposition is on offer that the game, socially and politically contested – in a word, the playground – is the foundation of all human meaning-making. Moreover, high levels of skill are intuitive; they outrun our capacity to think. Recall the image at the end of Chapter 9: we are not Cartesian minds contemplating the universe but centaurs, horses already jumping before our backward-looking rational faculties can catch up. Scratch, then, any group of experts – say recruiters, or High Court judges as described in Chapter 1 – and expect to find the playground. If doing selection better is our task, attentively inquiring into whether important qualities not so far articulated lurk behind crude them-and-us-ness, without relinquishing important values, will be more useful than a rush to judgement.

In the previous section we argued for the relevance of risk appetite as an important but often missing element in a person specification for a senior role. This was rooted in understanding the limitation of imagining selection as the measurement of candidates and in a more open grasping of the scale of the uncertainty faced in appointing any leader. However it links directly to making more systematically effective and accountable to the board that pursuit of diversity (in whatever sense) which the board wishes to prioritise. Succession planning should include the assignment of a provisional risk appetite to filling each role, should it fall vacant within the planning horizon. While when a vacancy arises in a fast-changing world the risk appetite should be debated before being confirmed, a systematic process of this kind would enable boards to consider with senior executives whether having 90 per cent of the organisation's senior management positions assigned as 'low risk appetite' (that is, we are scared) is right, and whether the positions where a higher risk appetite is proposed fall in the right places. More purposeful identification of where the higher risk appetite vacancies lie at any point in time should make recruiting more effective, because search firms can focus their energies better, and in turn be deployed to yield better value for money. It should also enhance accountability back to the board: how did the riskiness of the individuals appointed compare with the risk appetites judged in advance.

Conclusion

The way we choose leaders needs a new common sense. In closing the argument of this book, three suggestions for change have been offered, as part of proposing a period of wider (but disciplined) creativity on the part of all those to whom the quality of senior appointments matters. The car does not have to be stuck, and there are places worth going. Even if we suspect that the importance of leaders is exaggerated, there is still benefit in choosing them more insightfully, because in doing so we will undercut the growth of hype. Instead we will enact more grown-up versions of our own roles.

If the case for getting unstuck is accepted, the first thing we may notice is our own nervousness about change: a nervousness which being stuck in a ditch (in other words there are accepted ways of doing things) conveniently helped to cover over. The beach of unknowing is a lonely place and the capacity of events to swamp, with grave consequences, our limited tools and understanding is enormous. So it has been in human progress from the cave onwards.

In this place of uncertainty, the familiar rituals known to those close to power have their incantatory quality. The interview can be part science and part rain-dance, an invocation of a good harvest. There is a comfort in stuckness. Nervousness about change is allowed. But I hope you will be part of that change.

In this book we have stepped back to re-think the process of executive selection so that, returning to the beach of unknowing, we can light a fire of new meanings:

> *Reflection does not withdraw from the world towards the unity of consciousness as the world's basis; it steps back to watch the forms of transcendence fly up like sparks from a fire; it slackens the intentional threads which attach us to the world and thus brings them to our notice; it alone is consciousness of the world because it reveals that world as strange and paradoxical. (Merleau-Ponty, 2002: xv)*

PART V
Notes

12

Field Notes for Candidates

These notes address the situation of a candidate facing an example of a difficult senior management selection, namely applying for her first chief executive role. They can be read alongside the argument developed in the book (in particular, the longer-term implications for candidates proposed in Chapter 10) or independently. Practical advice is context-dependent, in this case multi-sectoral but British. It will date and have gaps. Therefore in actual situations the sense of the advice is as important as the letter.

Do You Want the Job?

The question's several aspects are all worth taking seriously. One is how much enthusiasm to express, another is researching the role. These are dealt with in separate sections below.

Perhaps only one chief executive role in the world could attract you and this is it. That situation is different from being in the market for a range of possible roles, either sequentially as they come up, or all at once because your present job is coming to an end. In either case, a further question is relevant to you but less appealing to your potential employer: compared with other possibilities, is this the chief executive job you want most?

In the sequential case, get as much advice as you can from experienced individuals who know you *well before* any selection process appears on the horizon. What characteristics should you look for and what should you avoid in your first chief executive role? Otherwise when opportunities do arise you will apply speculatively, dither or accept something prematurely. None of these is wise chief executive behaviour.

Speculative applications are not made whole-heartedly. Selectors will probably sense that and turn you down. Because you were not whole-hearted, the learning experience will not be deep. A few failed speculative applications further on and you will start to be seen as – and experience yourself as – not quite chief executive material. Alternatively, the learning experience may be deep but nearly fatal. Speculative candidates lacking prior chief executive experience are most likely to be appointed when more experienced candidates will not touch the situation with a barge-pole.

In the situation of pursuing several opportunities, playing up to a potential employer that you are likely to receive several offers works badly as a senior-level tactic. If you may need to decide on another offer on a particular timescale, deal with that factually and briefly (don't unveil it as a surprise), but don't harp on it. Appointing a chief executive is more like marrying than going out on a hot date.

Wanting the available job very badly is a dangerous situation. Thinking in that way often leads to not getting chosen, through behaviour (for instance not asking many searching questions) which marks you as unimpressive or desperate. Be excited about what you know, but more aware of your ignorance.[1]

Parading Enthusiasm

An immature but common enough game in advertised recruitment or internal promotion situations is that candidates are expected to show a high level of enthusiasm about the role at all stages. In any senior role there are always strategic or political factors which will not be paraded before multiple candidates in early stages of the process, so unqualified enthusiasm is foolish. However, in this game being too quizzical may mean you are not shortlisted. In these situations consider expressing excitement about the role; acknowledge that in making any appointment of this importance both sides have much to

---

[1] A rising executive in a major bank wanted very much to become chief executive of his own quoted financial services business. Some years after I met him, an ideal opportunity turned up: a business with a clear business model and a substantial track record of growth and profitability, delivered by a knowledgeable senior team which had stuck together over the years. The team and their shareholders were now ready to step up their ambitions. He took the role. His significant but not yet cashable bank stock options (a few million pounds' worth, representing most of his wealth) were converted into stock in his new company. Within months of joining he had to sack most of the management team and report them to the police (the long-running profit track record was not what it had seemed), the business proved unrescuable, his personal wealth was wiped out and he was unemployed and tainted by bad luck.

check out about each other; and express the hope that you will be the candidate with whom the employer most wants to have those final conversations. The structure of this game defers most important questions to the end; you can parade your enthusiasm while making clear that there will be questions at the end.

With headhunters who are known to you and command your confidence, be frank and expect frankness in return. If a position is of no interest to you, either in general or now, say so early on, and why. Otherwise the most useful stance is a frank version of qualified enthusiasm: I would be interested (or very interested) if X – X being if they have the capital to expand, if the board is united behind the strategy, if I can eyeball the minister to check that she is on the same page, if there is the opportunity from day one to own equity).[2] Everything you do is of course part of the selection process. Spelling out X, if the conditions are short and show that you are grasping the organisation's agenda as well as your own, increases your chances of being shortlisted.

Another viable stance (if true) is, I think this is a long shot but I'm willing to have a meeting if you think that's worthwhile; however I may not take it any further.

We can give the thumbs down to being chatty or coquettish but vague. If the opportunity is not a good match but you want to meet the headhunter because of future possibilities, consider saying that to the headhunter directly. Or say that you were impressed by some aspect of the headhunter's approach and would be interested to meet in a couple of months, when they can tell you what sort of person looks likely to get the role about which they have called you. You can be sure of a headhunter's attention if you have a search assignment you might give them, but don't bluff.

Getting Noticed by Headhunters

Some situations need to be considered individually, for example if the kind of chief executive role you seek is in a specialised field with a handful of specialist headhunters, or if all of your career to date has been within one large company.

---

2   In commercial situations where the headhunter claims they are unable in the initial stages to identify the hiring organisation by name, stipulate as part of X any organisations which you are not prepared to work for or to whom your details should not be provided, including any group of which your current organisation is a subsidiary. This is especially important if the group name and your organisation's trading name are unconnected.

In more generic situations the main reason why a good headhunter will come looking for you is because you have done something well which is relevant to their search. While it makes sense to invest 20 per cent of your career advancement effort in painting the rainbow in the sky (things like networking, having an appropriate web presence and presenting at conferences so people can notice you), keep 80 per cent of the effort on producing real gold (skills, achievements, track record and character) for headhunters to find once they have noticed you.

Some actions both paint the rainbow and dig for gold. For example, if you are in a large organisation and are looking to become chief executive of something smaller, try to join the board of a small or medium-sized business in a different field, or a public sector organisation or charity. Experiencing as a non-executive the actions of a chief executive can fill in one of your blind spots if your own organisation is too large for you to have much closeness to the board.

If You Are an Internal Candidate and the Favourite

In other words the chief executive vacancy is in your own organisation, in which you have spent a lot of your career, and you are seen as the front-runner. A loose estimate statistically which is truthful psychologically is that front-runners have a 40 per cent chance of winning. In other words, you might be far ahead your competitors (say five candidates with probabilities of 40 per cent, 15 per cent, 15 per cent, 15 per cent, 15 per cent) or more closely challenged (say four candidates on 40 per cent, 30 per cent, 15 per cent, 15 per cent), but the number to focus on is your 60 per cent chance of not winning.

For reasons which Bower (2007) explains, if change is needed, internal candidates can be best placed to bring it about. Recall the Brown Shoe Company in Chapter 3. However internal candidates face two hurdles: the selectors falling for the excitement of the stranger whose flaws they do not know, and, paradoxically, if they overcome this, nailing down as strong a mandate for change as an outsider would exact.

To address the first hurdle, if you have a year or two's warning, gain as much diverse externally focused experience as you can. Consider business school courses *outside* your main specialism, or finding an opportunity to join or to shadow for a year a quite different board (see the preceding section).

With the help of someone with board experience in a different organisation, work on your CV/application materials rigorously (do not assume that the selection panel know *anything* of the wealth of detailed information which your organisation has accumulated about your performance) and, again with their help, craft carefully what you will present as continuity and what you will present as change from the present chief executive, if you are appointed.

To address the second hurdle, if you are approaching being appointed, go back to the person who helped you with your CV and talk through with them what conditions you would stipulate before taking the role if you had the knowledge which you already have, but were two or three years into a successful chief executive assignment somewhere else. While remuneration might be relevant, your focus should be primarily on understandings or commitments which you want from the board. If your stipulations are grounded in what the business needs rather than in your ego, then you will not be bluffing; you will turn the promotion down if they are not met, and be right to do so. It will be difficult to recover from your first chief executive role being a failure, especially in an organisation you already know well.

This advice is especially needed in the public sector but hard for candidates to take, where there may be an ethos of being willing to serve wherever needed, and promotions may be in short supply. You are now sufficiently senior that your country may need you not only to serve but also to refuse to serve.

If You Are an Internal Candidate and Not the Favourite

Situations in which someone influential asks or advises you *not* to apply are tricky and need individual consideration; let us suppose instead that the responses to your informal soundings are positive but indicate that there is a front-runner. Again, the important number is their 60 per cent chance of not succeeding.

So apply with vigour but from the beginning plan to be generous in congratulating the winner. Avoid anything which will make people wonder about your team-playing if you are not chosen, such as an arrogant tone or loudly publicising your application to staff and colleagues. Think hard about the opportunity which an application presents to offer a distinctive vision of the business to your board or other superiors.

Getting Information about the Process

Before you can decide your strategy for getting information about the job, you need information about the selection process. If the person responsible cannot tell you much about it, that is not a good sign. Two kinds of process are common.

The first is structured. If so, write down the structure and the approximate timetable. Ask approximately how many candidates they hope to take through the main stages of the process; what are the intended opportunities for candidates to ask questions; and whether at a later stage the business plan or other confidential reading will be supplied (publicly available reading should be on the website).

The second kind is a less structured process mainly of one-to-one meetings. If so, ask approximately how many people and who may want to meet the candidates. (In some firms the number of such meetings could be between 10 and 20.) After one or two initial meetings, you may wish to influence the order of any following meetings, either to get earlier on information which matters to you or to establish the seriousness of the other side's interest.

In either case, establish whether initiating your own private conversations to find out more about the employer is expected or forbidden. Be equally clear about your own confidentiality requirements, especially if rumours about your candidacy could be damaging to you: how many people will be privy to the details of actual or potential candidates at the main stages? In sensitive situations in which the position to be filled will attract speculation, consider whether silence would be a tenable stance for you should the speculation include your name. If you would need to deny being a candidate, then invite the headhunter to propose a way of managing the situation.

Getting Information about the Job

Unless ruled out by the particular situation, all the normal avenues to find out more about organisations are open to you. However, for a chief executive role it is essential to have the opportunity of a substantial one-to-one conversation with the chair or line manager exploring expectations of each other, and in which you insist that any tricky issues (for example of board or senior management team functioning, parent organisation strategy or political context) are surfaced.

If the process does not include such a meeting at an appropriate stage, make clear from the outset that you will not accept any offer before such a meeting.

While your views may change as you learn more about the organisation, making surprise demands could harm your chances. Are there any other meetings which you wish to stipulate? These might not take place before you become the organisation's preferred candidate; it might be unworkable or undesirable for the employer to offer similar meetings to other candidates while they are still in the running. Here are some possibilities to think about, without implying that you should ask for them all.

Reading: CVs of the senior management team (were any of these candidates?); recent board minutes; the auditor's most recent management letter; the most recent risk register, including any significant possibilities of litigation and so on.

Meetings: an experienced non-executive director other than the chairman (for example the senior independent director, treasurer or chair of the audit committee according to organisation type); any dominant shareholder, funder or regulator; the current or most recent chief executive (depending on circumstances). Whether to meet with one or two, or all, senior management team members before accepting the role depends on circumstances and your management style. Often this happens once you have accepted the offer but before your appointment is announced. Be wary of such a meeting before you have a firm offer; you may be the pawn in a political game (for example around declared or undeclared internal candidates) of which you are unaware.

Referees

You may not be asked early on for referees. However, since you are likely to be competing against established chief executives, having significant backers can be of moderate help.[3] To have these cards to play you need enough exposure to the individual (for example through a project) for their opinion to mean something, as well as their consent. Play significant backers matter-of-factly and early, without exaggerating how well they know you. Withhold your consent for them to be approached by the employer or headhunter until an appropriately advanced stage of the process.

---

3   Their role is more important if you are associated with a prominent failure.

Money

Be clear when negotiation about money (and other important terms such as contract length or notice period) will take place. Usually this is at the end of the process, but if you have important 'red lines' (and if the information provided by the employer about remuneration has been vacuous and aspirational) these should be in writing from you not long after the start of the process. A short, polite email will suffice. Having disclosed your existing remuneration will *not* suffice: some private sector employers think nothing of proposing a cut.

If benefits are important to you, or for any very senior role, do not start the final negotiations without a draft contract or a letter setting out the main terms accompanied by an example senior management contract (for example your predecessor's or a senior management team member's, but with personal details redacted).

In public sector processes, confusingly both of the following patterns are known: no negotiation at all on any of the advertised terms; or a claim that the scale or rate for the job is fixed, but in practice some negotiation at the end. Normally, if the latter is the case there will be some reference to the possibility of negotiation or exceptional treatment in the fine print about the job. If this latitude exists it is unlikely to exceed 10–15 per cent of salary. Conventions both on amount of bonus (as a proportion of salary) and the likelihood of actually receiving maximum bonus are quite different in the private and public sectors. If in doubt, put your red lines in writing.

Applying and Preparing for Interview

Find out about your selectors: from the internet, from the employing organisation's website, for outside or non-executive selectors from the websites of any organisations which they run, or by asking your contacts or using internet networking tools to see whom you know who knows them.

If a CV (or résumé) is appropriate, with the exception of academic CVs,[4] keep it to two sides or pages with a one-page appendix (for example typical assignments) if needed. Drastically prune your early career (brief references to anything striking or particularly relevant are still useful). Dispense with an

---

4   The points below about quantifying responsibilities and achievements are however relevant to academic leadership or management roles.

opening paragraph on your 'transferable skills'. This book has argued that at senior levels there are limits to the transferability of skills, but more importantly, these paragraphs are typically riddled with unspecific over-claiming and are therefore not read by many selectors. Instead convert your three most relevant 'transferable skills' to points in a covering email or letter: each point should begin with something important which the employing organisation needs, and then cite your most relevant achievement.

Ensure that your responsibilities and achievements are clear and, in more recent jobs, quantified. To prepare for the interview, also follow the steps for a competency-based application through to the stage of the revised one-pager. Instead of competencies, focus on the abilities which you think the situation demands but also take into account any leadership attributes emphasised in the organisation's recent annual reports or on their website.

If a competency-based application is being used, before filling in any form provided make your own one-page table of the competencies which you are told (or infer) are sought. Against each, jot down brief phrases which remind you of your most relevant achievements (drawing from your whole career). Take time to explore with a friend, possibly one with an HR background, which examples carry most weight and what detail you need to provide – including context, quantification and outcomes – in order for them to carry that weight. Eliminate weaker examples: less is more. Quantification can be estimates from memory provided you either make this clear or err on the side of modesty. You now have a revised one-pager to use as your guide in completing any form, or from which to prepare your detailed application.

You are prepared for an interview if you have:

- prepared your opening presentation/closing remarks (see below);

- researched your selectors' backgrounds;

- dealt with separately or put down markers about your own information needs prior to accepting any offer, together with any 'red lines' on remuneration or other matters (all discussed above); and

- prepared the revised one-pager described in the preceding paragraph, to refresh your memory about your relevant achievements and experience ahead of the interview.

Dress

Let the interviewers see you in the role. Dress as you would if you had been appointed to the role and were going to your first meeting with a significant stakeholder.

Opening Presentation and Closing Remarks

If you are asked to open an interview for a chief executive job with a presentation, time yourself and keep it short. In most cases you are being invited to give the selectors five minutes to attune to your body language and the way you speak, while putting a few interesting thoughts into play which they might like to pick up with you in conversation. If you have a detailed manifesto (and think that is the right approach to doing the role), show the trailers and let them ask for more.

Unless the interview is scheduled to run for over an hour, be wary of presenting for more than seven or eight minutes, even if asked for 15 and a lot of detail. Sometimes the presentation task has been set without the selectors' knowledge. Watch their body language closely and be ready to drop parts of your presentation in favour of handing over copies of a two-page written summary.

If no presentation is requested, still be prepared if asked to open with three minutes on the three most important points which you want to leave in the selectors' minds. If no opportunity is given at the beginning, adapt the points for use at any opportunity at the close ('Do you have any questions?'). In any case you should have no closing questions (other than 'What timetable are you working to?' if this has not been explained already), because the information you need to accept a chief executive appointment needs to have been dealt with separately (see above).

If you have made an opening presentation, do not say anything at the close other than how pleased you would be to be part, with the board, of taking this organisation forward. Probably the selectors are running late.

Take into the interview a blank card (postcard size) and, if you were asked to supply a long and detailed application form, a copy of that. If you applied by a two-page CV, you are expected to know what you said. You can use the blank card's top face to write any notes to yourself (see next section). On the underside you can write keywords or phrases to remind you of the key points for your opening and closing remarks, which you can then either do from memory or after looking at the card. If you look at the card, do so unhurriedly.

If the interview is formal and there is no clock visible from where you are sitting, place your watch face down on the table, unless you can read it on your arm without awkwardness. Ensure your mobile phone is off. Do not place a BlackBerry or similar device on the interview table, even if you are only using it to tell the time.

Stumbles and Unexpected Questions

It is normal to stumble over one or two interview answers. You can say 'Let me try that again', and re-phrase. If you are in any doubt that your selectors have grasped your meaning, ask them.

You might do worse than stumble: it happens. Suddenly you have a mental blank. Don't keep floundering. Stop speaking, write the question (and who asked it) down on your card, and find your own words for, 'I'm not happy with that answer. If I may, I'll take two minutes at the end to come back and have another go.' Without fail you must then do that. Recapitulate the question accurately while facing the person who asked it.

For reasons explained in Chapter 13, hypothetical questions are generally to be avoided by selectors. However you may get them. You are entitled to ask a clarifying question and to take 30 seconds (a long time) to think. Make sure you state the obvious even if you go on to say something more advanced. Taking a typical case, the hypothetical question may want you to balance conflicting priorities but show decisiveness by choosing one. Typically, however, there is insufficient information to make a wise choice. The question may be a political test or simply a piece of poor-quality interviewing. You may have read the political game and spotted the 'right' answer. If not, summarise the conflicting priorities and say your choice would depend upon the situation, adding, 'When something a bit like that happened in my last job, I chose X.' The questioner will probably be too smug about her own scenario to probe yours. You will have shown decisiveness without committing yourself to an unknown.

Silences

After a nerve-jangling interview what usually follows is unexplained silence. You will imagine that they are negotiating with another candidate. It is possible, but it may also be that another candidate had an appendicitis scare or missed their flight. If headhunters have been engaged they should be attentive to your situation, but sometimes they are not. Sometimes clients are foolish enough to order their headhunters not to talk to any of the candidates. At a certain point your patience will (and should) run out – perhaps a week after the selectors had led you to expect contact – but otherwise save your energy and your imagination.

13

Field Notes for Selectors

Like the previous chapter, this one drills down to detailed practical advice in single selection situations. Our arguments have applied to senior roles in organisations large or small, regardless of sector. But detailed practical advice has to be particular. So here we pick out a lonely and difficult selection task – that of the board of a small or medium-sized organisation needing to appoint a chief executive. The scale of such an organisation makes all of the following likely: that external candidates must be attracted and considered; that internal candidates, important to the organisation in their current roles, may be disappointed by the selection outcome and leave; that the internal HR function (if any) lacks experience at this senior level; that external help looks very expensive; and the board dynamics pose challenges (which may be grave, recalling for example Patrick, the never-quite-departing chief executive in Chapter 1).

The notes can be read alongside the argument developed in the book (in particular, the approach to selection decision-making proposed in Chapter 11) or independently. Like the book, this chapter assumes some familiarity with basic selection good practice.[1] It does not cover legal issues.

Practical advice is context-dependent, in this case multi-sectoral but British. It will date and have gaps. Therefore in actual situations the sense of the advice is as important as the letter.

Succession Planning

Some issues arise, at least for the chair, two years or more in advance. Usually small or medium-sized organisations will need to consider external as well

---

1   Widely taught in early management training or see for example Wood and Payne (1998) or Dale (2006).

as internal candidates as chief executive, but this similarity masks important differences. Some organisations, while not large, have senior structures broad enough to support the weight of two or more strong internal candidates. Other organisations might be big enough to accommodate one strong internal candidate; yet others will have none. In the first group will be many medium-sized businesses and major hospitals or schools. In the middle category might be entrepreneurial businesses where one person is being groomed to succeed. In the last category we find some small organisations with well-known leaders (some think tanks or cultural organisations, and entrepreneurial businesses), where the gap in experience and skill between the chief executive and his lieutenants is large.

A chief executive transition may look easier to handle in one of these situations rather than another, but on close inspection all can be difficult. Having two high-performing successors-in-waiting sounds luxurious but a few months after you have made your choice, only one, and possibly neither, will still be with you. Internal candidates who may be keen rather than strong, yet have specialist knowledge which the organisation will not replace easily, may need a lot of managing. In juggling these complications the chair needs to be concerned with business continuity as well the likely calibre of his next chief executive, and with balancing fairness and rule-books against tailored approaches which treat key personnel according to their differing needs and preferences. Of course all this needs close co-operation with the existing chief executive; sometimes that is not possible.

Read Bower (2007). If the organisation has the necessary breadth, starting two years beforehand, give a group of internal candidates broader than just an obvious favourite the scope to surprise the board, for example by giving them opportunities to lead organisation-wide changes outside their usual remit. Then consider broadening experiences (see internal front-runners in Chapter 12).

Realistically, plans in smaller organisations are constantly biting the dust. The need to recruit a chief executive may arise with none of the above possible or done. It is still possible to carry out a high-quality selection process and get a high-quality result. But the very first steps which arise in launching the process are among the most perilous. When senior recruitments in which I have been involved have been cocked up, with hindsight the cock-up was made early on, before any candidate had been approached or any advertisement had appeared. These recruitment cock-ups – for example mistakes in choosing the selectors – have a time-delay fuse: they blow up at the end of the process.

Who Will Select?

This is a tricky jigsaw puzzle. Who needs to be involved, in terms of their experience or the politics of the board? What impression is the selection group likely to make on candidates, for example in terms of diversity (including of age)? Who has the time to spend getting alongside candidates in the final stages of the process, helping to land the one you want – the chair will have to be involved but does he need help? (Some chairs could not sell lifejackets on the *Titanic*; they have, we hope, other qualities. However if another board member is to help the chair with this, the two must sing in close harmony.) Who actually has any skill in interviewing? Who is the best listener on the board? Do you have some balance between analytic and intuitive decision-makers? The group of selectors also needs to be watertight in terms of confidentiality. Ideally the selection group should number between three and five.

This puzzle may bring on a headache. The composition of a board has to reflect many things, and the ideal line-up for recruiting a chief executive is not one of them. That is no embarrassment. But a brutally honest assessment of the board's needs and gaps is essential, and may feed into the decision on external help (below).

An effective group of selectors also needs the mandate to select, within objectives and parameters (including a person and risk appetite specification) approved by the board. An effective process is possible with the selection group empowered either to offer the role to its preferred candidate, or putting forward one candidate for a confirmation meeting with the full board. A large board doing its own selection is not buying a dog and barking itself, it is hiring a surgeon and operating itself.

Some selection groups have to include a compulsory external participant, representing perhaps a major shareholder, funder or government authority. Any such individual must make the time to play a sufficiently involved role. Someone who turns up to join a senior selection process on the final day, who has not been prepared to sign up to the agreed person specification and to join in the shortlisting discussion, puts the process at risk.

Senior management team involvement in the selection process is dealt with below. Much wider staff involvement in drawing up the person specification is helpful (subject to authority remaining with the board). However in choosing between candidates, the manifold problems of wide staff involvement (for example confidentiality) almost always swamp any 'wisdom of crowds'.[2] The selection group has a job of work to do which requires a small number of skilled individuals, committed to confidentiality and uninhibited discussion; all these might be problematic with junior or middle-level staff, who additionally cannot but be influenced by whether candidates seem sympathetic to the particular needs of their own part of the organisation. Exceptionally – for example where the organisation is owned by all the staff – staff involvement by full membership of representatives in the selection group is preferable, working to the agreed specification. Full membership entails the responsibilities (such as confidentiality) as well the rights of the role and is incompatible with being a separately mandated union delegate.

Timetable

As a first approximation, it will be between three and ten months (average six months) before your new chief executive arrives. The selection process itself, that is until the new chief executive is *announced*, will need three or four months, depending on whether you will advertise or proactively search for candidates, and major holiday periods. A difficult or highly international search will take longer. The time between your new chief executive being announced and starting will be zero to six months, depending upon your chosen candidate's notice period (zero if the candidate is internal or immediately available).

What's Going to be Most Difficult?

What is going to be most difficult in your recruitment? Spotting this and designing a process which commits your resources (money, your time and that of candidates) accordingly may be the smartest single call you can make in the whole process. Which of the following will be averagely difficult and which will be game-changing: working out what kind of person you should want;

---

2   Keeping the selection group small and tight is by no means the same as keeping it homogenous (see the beginning of this section) or a smug reliance on interview impressions (for example see below on using a psychologist and extensive referencing).

finding them; attracting them; or knowing reliably whether the man or woman in front of you is one of them?

Take the England football team (or the sporting equivalent of your choice) as an example of a small to medium-sized organisation with high complexity. If you had to recruit a new manager for the team today, which of the challenges just listed would you judge most difficult, and why?

External Help

In a small or medium-sized organisation the board may be lucky to have the help of an HR director or company secretary, but these individuals sometimes lack the experience of senior recruitment or are too close to some or all of their senior colleagues to provide critical advice. Equally the funds available for external help will be limited. In principle the cost of recruiting a chief executive should be spread over an estimate of their tenure (say four or five years) but in practice the cost usually comes as an unexpected single 'hit'. Some possible sources of help are listed below, cross-referenced in Table 13.1 against the potential need.

The recruitment industry includes (a) search firms, (b) selection firms, (c) specialist agencies and (d) freelance researchers. They charge differently, source candidates differently (by proactive search tailored to your needs, by advertising, by maintaining a database of candidates available for hire) and vary widely in their ethical standards and capacity to give advice. The recruitment industry – sprawling, opaque and with a closer resemblance to estate agents (realtors) than its practitioners would like you to think – spans large international firms and small boutiques, either of which can be excellent or a waste of money. The ability, experience, ethics and work ethic of the individuals who will do the work on your assignment are as important as the firm's size, name or corporate track record. A search firm which claims a large relevant corporate track record should disclose its off-limits policy (which organisations it cannot look in for candidates because they have been recent clients). Highly international search is particularly difficult to purchase well.

Other kinds of help include (e) psychologists specialising in senior executive selection (who can be solo, in independent firms or employed by search and selection firms) and (f) senior HR professionals with broad experience who are working solo or have 'gone portfolio'.

The internet offers many ways to find potential advisors (including the website of the international Association of Executive Search Consultants, www.aesc.org, and the commercial index Executive Grapevine) but for senior-level work, personal recommendation of individual firms and consultants is the most used route. If you want a search firm, the frequency of its appearance in advertisements or providing quotations in business news pages is largely meaningless.

Consider (at no cost other than time) inviting three contrasting recruitment firms to meet you for an exploratory conversation. Let them ask you questions for half an hour and then turn the tables: how would they attract candidates to your role; what remuneration do they anticipate you will need to offer; which parts of the recruitment process do they think will be most difficult (see the preceding section). They will then provide you with a written proposal for their services. You are not obliged to accept any of the proposals. If you are going to invite firms in to talk, do it early (you need not wait until the vacancy is public); you may well get advice which saves you grief later on (see cock-ups above).

Table 13.1   CEO recruitment: possible needs and sources of external help

Possible need	Possible sources
Designing the selection process including drafting the person specification	(a), (b), (f)
Assessing the candidate market and implications for remuneration or other terms	(a), (b), (c)
Finding candidates	(a), (b), (c), (d)
Assessing candidates	(a), (b), (c) – up to a point; (e), (f)
The selection decision	(a), (e), (f)
'Landing' your preferred candidate	(a), (f)
Dealing with internal board dynamics	(f)

Emotional Management

Not commonly mentioned, but an important task for the leader of the process is the emotional management of colleagues and (if you are not using headhunters) of candidates. Recruitment to a senior role is often an emotional roller-coaster. Elation and depression, fear and anger, can follow in bewildering succession. With colleagues, whatever early 'wins' or 'losses' appear in the process (for example a candidate perceived as a 'star' comes in or drops out), a purposeful, cautious emotional tone is most effective from the start until an offer has been accepted. (My description of the prudent emotional state for senior recruitment is 'No need to panic yet', from the start of the process until about two years after the appointed candidate has started work!)

A similar steady, measured tone but with more enthusiasm is needed with candidates. If disagreeable news about the role needs to be disclosed, this must be done fully and reasonably early; a disquieting drip-feed suggests incompetence and a late surprise bad faith. Candidates need to feel appropriately wanted throughout the process but avoiding premature excitement. Under the skin both colleagues and candidates are in an emotionally raw state. Sudden reversals of feeling will raise acute feelings of vulnerability which may hit reasoned consideration for six.[3]

Board Involvement

Determining the person specification and other important parameters for the appointment, such as remuneration and risk appetite, is a board responsibility of fundamental importance. However this requires thinking, wide experience and courage, followed by (once the specification has been agreed) a degree of keeping one's mouth shut. It is vastly less popular than gossip and opining on individual candidates.

Regular progress updates (a paragraph or two, candid but not identifying individual candidates) will be helpful to board members who are not part of the selection group. See emotional management above.

If board members wish closer involvement, invite them to attend the shortlisting meeting. While the shortlisting *decisions* should be reserved to the selection group, board members who attend will get a thorough immersion in how (and why) the field of candidates is shaping up as it is. Their reservations about or enthusiasms for individual candidates can be tested for relevance and evidential basis by the selectors. Board members taking advantage of this opportunity need to turn up and join a conversation with the purpose of listening as well as speaking. Evidence-free 'mortar bombs' lobbed in by email *in absentia* ('X is a ridiculous idea, I can't imagine who thought of him')

---

3   You may be told that any good enough chief executive will have a thick enough skin to take upsets in his stride. This is wrong. Even if the job does need a steel-skinned chief executive, an effective recruitment process aims to get under their skin (and yours).

should be ruled out of order; they prejudice the quality of discussion which the selectors need to have.

As noted earlier, presentation of a single candidate recommended by the selectors for ratification by the full board is a viable process.

Senior Management Team Involvement

Senior management team members (including in appropriate circumstances the departing chief executive) have a vital contribution to make to the process, particularly to the board's consideration of the person specification. That contribution is worth collecting individually and anonymously, and should then be discussed by the non-executives in private session.

Among the executives some jostling for succession may already occur, but the chair should discourage individuals from declaring themselves as candidates too early. The decision to be a candidate cannot properly be taken before they have seen the board's approved person specification. A deadline after that date should be set by which internal candidates declare themselves.[4]

If a senior management team member offers himself for appointment, he should not take part in any briefing meetings with shortlisted candidates, even if by that stage in the process he has changed his mind or been rejected by the selectors. Whatever his apparent or claimed state of mind, his subconscious state would be unpropitious. In some cases but not others an out-going chief executive can be an invaluable contributor to briefing meetings with shortlisted candidates; in no circumstances should the out-going chief executive attend or influence the selection group's interviews with candidates or subsequent decision-making. In the circumstances in which this principle bites hardest, such as a founding chief executive adored by much of the organisation, it is also the most necessary.

---

4   It is possible to imagine a small number of other models. For example, the selectors might take the initiative to have in-depth, individual meetings with all the senior management team, not simply seeking views and insights but also evidence of skills and achievements, and ask the individuals in effect to leave it to the selectors to invite the formal candidacy of one or more of them, if it seems in the best interests of the organisation to do so having met a number of external candidates. In some situations an arrangement like this could be seen as having benefits for team cohesion, overcoming shyness or minimising individuals' sense of failure. However to run a process in this way would need careful checks and balances and begs the question why the organisation would appoint as chief executive an individual who could not navigate the professional and emotional hurdles of straightforward candidature.

A potential internal candidate may play coy and offer to be a candidate if so invited by the selectors. Each situation and organisational context is different, but for 'the selectors' to respond in a formal sense is open to serious misunderstanding by the potential candidate and by all other candidates. Does the 'invitation' assure a place on the shortlist? Are the selectors anointing that candidate ahead of all other internal candidates (and if so, why)?

A senior manager who has worked in the organisation for some time might ask his chair informally, before the closing date for applications, whether his credentials are seen as a strong fit to the person specification, a partial fit or neither. This is a more nuanced situation in which the candidate keeps responsibility for his own decision. If he wishes the chair may give a personal opinion, underlining that he does not know the competitive field nor the opinion of his fellow selectors. Finally in some organisational situations a chair might proactively encourage a senior manager to enter the competition. If so, the chair bears all the more responsibility for not undermining the work of his fellow selectors, and excluding possible misinterpretations of that invitation by that candidate or his competitors.

Person Specification and Risk Appetite

In distilling all the board's background knowledge of the organisation together with all the inputs collected in connection with the vacancy into a person specification, the board undertakes possibly the most difficult part of the process. The main risks are that the person specification – the list of KSAOs of candidates which the board wants its selectors, recruiters or psychologists (if used) and potential candidates to focus on – will be too long and too inward-looking.

A long person specification with 20 or 30 points is a treacherous security blanket. It oozes thoroughness and appears to promise that the person appointed will be flawless. But few selection processes, and certainly none readily available to small or medium-sized organisations, can focus deeply on more than half a dozen dimensions. Therefore prioritising the half-dozen characteristics which (as the best the board can judge) will most sharply distinguish between excellence and adequacy is fundamental.[5]

---

5 Person specifications also need to distinguish essential characteristics from ones which are simply desirable, but there is no automatic link between this distinction and the characteristics which are most likely to discriminate between excellence and adequacy.

Also fundamental is balancing the likely inward focus of many internal stakeholders (concerned and a bit scared about who the next chief executive will be) with an informed assessment of change not only in the organisation's strategic environment but also in the relevant labour market. What is the likelihood of finding and attracting individuals with particular packages of experience?

An example of a person specification for one particular organisation (a trust with a small staff but a complex national influencing role and a high-profile board) is provided at the end of the chapter in Table 14.2. The prioritised characteristics are shown shaded.

Chapter 11 argued that, in addition to considering the person specification, the board should consider its risk appetite. The term 'risk appetite' underlines that risk is inseparable from opportunity, and that it can be as bad a mistake to be too risk-averse as it is to be too bold. A high risk appetite does not mean losing focus, being distracted impetuously away from the person specification: rather it means bearing in mind that the idea that the selection process is a 'measuring' of each candidate against an 'objective' specification can only take us so far. Buried in the idea of measurement is the misleading idea of one accurate answer.

Instead it is more realistic to represent the selectors' judgement of each candidate as a range of possibilities. The range is shaped not only by what (despite our best endeavours) we do not know about the candidate but by how a deeply complex and uncertain future may unfold. A high risk appetite would favour the choice of a candidate for whom the optimistic outcome is excellent, even if the pessimistic outcome is worrying, compared to a more mediocre candidate with less variance. In both cases it is the same person specification which drives the selectors' thinking and imagining process. See Chapter 11 for a fuller discussion.

Walk Your Proposed Process through in the Candidate's Shoes

You have the skills for which you are looking but already busy and doing well in a senior role. Would you make the time to go through your proposed process as a candidate? If not, how can you change the process to be a win-win for candidates and selectors alike? From the outset, be clear who will have the lead role at the end in persuading your preferred candidate to take the role and ensure that their part in the process puts them in a good position to do this.

Three Common Types of Process

A process may be *headhunter-driven*, with minimal administrative burden on you, in which you only meet a small number of shortlist quality (in other words appointable, with some variation between obvious matches to the specification and longer shots). This kind of process can offer speed and efficient use of your time but depends heavily on the headhunter and may leave you unclear as to how well the field has been covered.

Either of the other two common processes can involve a headhunter but you can also do them yourself. A *shortlist* process goes in one stage from a whole field of applicants to perhaps six whom you meet. In a *longlist and shortlist* process, you review the whole field to select perhaps a dozen who may be given more information and about whom more information is gathered. This could be done by an interview or by an exchange of written information – for example you might send the longlisted candidates fuller information about your business plan and you might ask them to send you a short critique of it, together with more detailed accounts of their most relevant achievements.

If the Field of Applicants is Very Large

This can mean that the person specification was too vague but in other cases it reflects the attractiveness of the role. Rather than being good news, a very large field of applicants may be like inheriting a large tract of empty land with scattered mineral deposits: the size of the field encourages you to believe that you've got something valuable, but where? This is a problem if (which is quite likely in a chief executive role for a small or medium-sized organisation) some of the criteria which you have prioritised as discriminating excellence are hard to judge on paper.

The challenge needs to be broken into an elimination phase and a balanced judgement phase. Identify a subset of criteria in your person specification which can more reliably be evidenced on paper (for example size of management responsibility, industry or professional relevance, experience of managing internationally or launching new ventures as opposed to teamwork, ability to work with non-executives, energy). Avoid raising the bar on particular criteria to extremes (for example first class honours degrees) if these are not justified by the role and will make the field of candidates left for discussion too homogenous. In the elimination phase, focus only on this subset of criteria.

If you are using recruiters, ask them to carry out the elimination phase based on an agreed subset of criteria, leaving you and other selectors free to concentrate on a more balanced discussion of a smaller number of candidates. If you are doing the elimination yourself, ask each selector to come to the meeting with a list of (say) the eight candidates which they most think merit discussion. Then discuss on equal terms all the candidates listed by at least one selector. A procedure like this prompts all the selectors to have read all the applications before the meeting and enables you to have a manageable amount of discussion. It also allows a more nuanced collective judgement to be made of striking but less conventional against more obvious candidates than (for example) adding up numerical scores for each candidate against each criterion.

What Kinds of Interview?

By the time of final decision-making, the following tasks should have been completed:

 a) each candidate should have had an opportunity to talk through key parts of their career (including their present situation) in an informal, narrative way. This is important to knowing how the candidate understands themselves, to gauging how committed they are to new learning, and to cross-checking what they say more formally about their values and motivation;

 b) each candidate's career should have been reviewed for missing details and unexplained job moves;

 c) at least two of each candidate's most challenging and relevant achievements should have been explored in significant factual detail (to elicit potential overstatement, particularly the hijacking of credit belonging to others and more generally illuminate the candidate's way of working with colleagues and stakeholders; to bring into focus the context, supporting resources or strokes of luck on which the achievement may have relied);

d)   evidence should have been sought and probed on all the prioritised dimensions of the person specification;

e)   each candidate should have had a substantial, private opportunity to ask questions of the chair (and possibly a small number of other individuals); and

f)   after (e), the candidate should have had the chance to explore with the selectors what conclusions the candidate is beginning to draw for moving the organisation forward.

That is a lot but, even in a shortlist-only process, can be accomplished in two interviews provided sufficient time (say an hour) is allocated to each: first a one-to-one meeting with the chair, covering (a), (b) and (e), followed by a group interview covering (c), (d) and (f), with different selectors taking the lead in exploring different aspects.

Interview Questions

Interview questions should follow a structure but allow for some flow of conversation, rather than being mechanical. Answers which are unclear, or which suggest that the question has been misinterpreted, should be explored further. The selector's tone should be courteous and interested, with engaged body language throughout. Virtually all questions should include, directly or as a supplementary, a request for pertinent examples from the candidate's experience. Hypothetical questions are no guide to what the candidate would actually do in a real situation, and invite game-playing.

Be aware of initial impressions, and strong impressions which form during the course of the interview: neither reject nor accept them but interrogate and try to challenge them. On what might these intuitions be based? What achievements could you ask the candidate to tell you about which might show your intuition to be mistaken? How might a strong negative impression be affecting the candidate through your phrasing or eye contact?

Since interviews are conducted through words, they depend on candidates' communication skills. All chief executive jobs require some communication skill, and in some cases a lot, but beware generating a halo effect around a particularly skilled communicator (for example someone who establishes early and deft rapport, and sustains it). An adroit communicator will present their own achievements adroitly; therefore in comparison the achievements outside the communication arena of more halting, diffident candidates are likely to be greater than they seem.

Taking References

This is a complex subject, however in the current British context the following are (relatively) fixed points.

The most informative references are oral, where the referee has a copy of the person specification, has made clear for how long and in what capacity he has known the candidate and where the reference-taker is attentive to silences and asks follow-up questions based on having met the candidate (or, seeks agreement at the outset to come back with any follow-up questions once he has met the candidate). Unpractised selectors over-interpret interviews to answer questions which, in the case of experienced candidates, would be better answered by asking the candidate for more or different referees, such as individuals who have worked for them.

With a talkative referee who is supportive of candidate X, the answer to 'If X is appointed, how would you advise us to get the best out of him?' can be illuminating. Still, some referees are not forthcoming at all about the candidate's weaknesses. In this situation, if you suspect a particular weakness (say a bullying manner), then consider putting this to the referee as a suggestion rather than a question: 'It's been suggested that X sometimes bullies people. Have you seen that?' If the suggestion is manifestly absurd, the referee's answer will tell you this. Conversely you can dig for specific examples if they reply, 'Oh, I don't think so. I mean some people find his management style a bit strong, but I've always found it appropriate.'

A written reference from the last one or two employers is advisable to confirm periods of employment and positions held, and possibly sickness and disciplinary record, but their usefulness beyond this is limited.

Taking references needs the candidate's agreement, but by all means at an appropriate stage in the process ask for additional referees to those the candidate has suggested, or propose someone you know whom you think knows the candidate.

Postscript

The themes of this book inform this chapter's suggestions. Gathering data widely, and resisting being bewitched by the interview-as-theatre, is scientific. The rejection of skilled agents as simply rational choosers of their own actions, spelled out further in the ideas of *habitus* and misrecognition, shows up hypothetical interview questions as hollow. Intuitions honed by challenging experience enrich the decision-making process, but submit themselves to argument and contrary evidence. The ideas of risk appetite and sketching a range of possibilities for each candidate, in which we acknowledge that our own actions (and those of the hiring organisation more widely) will influence the outcome, replace the idea of measuring an unchanging object. Focussing the selection task on a small group with relevant skills is an inextricably political act, open to abuse but also in most situations necessary to avoid irresponsible political behaviour running amok.

In the children's game of 'stone, paper, scissors', any of the three possible elements can be beaten by one of the others. This book has argued that science, politics and intuition are the stone, paper, scissors not only of executive selection but also of all skilled human action. Each can do good; each can do harm. We need to work with the whole set.

Table 13.2   A person specification for the CEO of a small, complex organisation

	Candidate	vv, v, ?, X	Comments
Drives and values	Energy, ambition, persistence		
	Importance of P and Q[1] in society (nature of excellence, regional commitment)		
Track record	Organisational and financial management		
	Leadership of innovation		
	Sufficient[2] experience across more than one of: P; Q; marketing; influencing government		
Skills (strengths)[3]	Sensitive, tactful, persuasive with a wide range of people		
	Speaking to small and large groups		
Skills (balanced)[4]	*Decision-making* Imagination focus risk-taking (vs) discipline		
	Managing staff Personal touch results motivating firmness flexible (vs) fair, consistent		
	Trustee relations Will take can lead, direction from motivate, the board (vs) use trustees		

All ten attributes are important but the (suggested) highest-priority five are shaded.

Notes

1   P and Q refer to the two main fields within which the Simon Trust works. The fields are large (each with several types of sub-specialist expert).

2   'Sufficient': how likely to be effective across all the areas, and accomplished in some, within one year?

3   More is good (cf 'balanced' below).

4   A skilled balance of opposites/complements is required.

14

Academic Notes

The following notes supplement the chapters referred to by providing additional sources, detail and perspectives.

PART I: FROM BAD TO GOOD TO STUCK

Chapter 1: From Bad …

Readers are assumed to have had some basic training and experience in selection. A good introductory guide to practice is Dale (2006).

For overviews of selection research and good practice see, for example, Schmitt and Chan (1998), Posthuma, Morgeson and Campion (2002), Hollenbeck (2009) and Silzer and Jeanneret (2011).

The preceding research is mostly scientific (in particular psychological) in orientation. Other kinds of research into senior selection are isolated and do not form a cohesive and influential body of work. One purpose of this book is to argue for this to change: in particular for psychologists (particularly consulting psychologists who practise executive assessment and research psychologists) to engage in multi-disciplinary dialogue. This is in line with Hollenbeck's call above.

The study by Silverman and Jones (1973) quoted in the chapter is an example of a study from a different research perspective, in this case ethnomethodological. They note:

> The theoretical focus of this paper is that an account of any reality derives its rationality not from its direct correspondence with some objective world but from the ability of its hearers (readers) to make sense

of the account in the context of the socially organized occasions of its use (and, thereby, to treat it as corresponding to an objective world). (Silverman and Jones, 1973:63–64)

They conclude their study in a subsequent book (1976). An example of a study which draws on their work as well as that of Bourdieu in looking at interviews for front-line employment as well as exchanges in vocational education classrooms is Roberts and Sarangi (1995).

The suggestion that personnel selection researchers should pay attention to research into the fallibility of other, in particular clinical, processes of judgement was made in Arvey and Campion's seminal review (1982), referring back to work by Kahneman and Tversky (1973).

There is an extensive literature on bounded and biased rationality in human decision-making: Thaler and Sunstein provide a popular introduction and a guide to academic sources (2008). The dominant approach taken in such literature is to measure differences between practical human judgements and theoretical rationality. There are other important ways of thinking about the relationship between these ideas, for example Gigerenzer (2000) to which we will return in Part III. At that point, as noted above, this book will particularly take up Bourdieu's logic of practice and contrast it with Weick's concept of sensemaking (1995).

The annual reports and other publications of the Commission for Judicial Appointments, including its reports into the 2003 High Court and QC competitions, are available as archived web documents.[1]

The Commission should be distinguished from its successor body with appointing powers (the Judicial Appointments Commission). The discussion here about the social–professional process of assessment within groups is preliminary. The underlying issues are taken up substantively in Chapter 8.

---

1   http://www.webarchive.org.uk/wayback/archive/20070220173847/, http://www.cja.gov.uk/reports.htm (accessed 4 March 2012): The Commissioners' First Annual Report, The Commissioners' Annual Reports 2003, 2004, 2005, 2006; The Commissioners' Audit of Silk 2003; The Commissioners' Audits of the High Court Competition 2003, 2005.

Chapter 2: ... To Good

As well as Wood and Payne (1998), readers wishing to inquire further into what is contemporary good practice are referred for example to Howard (2007), Dale (2006), Guion and Highhouse (2006) and Turner (2004). For example Howard cites upper limits of validity of 0.67 for highly-structured interviews and 0.34 for unstructured.

This chapter is neither a substitute for interview training nor an attempt to establish that the steps advocated improve selection outcomes. Instead it is a description of what widely recognised contemporary good practice is. Other practitioners and researchers should test this description against their own understandings as well as literature such as that above and industry-standard training (for example courses such as 'Recruitment, Selection and Resourcing Talent' offered over three days by the Chartered Institute of Personnel and Development).

Boyatzis (1982) takes his definition of a competency from Klemp (1980), as follows:

> ... *an underlying characteristic of a person which results in effective and/or superior performance in a job. (Boyatzis, 1982: 21)*

Looking at his work critically, three initial points might strike the practitioner. Firstly, the private sector did not allow in-depth behavioural event interviews to be done with poor performers. Unlike the public sector, the companies only wished superior and average performers to be studied in this detailed way, on the argument that poor performers would be leaving the company shortly (Boyatzis, 1982: 46). One's eyebrows might rise at this.

Secondly, to a significant extent Boyatzis assumes (or constructs) the very generalizable/portable picture of 'general management skills' which emerges from his study. He fully acknowledges that whether 'effective managerial performance' is something that can be measured in a comparable way across different organisations is a major question. I will quote a significant part of his response because the extent to which we can abstract skills from their specific contexts and treat them as portable is fundamental both to the contribution which competencies have made to HR management and to the argument of this book.

It was concluded that a basis for comparability across organizations and specific jobs had been established. For example, suppose that we could construct an absolute scale of managerial performance ranging from 1–10. The average performance rating of middle-level manufacturing managers of The Plastics Company may be 6, while the average performance rating of middle-level manufacturing managers in Computer Wizards Incorporated may be 8. Through the use of ordinal classification of performance [that is focussing only on the relativity within each company of superior compared to average and poor], we would probably find that the superior middle-level manufacturing managers of The Plastics Company varied in ratings from 6–10, with an average of 8. We might also find that the superior middle-level manufacturing managers of Computer Wizards Incorporated varied in ratings from 7–10, with an average of 9. A category of 'superior' middle-level manufacturing managers across both organizations might be considered to include managers with ratings of 7–10. There might be a few managers from The Plastics Company who would be classified as superior performers who would not be so classified if they were working for Computer Wizards Incorporated, but they would be relatively few.

In this manner, an ordinal classification removes a good deal of the variation across organizations and specific jobs. From a methodological view, this is more desirable than comparisons of interval performance assessments, which would raise the question of whether the difference between an 8 and a 9 rating were the same in both organizations …

It should be remembered that the purpose of the study was to determine differences in competencies of managers from various organizations and jobs that could be considered generic, or common, managerial competencies. (Boyatzis, 1982: 46–47)

I do not disagree with Boyatzis's way of carrying out his study but the extent to which his study can be taken to demonstrate that managerial competencies can sensibly be taken as generic must be qualified. The obverse of Boyatzis's stance on this issue is that he treats specialised knowledge as discrete data downloadable into any effectively thinking and reasoning general manager:

Specialized knowledge is defined as a usable body of facts and concepts. Literally, knowledge refers to the retention of information, whether that information is technical or a method of communication (e.g.

a language). The ability to utilize knowledge effectively is the result
of other competencies that involve ways of thinking or reasoning.
(Boyatzis, 1982: 26)

I will break sharply with this understanding of knowledge in Chapters 7 and 8.

Thirdly, the organisations studied were all large, American and studied over a number of years leading up to 1982.

Wood and Payne (1998: 29–32) highlight a number of criticisms of competencies made by one of their colleagues, Kandola (1996). Three of these (summarised by Wood and Payne as living in the past, cloning and the difficulty of turning a tanker) can be subsumed into the Maginot Line argument made in Chapter 2. Kandola also highlights the methodological point that the comparisons between successful, average and poor groups of performers within one organisation may throw up as indicators aspects which have nothing to do with performance, for example age; and to criticise the frequently shoddy execution of competency frameworks in practice.

A different kind of critique has been offered by Peter Vaill (1989) of the competency movement. His central concern is that competencies are reifications or abstractions

> *... of a very tricky sort for they involve splitting action from*
> *consciousness. Managing of any sort, let alone highly effective*
> *managing, is a very personal intertwining of consciousness and action*
> *... The [competency movement's] idea of what is real is an abstraction*
> *twice-removed for in its creation of a competency it has aggregated the*
> *visible action-capabilities of many actors, smoothing out the differences*
> *of energy-level, personal style and cultural attunement which individual*
> *actors manifest. (Vaill, 1989: 45–46)*

I would make an overlapping point, which is that although Boyatzis builds a multi-level concept which is more than behaviour and result, it is not clear that his model is capable of doing justice to human action. Thus quite complex motivations are ultimately reduced through his competency framework to stimulus-response. For example:

> *When people with a high achievement motive encounter a situation*
> *in which their performance can be measured and a goal can be stated,*

> *their achievement motive is aroused. Once aroused, the motivated*
> *thought directs and selects their behavior. (Boyatzis, 1982: 28)*

 Finally, although Boyatzis builds social role into his concept, quite rapidly he breaks with (or heavily circumscribes) the importance of the social context. He notes:

> *In his framework, Bales has described the roles that a person may*
> *take in a particular group. The role is determined by the interactions*
> *of the person with others in the group. The social role level of the*
> *competencies is a distinction based on the* contention *that individuals*
> *will demonstrate a degree of consistency in the roles that they will take*
> *in various groups at work and in their lives. (Boyatzis, 1982: 30–31,*
> *emphasis added)*

On the British Civil Service Selection Board, the study by Anstey (1977) used a sample of 301 employees and compared the Selection Board's assessment of them with the Civil Service ranks they had reached 30 years later. Anstey found a validity coefficient of 0.35 which, when corrected for restriction of range, rose to 0.66. The Board does not exist under that name any more but there continues to be an assessment centre in the equivalent high-potential graduate recruitment scheme. The procedures currently set out by the Cabinet Office (2010) testify to the advance of competencies (as well as the internet and pressures to reduce time and costs):

> *Candidates are first asked to complete an online self-assessment of*
> *suitability. The first stage of the actual selection process consists of*
> *on-line tests of Verbal and Numerical Reasoning and a Competency*
> *Questionnaire. This stage of the selection process can be completed*
> *on any PC with internet access. If candidates reach the required level,*
> *they progress to an electronic in-tray test (the e-Tray) held in centres*
> *throughout the United Kingdom. The best performers in the e-Tray*
> *exercise are invited to the Fast Stream Assessment Centre (FSAC), a*
> *day-long process at which their potential in a range of key competencies*
> *is assessed. (Cabinet Office, 2010: section 1.5.3)*

Chapter 3: ... To Stuck

My scope has not extended to studying why senior selection practices divide in the way I have suggested between the private and public, academic and voluntary sectors. My surmise as a practitioner is that organisations in the latter sectors have multiple stakeholders and accountabilities, which is taken to require a decision by committee. Very often that is also taken to require interviewing by committee. At this point the intense practical difficulty of bringing diaries together means that a half-day or day is chosen, which in turn means – if five or six candidates are to be interviewed[2] – at most 50-minute interviews and nothing resembling a conversation. The advantages of a well-conducted committee or panel process with a small membership include a disciplined timetable for the recruitment process and the possibility of panel members challenging each other's interpretations of particular question and answer exchanges which all of them have observed. The disadvantage is that the whole process resembles the recruitment version of the descent into the First World War, supposedly dictated by the inflexibility of railway timetables.

At most levels in the private sector below the board, decision by committee is eschewed in favour of individual accountability. Therefore most meetings with the candidates are one-to-one with the possibility, though by no means the assurance, of an extended two-way conversation: the hiring organisation realises it is selling as well as buying. A sequence of one-to-one meetings is more flexible (and by the same token less disciplined) in terms of the shifting diaries of both hirers and candidates, who may need to fly to other parts of the world at short notice, and in terms of accommodating late or unexpected candidates. However one-to-one meetings may become chaotically unstructured or repetitive of ground covered several times before in previous one-to-one meetings; note-taking is poor to non-existent; and there is no possibility of an interviewer's interpretation of an exchange being challenged. The whole process can be so undisciplined in terms of time that expensively wooed candidates withdraw disillusioned.

At board level in the private sector the appointment of a CEO is the responsibility of a committee. However the cultural preference for one-to-one meetings may continue to apply: for example in Brown Shoe, the committee decided that the final shortlist should first be interviewed by Bower alone

---

2   Which is wise if there is any risk of the committee operating in primitive mode, with each member or representative interest seeking proof of being heard by dismissing at least one of the candidates as unappointable.

(Bower, 2007: 43). This lack of practice in group interviews might contribute to why, according to Khurana (2002), interviews of CEO candidates by board committees are so stilted or obsequious when they do take place.

A major difference between senior appointments in the private sector (worldwide) and the public sector (at least in Britain) is the strong expectation that they will, respectively, not be advertised and be advertised. The factors here are complex but include that many senior private sector searches are commercially confidential (for example the search firm will commonly be expected to conceal which retailer is looking for someone to head up a new e-venture or expansion overseas), and this culture, together with the self-interest of search firms in amplifying the ineffectiveness of advertising in producing good candidates at senior levels, carries through even where the vacancy is not competitively sensitive or a matter of public record.

My research (Board, 2010a) included a further argument for senior selection's stuckness. I noted that a significant part of the function of senior selection processes and of professional advisers may lie in reducing (or covering over) to the point of manageability the anxiety about the unknown which arguably ought to accompany changing leaders. Viewed in this way senior selection processes may function like a witch doctor's rituals. I take this point seriously, and one of its consequences is that once an elite group have become familiar with a certain pattern of process, changing or unsticking that process may prove very difficult. Its familiarity to those 'in the know' reduces anxiety and contributes to defining membership of the elite. However neither the force of the argument (including the extent to which we are acting into the unknown) nor the point that the argument is not reductive (self-serving rituals whose content is misrecognised by those who carry them out may still carry out valid disinterested work) depend on positing a sociological frame of thought which the book does not begin to reach until Chapter 8.

PART II: WHAT'S DIFFERENT ABOUT SENIOR ROLES?

Chapter 4: Complexity, Humility and Responsibility

An issue about currently available intelligence tests is their adverse impact on some racial groups. Howard (2007) notes 'the strong adverse impact of cognitive tests' (Howard, 2007: 30). Furnham (2010) acknowledges their differential racial impact but, citing *inter alia* support from over 50 'experts on intelligence' writing in the *Wall Street Journal* in 1994, argues that 'IQ scores predict equally accurately for all [native-born English-speaking] Americans, regardless of race and social class' (Furnham, 2010: 210–211). Furnham describes this as perhaps an irreconcilable clash of values in which, for him, the role of science is to point to intelligence's objectively demonstrated strengths.

From 1981 until 2005 Professor Gillian Stamp was Director of the Brunel Institute of Organisation and Social Studies (BIOSS), a self-financing research institute founded at Brunel University in the UK and now a community of daughter institutes present in more than 20 countries. A significant part of BIOSS's work is proprietary. I am grateful to Professor Stamp for making time to introduce this work and for the opportunity to discuss it with two senior clients in the private and public sectors. The description of BIOSS levels is informed by private communications from Professor Stamp to clients about 'capability' between November 2008 and January 2011 but the interpretations given are abbreviations of mine. Professor Stamp notes that research shows that BIOSS's concept of capability is not dependent on education, ethnicity or gender.[3]

The 'ulcer quotient' is speculative. It would require some measure of the stressful intensity of extreme events survived during a period of past time, or prudently anticipated. Applying this calculation to the candidate's life and to the candidate's expected tenure in the position to be filled would produce the bottom and the top of the quotient respectively. The event contents would not be relevant. An example of a significant adverse ulcer quotient: Miss Kate Middleton on her marriage to HRH Prince William. Obvious difficulties stand in the way of testing the concept. An analysis might be possible with a sufficiently detailed data set spanning life and work stressors as well as work success over many years. Any variation due to individual resilience (as a relatively stable personal trait) as well as individual skill would, ideally, be removed from the data.

A more general comment on method. The approach taken in this chapter is practice-led, that is to say I take seriously the lessons learned from working with fellow practitioners (selection professionals, clients and candidates). This does not mean accepting practical insights unquestioningly or ignoring contrary perspectives from research, as witness the discussion on intelligence.

---

3   For more information see www.bioss.com

More precisely it means when I express a view which I know to be a minority one among practitioners, I should make this apparent. In general I do this by restricting such potentially idiosyncratic points to Chapters 12 and 13; an exception is the 'ulcer quotient'. Thus claims made in this chapter can be tested at least as to their prevalence by readers examining their own experience and reading of other practice-based literature. It also means that the general course of my argument – which questions seem worth pursuing and to what length – is shaped by an understanding of what seems important or unimportant or 'common sense' – derived from experience.

From one academic point of view this kind of discussion is valueless or counterproductive, in which case this chapter can be omitted. The conclusion to which this Part leads can be judged simply on the basis of Chapter 5. Alternatively Chapter 4 could be considered as a kind of 'data'. On this view, to the extent that this chapter reflects well more than one practitioner's world view, it forms part of what an inquiry might try to explain: what is *really* going on which leads those who take part in choosing leaders to see the world in the way presented here? The invitation which I prefer to extend is neither of these, but an invitation to make a shared journey – to think together about the issues, neither disparaging practice nor throwing away radical critique. The theoretical challenge to the 'everyday obvious' will become significant in Part III. Our train of thought will be impoverished and the chances of theoretical challenge making a difference to practice will be much reduced if practitioners are thrown off that train here.

Chapter 5: Power and Politics

This chapter starts by inviting the reader's attention to power and politics as a central feature of senior selection (and senior management), and to the absence of this feature from virtually all selection literature (and much management literature). The argument is then developed by paying attention to how power is treated in management literature and (in Chapter 6) within a broad strand of sociology, political science and philosophy.

The discussion of Kim and Mauborgne (2005) illustrates that literature on change management has to deal with the idea of opposition. An example of a reading of organisations in which the necessity (and healthiness) of conflict and the role of leaders in resolving conflict is unusually explicit is Galbraith (2005). Here, alternative organisation designs are seen as different ways of intending conflict to arise and be managed. However, even here the implied role of conflict is rationalised and de-politicised. Managers are expected to argue for, and in important cases escalate up the organisational structure, the interests for which their part of the organisation is by design the advocate. The most senior managers then decide in the organisation's interest. But even here any ethical aspects, as well as the extent to which one's clout in an organisation emerges politically, bound up in part with what one is seen to have argued for (and with hindsight wisely not argued for) in the past, whom one has annoyed in that process, and the implication of this whole dance for the subject of this book – who gets chosen to fill the next senior management vacancy – are left unsaid.

The discussion in this chapter stops short of what will be identified (and taken up) in Chapter 8 as a radically social perspective. An example of the difference is provided when the reader is invited to consider religious organisations which subscribe to a single supreme interpreter (called here monarchical interpretation), for example the Roman Catholic Church or the Iranian Government. From the perspective of Chapter 8, even in these cases interpretation is necessarily political because human action and identity are necessarily political. However the answer given in this chapter is pragmatic.

Pfeffer attributes the 'just-world hypothesis' to Lerner (1980). The view is characterised as the belief that people get what they deserve. Good people are likely to be rewarded and the bad punished. Moreover, if someone prospers or suffers setbacks, there is a social psychological tendency to consider that what happened was deserved.

Chapter 6: A Deeper Crisis

The exploration of the atomistic nature of thinking about power and the political nature of knowledge and science is presented in more detail in Board (2010a: 34–67), looking particularly at Dahl, Lukes, Foucault and Arendt. The comments on French and Raven (1959) have been added subsequently.

The notion of loud power (versus soft) connects not only to deterrent effects but to commitment strategies more generally, such as an invading force burning its boats on landing. A connected but more subtle distinction is de Certeau's (1984) between what he calls strategies (the ways of operating open to an agent with a base of its own) and tactics (the more opportunistic, guerrilla-style ways of operating open to an agent lacking such a base) (de Certeau, 1984: xix–xx).

In part, the chapter invites an engagement with contemporary philosophy – a sprawling subject with numerous points of entry in which I do not claim any credentials. But an example of a point of entry from a distinguished philosopher in his own right, which opens up a range of questions and connections with many twentieth-century thinkers, is Taylor (1997).

The argument for the death of science (in the sense of 'the death of God' as described in the chapter) is a version of a wider argument about the death of grand theories and incredulity towards metanarratives prominently associated with Lyotard (1984).

An example of a relevant analysis of power and identity in contemporary scholarship which is beyond the scope of this chapter is that due to Axel Honneth (1995; 2007), who has argued for the constitutive nature of social processes of recognition as part of human identity. In this context recognition is a radically social process unlike (for example) mechanical pattern recognition: instead it refers to the complexity of relations and assessments entailed in situations such as the following. For *A* to experienced being recognised by *B* as, say, a world-class photographer, not only must *B* make and intend to be taken seriously a gesture or comment which indicates this, but *A* must recognise *B* as competent to know a world-class photographer when she sees one. In this sentence one could also substitute 'human being' for 'world-class photographer'. The perspective taken is deeply social, in contrast to the signal-processing version of the human recognition question (the Turing test).

Rather than detecting the impact of power through the violation of the individual's wishes, interests or rights, Honneth proposes three strands to the successful development of the self: self-confidence, self-respect and self-esteem (Honneth, 1995: 129). Self-confidence refers to the recognition of one's physical integrity and basic needs, and is founded primarily in emotional relations. Self-respect refers to the recognition of one's capacity and responsibility as a moral agent, and one's legal rights. At this level equality is fundamental. Self-esteem refers to social recognition of one's value which springs not from being equal but from being different:

> *Persons can feel themselves to be 'valuable' only when they know*
> *themselves to be recognized for accomplishments that they precisely*

do not share in an undifferentiated manner with others. (Honneth, 1995: 125)

This analysis appears highly pertinent to selection which, in terms of good practice and legality, remains strongly focused on rights and equality when differentiation is selection's purpose. The links between recognition and power are explored in a collection of critiques edited by van den Brink and Owen (2007). Exploring the connections between recognition and personnel selection is work which remains to be done.

PART III: RE-THINKING FUNDAMENTALS

Chapter 7: Skill and Intuition

Notable authors who have underlined the close connection between emotion and reason include the neuroscientist Antonio Damasio (2006) and the philosopher Martha Nussbaum (2001). The twentieth-century philosopher most noted for emphasising the corporeality of existence and thought against the disembodied Cartesian mind was Maurice Merleau-Ponty (2002).

Dreyfus and Dreyfus (1986) provide the following summary of their model.

Table 14.1   The Dreyfus model of expertise

Skill level	Components	Perspective	Decision	Commitment
1. Novice	Context-free	None	Analytical	Detached
2. Advanced beginner	Context-free and situational	None	Analytical	Detached
3. Competent	Context-free and situational	Chosen	Analytical	Detached understanding and deciding. Involved in outcome
4. Proficient	Context-free and situational	Experienced	Analytical	Involved understanding. Detached deciding
5. Expert	Context-free and situational	Experienced	Intuitive	Involved

McPherson (2005) provides a valuable philosophically-grounded critique of the Dreyfus model, and addresses the significance of two additional stages of learning, mastery and practical wisdom, which (Hubert) Dreyfus added later (2001). McPherson comments that:

> ... the two 'new stages' make better sense if they are interpreted as concerned with features of learning already present at earlier stages, but which now need to be made more explicit ... (McPherson, 2005: 711)

These features concern issues of human identity, ethics, social cohesion and reflexivity which we will instead address beginning in Chapter 8 using the thought of Pierre Bourdieu. Therefore, and in order to provide in Chapter 7 an intermediate step between everyday ideas of skill and those to be explored in Chapter 8, Dreyfus' original five-stage model of expertise is used.

The Dreyfus's conceptualisation of fluid, expert action can usefully be compared with the idea of flow, which is well-known in its own right and is drawn on in the BIOSS framework of levels of complexity referred to in Chapter 4. The idea of flow was developed by psychologist Mihaly Csikszentmihalyi (2002). Pursuing the idea of happiness or optimal experience, Csikszentmihalyi posited that it could be found in experiences where the challenges faced by an agent were sufficiently well-matched against the agent's skills to produce absorption in the task, forgetfulness of self and progression towards higher levels of skill (marked by ability cope with greater complexity). On either side of these experiences of flow lay anxiety (where the challenges were too great relative to the agent's skills) or conversely boredom. This analysis shares some ground with the Dreyfus's model of expertise, or the idea of intuition more generally, but is differently oriented. Csikszentmihalyi wishes to emphasise the inward pursuit of happiness, in particular the ability of individuals to re-interpret their circumstances (however unrewarding these may be objectively) to create for themselves happiness or flow. One among several accounts which Csikszentmihalyi (2002: 91–92) cites is that of hundreds of Hungarian intellectuals imprisoned in Visegrád jail, who occupied themselves for several months in a secret poetry translation contest, even though they had no books or paper. By contrast with this turning inside an individual to find what Csikszentmihalyi calls the autotelic personality, we will emphasise in Chapter 8 the social process aspects of meaning-creation and its relationship to skill.

Chapter 8: Games, Skill and Belonging

In place of the argument in the first part of this chapter (until 'The Logic of Games') academic readers should refer to Medina (2003). While the responsibility for misleading interpretations or illustrations is mine, the underlying argument is borrowed from Medina's paper, which he summarises as follows:

> This paper is a critical examination of Wittgenstein's view of the limits of intelligibility. In it I criticize standard analytic readings of Wittgenstein as an advocate of transcendental or behaviourist theses in epistemology; and I propose an alternative interpretation of Wittgenstein's view as a social contextualism that transcends the false dichotomy between Kantianism and psychologism. I argue that this social contextualism is strikingly similar to the social account of epistemic practices developed by Pierre Bourdieu. Through a comparison between Wittgenstein's and Bourdieu's and an analysis of the notion of habitus, I try to show how social contextualism can account for the distinction between sense and nonsense without falling into transcendental constructivism or social behaviourism. (Medina, 2003: 293)

Of more general relevance are Bourdieu (1977; 1990; 1998), Taylor (1997) and Board (2010a). What is introduced in this chapter as 'the grammar of games' is referred to by Bourdieu as the logic of practice. Readers unfamiliar with his ideas but familiar with the concept of sensemaking as developed by Karl Weick (1995) might find Board (2011) helpful. A fuller treatment than this chapter permits would say more about the break from a solitary mind posited in the Cartesian picture towards a radically social perspective, that is to say not one in which individual identities are treated as atomic and society is the interaction of atoms but one in which individual identity and society emerge inseparably from interaction. This would include underlining the contribution of Mead (1934) and Elias (1978; 1987), particularly the latter's development of the notion of *habitus*, which overlaps Bourdieu's. For such a discussion, as well as a discussion of the distinction between Bourdieu's thought and structuration theories as posited by Giddens (1979), see Board (2010a: 119–135).

To follow academic convention within this chapter would mean so far as possible identifying each point made with thinkers who made similar points during philosophy's long development, at the same time noting major and minor differences, as well as using terms which are well recognised in the discourse (such as transcendental or epistemic). Not only would I fail to do this task justice but also I would defeat one of the chapter's primary objectives, which is to give as many general readers as possible the confidence to relate the debates described to their own experience and interpretation of the world.

Chapter 9: Re-thinking Science and Leader Selection

This chapter's focus is on science and leader selection understood as Bourdieusian games, and rather than understanding human identity in this way. However the latter perspective is very pertinent.

Feminist thinkers such as Butler (1999), Krais (1993) and McNay (1999) have taken up Bourdieu's logic of practice and his explicit consideration of gender (2001). Such thinkers particularly notice Bourdieu's emphasis on situations in which *habitus* and field mesh seamlessly and raise questions about situations of disruption, for example in gendered identity. For Butler Bourdieu's framework underestimates agents' scope to make radical change, while McNay sees the constraining effect of *habitus* and field as a realistic consequence of embodiment. The comparison of Bourdieu and Weick later in this chapter also explores situations of radical change and disruption in the selection of leaders.

Another aspect of identity is its narrative construction, which is particularly pertinent when considering selection processes (such as interviews of senior individuals) in which narrative often plays a vital part. This is discussed by Board (2010a: 152–158) which considers critically Bourdieu's assault on *The Biographical Illusion* (Bourdieu, 2000a) alongside the exploration of human identity as social and narrative in nature offered by Ricoeur (1992). Bourdieu's jibe at biographical identity as, in Shakespeare's language, a meaningless tale told by an idiot hits the mark when the narrative is a thin (linear, coherent, self-serving) account offered by a leader for public consumption but Ricoeur focuses on the essence of narrative as thick with tensions, contradictions and accidents which are wrestled with alongside purpose.

For a discussion of the critique of Bourdieusian practice by Dreyfus and Rabinow (1993) and Sayer (1999) see also Board (2010a: 129–135).

The comparison between Bourdieusian practice and Weickian sensemaking is developed in Board (2011), from which the following summary table (Table 14.2) gives the main points.

Table 14.2   Comparison of sensemaking and practice

	Weick – sensemaking	Bourdieu – practice
Purpose of account	To articulate how intelligent human action and social order arise together from action in practice.	
Unit (atom) of explanation	The individual (in society).	The game (a process involving multiple individuals whose stakes are self-evident to participants and opaque to outsiders).
The driving force behind action	To make the environment intelligible (reduce ambiguity). To account for oneself. In so doing to enhance one's sense of existence and capacity to act.	To accrue symbolic profits (whatever is valued in the game). In so doing to enhance one's sense of existence and capacity to act.
The environment	Enacted by agents and relatively malleable: by choice or accident agents can often enact different environments.	Also called the field. Enacted by agents but may be hard to change (e.g. class structure): socially constructed out of repeated, habitual actions whose significance individuals cannot fully grasp, and intrinsically political. Agents in different positions in the field do not have the same capacity to act.
What simplifies (interprets) the environment for the agent?	Prominence given to the agent's own committed actions (public, irrevocable, volitional) and values – especially self-fulfilling prophecies – alongside shared stories, common and individual cause-maps.	*Habitus* – the 'common sense' of the game carried in the bodies of experienced participants, which, without constructing a mental model, anticipates the flow of play and makes one or a small number of next actions feel possible/obvious (and excludes a large number of unnoticed other actions as inappropriate).
The place of conscious thought	The individual's mind (in society). The individual's choices can be highly significant – e.g. to act, to create self-fulfilling prophecies. Surprises, discrepancies are of more interest than repetitions or habits because they engage conscious thought.	In embodied social process, emerging particularly strongly in certain games with relevant stakes (such as science). The significance of individual rational choice is acknowledged but played down.
The place of repetition, habit	Acknowledged as the way the social world is mostly constructed, but not of primary interest.	Crucial to the construction of the social world and individuals within it, and of primary interest.
Significance of the agent's self-understanding	Relevant to understanding agents' practices but flawed – subject to memory loss/bias and *post hoc* rationalisation in Weick's account, or to necessary misrecognition in Bourdieu's.	
Advice to the agent?	Act!	Reflect (as part of a community of practice)!
Time orientation	Retrospective.	Anticipatory.

PART IV: SO WHAT?

Chapter 10: The Candidate's Perspective

On the need for more writers to take up in a philosophically deeper way the ethical challenges of contemporary management, Griffin (2002) and Steare (2006) are both philosophers steeped in management practice. There is a wider spectrum of concern among management scholars about the 'scientisation' or ethical improverishment of management studies. Two examples, both of whom take up the role played by business schools in this process, are Ghoshal (2005) and Khurana (2007). The literature within philosophy is of course prodigious but some points of entry with connections to the themes of this book include MacIntyre (1997), Joas (2000) and Taylor (1989; 2007).

In the discussion which opens the chapter's final section of the goal of my career advice work, 'energy' is the word which makes most sense at a practical level. From an academic perspective it may be that I am describing an increased sense of agency, that is, experiencing myself able to make sufficient sense of my world to take meaningful actions within it (Weick). See also the discussion in the notes above on Chapter 7 of flow (Csikszentmihalyi). In terms of my interpretation of Bourdieu, career change partakes of the idea of changing or re-inventing some of the games in which one plays, and the discussion in Chapter 9 about the interpretative advantages which Weick's sensemaking offers compared with *habitus* is relevant. However there is more thinking to do here. In holding myself out as an adviser on career change, am I not inviting recognition of career transition as a game in itself; indeed this complements the work I do with clients to uncover, and make useable for this new purpose, resources which they already possess (by all means people, knowledge and skills but also memories re-interpreted or re-invigorated, and what to take as 'common sense' or obvious in the new activity); as well as with which of their friends and acquaintances they describe themselves as searching (between games), searching (in a new game), or neither. This lack of clarity suggests a direction for further work.

An issue not explored here is the extent to which perspectives which emphasise the social nature of identity (whether atomic–interactionist or radically social in their foundations) are taken up in different international cultures. For example Tokihiko Enomoto, a professor at Tokai University notes:

> *[Follett] sees individuals not as independent selves going their separate ways, but as interdependent, interactive and interconnecting members of the groups to which they belong. This is something close to the Japanese ethos. We can fully agree with Follett when she writes that 'the vital relation of the individual to the world is through his groups'. (Graham, 1995: 243)*

Similarly an important cultural concept found in Africa is *ubuntu,* that each of us only has our being through each other.

A readable and practical book which illuminates a social way of thinking about career change is Ibarra (2003).

Chapter 11: The Selector's and Society's Perspective

For a discussion of narrative-based participant research by senior managers see Warwick and Board (2011).

Works Cited

Anstey, E. (1977). A 30 year follow-up of the CSSB procedure, with lessons for the future. *Journal of Occupational Psychology, 50*, 149–159.

Archbishops' Council: Ministry Division. (2010). *Going to a Bishops' Advisory Panel: Selection for Training for Ordained Ministry.* Retrieved May 17, 2011, from http://www.churchofengland.org/clergy-office-holders/ministry/selection/ddos.aspx.

Arvey, R., & Campion, J. (1982). The employment interview: a summary and review of recent research. *Personnel Psychology, 35*(2), 281–322.

Bechara, A., Damasio, H., Tranel, D., & Damasio, A. (1997). Deciding advantageously before knowing the advantageous strategy. *Science, 275*(5304), 1293–1295.

Board, D. (2010a). *Senior Selection Interviewing: From Individual Skill and Intuition to Habitus and Practice.* Hatfield, UK: University of Hertfordshire.

Board, D. (2010b). Leadership: the ghost at the trillion dollar crash. *European Management Journal, 28*(4), 269–277.

Board, D. (2011). Practice and sensemaking: rethinking senior selection with Bourdieu and Weick. *International Journal of Learning and Change, 5*(1), 1–15.

Bourdieu, P. (1977). *Outline of a Theory of Practice.* Cambridge, UK: Cambridge University Press.

Bourdieu, P. (1990). *The Logic of Practice.* Cambridge, UK: Polity Press.

Bourdieu, P. (1991). *Language and Symbolic Power.* Cambridge, UK: Polity Press.

Bourdieu, P. (1993). Concluding Remarks: For a Sociogenetic Understanding of Intellectual Works. In C. Calhoun, E. LiPuma, & M. Postone (Eds), *Bourdieu: Critical Perspectives* (pp. 263-274). Cambridge, UK: Polity Press.

Bourdieu, P. (1998). Is a Disinterested Act Possible? In P. Bourdieu, *Practical Reason: On the Theory of Action* (pp. 75–91). Cambridge, UK: Polity Press.

Bourdieu, P. (2000a). The Biographical Illusion. In P. du Gay, J. Evans, & P. Redman (Eds), *Identity: A Reader* (pp. 297–303). London: Sage.

Bourdieu, P. (2000b). *Pascalian Meditations.* Cambridge, UK: Polity Press.

Bourdieu, P. (2001). *Masculine Domination*. Stanford, CA: Stanford University Press.

Bourdieu, P. (2004). *Science of Science and Reflexivity*. Cambridge, UK: Polity Press.

Bourdieu, P and Wacquant, L. (1992). *An Invitation to Reflexive Sociology*. Cambridge, UK: Polity Press.

Bower, J. (2007). *The CEO Within: Why Inside Outsiders are the Key to Succession Planning*. Boston, MA: Harvard Business School Press.

Boyatzis, R. (1982). *The Competent Manager: A Model for Effective Performance*. New York: John Wiley & Sons.

Bozionelos, N. (2005). When the inferior candidate is offered the job: the selection interview as a political and power game. *Human Relations, 58, 1605-1631.*

Brown, A. (1997). Narcissism, identity and legitimacy. *Academy of Management Review, 22*(3), 643–686.

Burnett, J., & Motowidlo, S. (1998). Relations between different sources of information in the structured selection interview. *Personnel Psychology, 51*(4), 963–983.

Butler, J. (1999). Performativity's Social Magic. In R. Shusterman (Ed.), *Bourdieu: A Critical Reader* (pp. 113–128). Oxford, UK: Blackwell Publishers Ltd.

Cabinet Office, London. (2010, November 14). *Civil Service Management Code, Chapter 1 – Taking up Appointment*. Retrieved May 6, 2011, from http://www.civilservice.gov.uk/about/resources/civil-service-management-codeCampbell, A., Goold, M., & Alexander, M. (1995). Corporate strategy: the quest for parenting advantage. *Harvard Business Review*, March–April.

Christie, R., & Geis, F. (1970). *Studies in Machiavellianism*. London: Academic Press.

Collins, J. (2001). *Good To Great: Why Some Companies Make the Leap and Others Don't*. New York: HarperCollins.

Commission for Judicial Appointments. (2003). *Annual Report*. London.

Cookson, R. (2011). Bolton's China fund suffers. *Financial Times*, June 17, p. 17.

Csikszentmihalyi, M. (2002). *Flow: The Classic Work on How to Achieve Happiness*. London: Rider.

Dahl, R. (1957). The Concept of Power. *Behavioral Science, 2*(3), 201–205.

Dahl, R. (1986). Power as the Control of Behavior. In S. Lukes, *Power* (pp. 37–58). New York: New York University Press.

Dale, M. (2006). *The Essential Guide to Recruitment: How to Conduct Great Interviews and Select the Best Employees*. London: Kogan Page.

Damasio, A. (2006). *Descartes' Error*. London: Vintage.

Damhorst, M., & Reed, A. (1986). Clothing color value and facial expression: effects on evaluations of female job applicants. *Social Behavior and Personality, 14*(1), 89–98.

Dane, E., & Pratt, M. (2007). Exploring intuition and its role in managerial decision-making. *Academy of Management Review, 32*(1), 33–54.

Davies of Abersoch, Lord (2011). *Women on Boards*, February. Retrieved May 17, 2011, from http://www.bis.gov.uk/assets/biscore/business-law/docs/w/11-745-women-on-boards.pdf.

de Certeau, M. (1984). *The Practice of Everyday Life*. Berkeley, CA: University of California Press.

DeGroot, T., & Motowidlo, S. (1999). Why visual and vocal interview cues can affect interviewers' judgments and predict job performance. *Journal of Applied Psychology, 84*(6), 986–993.

Descartes, R. (1994). *A Discourse on Method: Meditations and Principles*. London: J. M. Dent.

Dipboye, R. (1982). Self-fulfilling prophecies in the selection-recruitment interview. *Academy of Management Review, 7*(4), 579–586.

Dreyfus, H. (2001). *On the Internet*. London: Routledge.

Dreyfus, H., & Dreyfus, S. (1986). *Mind Over Machine: The Power of Human Intuition and Expertise in the Era of the Computer*. New York: The Free Press.

Dreyfus, H., & Rabinow, P. (1993). Can there be a science of existential structure and social meaning? In C. Calhoun, E. LiPuma, & M. Postone, *Bourdieu: Critical Perspectives* (pp. 35–44). Cambridge, UK: Polity Press.

Einhorn, H., & Hogarth, R. (1978). Confidence in judgment: persistence of the illusion of validity. *Psychological Review, 85*(5), 395–416.

Elias, N. (1978). *What is Sociology?* New York: Columbia University Press.

Elias, N. (1987). *Involvement and Detachment*. Oxford, UK: Blackwell.

Elkind, P., & McLean, B. (2004). *The Smartest Guys in the Room: The Amazing Rise and Scandalous Fall of Enron*. London: Penguin.

Fletcher, C. (2005). *Final Report On A Research Study Relating To Effective Selection Of Staff For Senior Posts In The Civil Service* . London: HMSO.

Flyvbjerg, B. (1998). *Rationality & Power: Democracy in Practice*. Chicago, IL: The University of Chicago Press.

Flyvbjerg, B. (2001). *Making Social Science Matter: Why Social Inquiry Fails and How it Can Succeed Again*. Cambridge, UK: Cambridge University Press.

Foucault, M. (1984). *The Foucault Reader: An Introduction to Foucault's Thought*. (P. Rabinow, Ed.) London: Penguin.

Foucault, M. (1986). Disciplinary Power and Subjection. In S. Lukes, *Power* (pp. 229–242). New York: New York University Press.

French, J., & Raven, B. (1959). The Bases of Social Power. In Cartwright, D. (Ed.) *Studies in Social Power* (pp. 150–167). Michigan, MI: University of Michigan Press.

Furnham, A. (2010). *The Elephant in the Boardroom: The Causes of Leadership Derailment.* Basingstoke, UK: Palgrave Macmillan.

Galbraith, J. (2005). *Designing the Customer-Centric Organization: A Guide to Strategy, Structure, and Process.* San Francisco, CA: Jossey-Bass.

Ghoshal, S. (2005). Bad management theories are destroying good management practices. *Academy of Management Learning and Education, 4*(1), 75–91.

Giddens, A. (1979). *Central Problems In Social Theory: Action, Structure and Contradiction in Social Analysis.* Basingstoke, UK: Palgrave Macmillan.

Gigerenzer, G. (2000). *Adaptive Thinking: Rationality in the Real World.* Oxford, UK: Oxford University Press.

Girard, R. (1979). *Violence and the Sacred.* Baltimore, MD: Johns Hopkins University Press.

Gladwell, M. (2005). *Blink: The Power of Thinking Without Thinking.* London: Penguin.

Goleman, D. (1996). *Emotional Intelligence: Why It Can Matter More Than IQ.* London: Bloomsbury Publishing.

Graham, P. (Ed.) (1995) *Mary Parker Follett: Prophet of Management.* Frederick, MD: Beard Books.

Griffin, D. (2002). *The Emergence of Leadership: Linking Self-organization and Ethics.* London: Routledge.

Groysberg, B., McLean, A., & Nohria, N. (2006). Are leaders portable? *Harvard Business Review,* May, 92–100.

Guion, R., & Highhouse, S. (2006). *Essentials of Personnel Assessment and Selection.* Mahwah, NJ: Lawrence Erlbaum Associates.

Heidegger, M. (1962). *Being and Time.* Malden, MA: Blackwell.

Hollenbeck, G. (2009). Executive selection – what's right and what's wrong. *Industrial and Organizational Psychology, 2,* 130–143.

Honneth, A. (1995). *The Struggle for Recognition: The Moral Grammar of Social Conflicts.* Cambridge, UK: Polity Press.

Honneth, A. (2007). *Disrespect: The Normative Foundations of Critical Theory.* Cambridge, UK: Polity Press.

Howard, A. (2007). Best Practices in Leader Selection. In J. Conger, & R. Riggio (Eds), *The Practice of Leadership: Developing the Next Generation of Leaders* (pp. 11–40). San Francisco, CA: Jossey-Bass Inc.

Huguenard, T., Sager, E., & Ferguson, L. (1970). Interview time, interview set, and interview outcome. *Perceptual and Motor Skills, 31*(3), 831–836.

Ibarra, H. (2003). *Working Identity: Unconventional Strategies for Reinventing Your Career.* Boston, MA: Harvard Business School Press.

Joas, H. (2000). *The Genesis of Values.* Cambridge, UK: Polity Press.

Judge, T., & Cable, D. (2004). The effect of physical height on workplace success and income: preliminary test of a theoretical model. *Journal of Applied Psychology, 89*(3), 428–441.

Judge, T., & Cable, D. (2011). When it comes to pay, do the thin win? The effect of weight on pay for men and women. *Journal of Applied Psychology, 96*(1), 95–112.

Kahneman, D., & Tversky, A. (1973). On the psychology of prediction. *Psychological Review, 80*(4), 251–273.

Kandola, R. (1996) Putting competencies in perspective. *Competency, 4*(1), 31-34.

Kanter, R. (2009). *Supercorp.* London: Profile Books.

Kaplan, S., Klebanov, M., & Sorensen, M. (2008). Which CEO characteristics and abilities matter? *Swedish Institute for Financial Research Conference on the Economics of the Private Equity Market, AFA 2008 New Orleans Meeting Paper,* July. Available at SSRN: http://ssrn.com/abstract=972446.

Kellerman, B. (2004). *Bad Leadership.* Boston, MA: Harvard University Press.

Khurana, R. (2002). *Searching for a Corporate Savior: The Irrational Quest for Charismatic CEOs.* Princeton, NJ: Princeton University Press.

Khurana, R. (2007). *From Higher Aims to Hired Hands: The Social Transformation of American Business Schools and the Unfulfilled Promise of Management as a Profession.* Princeton, NJ: Princeton University Press.

Kim, W., & Mauborgne, R. (2005). *Blue Ocean Strategy: How to Create Uncontested Market Space and Make the Competition Irrelevant.* Boston, MA: Harvard Business School Press.

Kirby, J. (2011). *Jack Griffin's 'ouster': lessons from a failed change agent,* February 18. Retrieved March 3, 2011, from *Harvard Business Review* http://blogs.hbr.org/hbr/hbreditors/2011/02/jack_griffins_ouster_lessons_f.html

Klemp, G. (1980). *The Assessment of Occupational Competence.* Washington, DC: National Institute of Education.

Kotter, J. (1988). *The Leadership Factor.* New York: The Free Press.

Krais, B. (1993). Gender and Symbolic Violence: Female Oppression in the Light of Pierre Bourdieu's Theory of Social Practice. In C. Calhoun, E. LiPuma, & M. Postone (Eds), *Bourdieu: Critical Perspectives* (pp. 156–177). Cambridge, UK: Polity Press.

Kuhn, T. (1970). *The Structure of Scientific Revolutions.* Chicago, IL: University of Chicago Press.

Lerner, M. (1980). *The Belief in a Just World: A Fundamental Delusion.* New York: Plenum.

Lewin, K. (1947). Frontiers in group dynamics. *Human Relations, 1*(2), 5–41.

Lewis, D. (1997). *Hidden Agendas: Politics, Law and Disorder.* London: Hamish Hamilton.

Lukes, S. (1974). *Power: A Radical View.* London: Macmillan Press.

Lyotard, J.-F. (1984). *The Postmodern Condition: A Report on Knowledge.* Manchester, UK: Manchester University Press.

Machiavelli, N. (2005). *The Prince.* Oxford, UK: Oxford University Press.

MacIntyre, A. (1997). *After Virtue: A Study in Moral Theory.* London: Gerald Duckworth & Co.

McCall Jr, M., & Hollenbeck, G. (2007). Getting Leader Development Right: Competence Not Competencies. In J. Conger, & R. Riggio (Eds), *The Practice of Leadership: Developing The Next Generation of Leaders* (pp. 87–106). San Francisco, CA: Jossey-Bass Inc.

McNay, L. (1999). Gender, habitus and field: Pierre Bourdieu and the limits of reflexivity. *Theory, Culture & Society, 16*(1), 95–117.

McPherson, I. (2005). Reflexive learning: stages towards wisdom with Dreyfus. *Educational Philosophy and Theory, 37*(5), 705–718.

Mead, G. (1934). *Mind, Self & Society from the Standpoint of a Social Behaviorist.* Chicago, IL: The University of Chicago Press.

Medina, J. (2003). Wittgenstein and nonsense: psychologism, Kantianism and the habitus. *International Journal of Philosophical Studies, 11*(3), 293–318.

Merleau-Ponty, M. (2002). *Phenomenology of Perception.* London: Routledge Classics.

Moss Kanter, R. (2010). *Supercorp: How Vanguard Companies Create Innovation, Profits, Growth and Social Good.* London: Profile Books.

Motowidlo, S., & Burnett, J. (1995). Aural and visual sources of validity in structured employment interviews. *Organizational Behaviour and Human Decision Processes, 61*(3), 239–249.

Nagourney, A. (2011). *Madonna's charity fails in bid to finance school,* March 25. Retrieved April 7, 2011, from *The New York Times* http://query.nytimes.com/gst/fullpage.html?res=9801E2DF1131F936A15750C0A9679D8B63&ref=adamnagourney.

Nietzsche, F. (2006). *The Gay Science.* Mineola, NY: Dover Publications .

Nussbaum, M. (2001). *Upheavals of Thought: The Intelligence of Emotions.* Cambridge, UK: Cambridge University Press.

Parikh, J., Neubauer, F., & Lank, A. (1994). *Intuition: The New Frontier in Management.* Cambridge, MA: Blackwell.

Pears, D. (1971). *Wittgenstein.* London: Fontana.

Peter, L. (1985). *Why Things Go Wrong.* London: Unwin.

Pfeffer, J. (2010). *Power: Why Some People Have It – And Others Don't*. New York: HarperCollins.

Posthuma, R., Morgeson, F., & Campion, M. (2002). Beyond employment interview validity: a comprehensive narrative review of recent research and trends over time. *Personnel Psychology, 55*(1), 1–81.

Raven, B. (1992). A power/interaction model of interpersonal influence: French and Raven thirty years later. *Journal of Social Behavior and Personality, 7*(2), 217–244.

Ricoeur, P. (1992). *Oneself as Another*. Chicago, IL: University of Chicago Press.

Roberts, C., & Sarangi, S. (1995). 'But are they one of us?': managing and evaluating identities in work-related contexts. *Multilingua, 14*(4), 363–390.

Rosenthal, S., & Pittinsky, T. (2006). Narcissistic leadership. *Leadership Quarterly, 17*(6), 617–633.

Russell, C. (1990). Selecting top corporate leaders: an example of biographical information. *Journal of Management, 16*(1), 73–86.

Sadler-Smith, E. (2008). The role of intuition in collective learning and the development of shared meaning. *Advances in Developing Human Resources, 10*(4), 494–508.

Sayer, A. (1999). Bourdieu, Smith and disinterested judgement. *The Sociological Review, 47*(3), 403–431.

Scherbaum, C., & Shepherd, D. (1987). Dressing for success: effects of color and layering on perceptions of women in business. *Sex Roles, 16*(7-8), 391–399.

Schmitt, N., & Chan, D. (1998). *Personnel Selection: A Theoretical Approach*. Thousand Oaks, CA: Sage.

Schroeder, A. (2011). *Buffett must show his sage side on succession*, February 25. Retrieved April 7, 2011, from *The Financial Times* http://www.ft.com/cms/s/0/fd646b8a-4053-11e0-9140-00144feabdc0.html.

Silverman, D., & Jones, J. (1973). Getting In: The Managed Accomplishment of 'Correct' Selection Outcomes. In J. Child (Ed.), *Man and Organization* (pp. 63–106). London: George Allen and Unwin.

Silverman, D., & Jones, J. (1976). *Organisational Work: The Language of Grading/ The Grading of Language*. London and New York: Collier/Macmillan.

Silvester, J. (2008). The Good, the Bad and the Ugly: Politics and Politicians at Work. In G. Hodgkinson, & J. Ford (Eds), *International Review of Industrial and Organizational Psychology* (pp. 107–148). Chichester, UK: John Wiley & Sons.

Silzer, R., & Jeanneret, R. (2011). Individual psychological assessment: a practice and science in search of common ground. *Industrial and Organizational Psychology, 4*(3), 270–296.

Sokal, A. (1996a). Transgressing the boundaries: toward a transformative hermeneutics of quantum gravity. *Social Text, 46/47*, 217–252.

Sokal, A. (1996b). A physicist experiments with cultural studies. *Lingua Franca*, May/June, 62–64.

Sokal, A. (1996c). Transgressing the boundaries: an afterword. *Dissent, 43*(4), 93–99.

Spengler, P., Strohmer, D., Dixon, D., & Shivy, V. (1995). A scientist-practitioner model of psychological assessment: implications for training, practice and research. *The Counseling Psychologist, 23*(3), 506–534.

Springbett, B. (1958). Factors affecting the final decision in the employment interview. *Canadian Journal of Psychology, 12*, 13–22.

Steare, R. (2006). *Ethicability: How to Decide What's Right and Find the Courage to Do It.* London: Roger Steare Consulting.

Tanner, M. (2000). *Nietzsche: A Very Short Introduction.* Oxford, UK: Oxford University Press.

Taylor, C. (1989). *Sources of the Self: The Making of the Modern Identity.* Cambridge, UK: Cambridge University Press.

Taylor, C. (1997). *Philosophical Arguments.* Cambridge, MA: Harvard University Press.

Taylor, C. (2007). *A Secular Age.* Cambridge, MA: The Belknap Press.

Taylor, L. (2010). Why Are CEOs rarely fired? Evidence from structural estimation. *The Journal of Finance, LXV*(6), 2051–2087.

Thaler, R., & Sunstein, C. (2008). *Nudge: Improving Decisions about Health, Wealth and Happiness.* New Haven, CT: Yale University Press.

Tucker, D., & Rowe, P. (1977). Consulting the application form prior to the interview: an essential step in the selection process. *Journal of Applied Psychology, 62*(3), 283–287.

Tuckman, B. (1965). Developmental sequence in small groups. *Psychological Bulletin, 63*(6), 384–399.

Turner, T. (2004). *Behavioral Interviewing Guide: A Practical, Structured Approach for Conducting Effective Selection Interviews.* Victoria, BC: Trafford Publishing.

Vaill, P. (1989). *Managing as a Performing Art: New Ideas for a World of Chaotic Change.* San Francisco, CA: Jossey-Bass .

van den Brink, B., & Owen, D. (eds). (2007). *Recognition and Power: Axel Honneth and the Tradition of Critical Social Theory.* Cambridge, UK: Cambridge University Press.

Walzer, M. (1983). *Spheres of Justice: A Defence of Pluralism and Equality.* New York: Basic Books Inc.

Warwick, R., & Board, D. (2011). Reflexivity as methodology: an approach to the necessarily political work of senior groups. *First International Conference on Emerging Research Paradigms in Business and Social Sciences.* Dubai: Middlesex University.

Weick, K. (1995). *Sensemaking in Organizations*. Thousand Oaks, CA: Sage Publications.

Weick, K. (2001). *Making Sense of the Organization*. Malden, MA: Blackwell.

Weick, K. (2009). *Making Sense of the Organization: Volume Two: the Impermanent Organization*. Chichester, UK: John Wiley & Sons.

Williams, M. (1999). *Wittgenstein, Mind and Meaning*. London: Routledge.

Wood, R., & Payne, T. (1998). *Competency Based Recruitment and Selection: A Practical Guide*. Chichester, UK: John Wiley & Sons.

Zaleznik, A. (1978). Managers and leaders: are they different? *McKinsey Quarterly*, Spring, 2–22.

Index

Page numbers in **bold** refer to tables.

If you have found this book useful you may be interested in other titles from Gower

Women in Management Worldwide
Progress and Prospects
Edited by Marilyn J. Davidson and Ronald J. Burke
Hardback: 978-0-566-08916-9
Ebook: 978-0-566-08917-6

Complex Adaptive Leadership
Embracing Paradox and Uncertainty
Nick Obolensky
Hardback: 978-0-566-08932-9
Ebook: 978-0-566-08933-6

Rethinking Management
Radical Insights from the Complexity Sciences
Chris Mowles
Hardback: 978-1-4094-2933-3
Ebook: 978-1-4094-2934-0

Assessment Centres and Global Talent Management
Edited by Nigel Povah and George C. Thornton III
Hardback: 978-1-4094-0386-9
Ebook: 978-1-4094-0387-6

Visit **www.gowerpublishing.com** and

- search the entire catalogue of Gower books in print
- order titles online at 10% discount
- take advantage of special offers
- sign up for our monthly e-mail update service
- download free sample chapters from all recent titles
- download or order our catalogue